Indian Agriculture after the Green Revolution

The Green Revolution turned India from a country plagued with chronic food shortages into a food grain self-sufficient nation within the decade of 1968–1978. By contrast, the decade of 1995–2005 witnessed a spate of suicides among farmers in many parts of the country. These tragic incidents were symptomatic of the severe stress and strain that the agriculture sector had meanwhile accumulated. The book recounts how the high achievements of the Green Revolution had overgrown to a state of 'agrarian crisis'. In the process, the book also brings to fore the underlying resilience and innovativeness in the sector which enabled it not just to survive through the crisis but to evolve and revive out of it. The need of the hour is to create an environment that will enable the agricultural sector to acquire the robustness to contend with the challenges of lifting levels of farm income and with climate change. To this end, a multi-pronged intervention strategy has been suggested. Reviving public investment in irrigation, tuning agrarian institutions to the changed context, strengthening market institutions for better farm-to-market linkage and financial access of farmers, and preparing the ground for ushering in technological innovations should form the major components of this policy paradigm.

Binoy Goswami is Assistant Professor in the Faculty of Economics, South Asian University, New Delhi, India.

Madhurjya Prasad Bezbaruah is Professor in the Department of Economics, Gauhati University, Guwahati, India.

Raju Mandal is Assistant Professor in the Department of Economics, Assam University, Silchar, India.

Routledge Studies in the Modern World Economy

For a full list of titles in this series, please visit www.routledge.com/series/SE0432

Indian Agriculture after the Green Revolution

Changes and Challenges

**Edited by Binoy Goswami,
Madhurjya Prasad Bezbaruah
and Raju Mandal**

Routledge
Taylor & Francis Group

LONDON AND NEW YORK

First published 2018 by Routledge

2 Park Square, Milton Park, Abingdon, Oxfordshire OX14 4RN

52 Vanderbilt Avenue, New York, NY 10017

Routledge is an imprint of the Taylor & Francis Group, an informa business

First issued in paperback 2019

British Library Cataloguing-in-Publication Data
A catalogue record for this book is available from the British Library

Library of Congress Cataloging-in-Publication Data
Names: Goswami, Binoy, 1983– editor. | Bezbaruah, Madhurjya
    Prasad, 1959– editor. | Mandal, Raju, 1980– editor.
Title: Indian agriculture after the green revolution : changes and
    challenges / edited by Binoy Goswami, Madhurjya Prasad
    Bezbaruah and Raju Mandal.
Description: Abingdon, Oxon ; New York, NY : Routledge, 2018. |
    Series: Routledge studies in the modern world economy ; 172 |
    Includes bibliographical references and index.
Identifiers: LCCN 2017031922 | ISBN 9781138286290 (hardback) |
    ISBN 9781315268538 (ebook)
Subjects: LCSH: Agriculture—Economic aspects—India—History. |
    Agriculture—India—History.
Classification: LCC HD2072 .I5268 2018 | DDC 338.10954—dc23
LC record available at https://lccn.loc.gov/2017031922

ISBN: 978-1-138-28629-0 (hbk)
ISBN: 978-0-367-37483-9 (pbk)

Typeset in Galliard
by Apex CoVantage, LLC

Contents

Figures

Tables

Contributors

Amarendra Das is Assistant Professor in the School of Humanities and Social Sciences, National Institute of Science Education and Research (NISER), HBNI, Off Campus Centre, Bhubaneswar, India.

Anirban Dasgupta is Associate Professor in the Faculty of Economics, South Asian University, New Delhi, India.

Anup Kumar Das is Assistant Professor in the Department of Economics, Rajiv Gandhi University, Itanagar, India.

Arindam Laha is Assistant Professor in the Department of Commerce, University of Burdwan, Burdwan, India.

Bibhunandini Das is Assistant Professor in the School of Management, Centurion University of Technology and Management, Bhubaneswar, India.

Binoy Goswami is Assistant Professor in the Faculty of Economics, South Asian University, New Delhi, India.

Hiranya K. Nath is Professor in the Department of Economics and International Business, College of Business Administration, Sam Houston State University, Huntsville, USA.

Jitu Tamuli is Assistant Professor in the Department of Economics, T.H.B. College, Jamugurihat, India.

Kiril Tochkov is Associate Professor in the Department of Economics, Texas Christian University, Fort Worth, USA.

Kirtti Ranjan Paltasingh is Assistant Professor in the Department of Economics, SMVD University, Jammu, India.

Mofidul Hassan is Assistant Professor in the Department of Economics, Pandit Deendayal Upadhyaya Adarsha Mahavidyalaya, Bongaigaon, India.

M. P. Bezbaruah is Professor in the Department of Economics, Gauhati University, Guwahati, India.

Mrinal Kanti Dutta is Professor in the Department of Humanities and Social Sciences, Indian Institute of Technology, Guwahati, India.

Murali Kallummal is Associate Professor at the Centre for WTO Studies, Indian Institute of Foreign Trade, New Delhi, India.

Phanindra Goyari is Professor in the School of Economics, University of Hyderabad, Hyderabad, India.

Pravat Kumar Kuri is Professor in the Department of Economics, University of Burdwan, Burdwan, India.

Rajib Sutradhar is Assistant Professor at the OKD Institute of Social Change and Development, Guwahati, India.

Raju Mandal is Assistant Professor in the Department of Economics, Assam University, Silchar, India.

Smitha Francis is an economist based in New Delhi.

Surya Bhushan is Associate Professor at the Development Management Institute (DMI), Patna, India.

Udayan Rathore is Research Associate at the Indira Gandhi Institute of Development Research, Mumbai, India.

Upasak Das is a Post-Doctoral Fellow at the University of Pennsylvania and primarily based in New Delhi.

Preface

A good part of the recent literature on India's agriculture sector naturally dwells upon the 'agrarian crisis' which drew wide public attention from its manifestation in the form of a spate of suicides among farmers reported from several parts of the country since the mid-1990s. Many of these writings sought to locate the root cause of the crisis in the market-oriented economic reform introduced in 1991. In viewing the phenomenon as a fall out of the 'neoliberal' reforms, these works often overlooked the fact that the genesis of the problem lied in the policies that made the Green Revolution a success back in the late 1960s through the 1970s. Further, few studies appreciated the resilience and innovativeness displayed by India's farm sector in surviving through the decade of crisis, diversifying in response to changing consumer preference and largely recovering its lost ground to be back on the path of growth. To put the record straight, it was therefore necessary to look closely at the entire life cycle of the crisis, from its germination in the womb of the Green Revolution, to its aggravation due to absence of timely policy corrections, to its accentuation in the process of economic reforms and finally its mitigation initiated by inner dynamism in the sector and aided by supportive policy measures from the government. Motivated by this necessity, this book is an attempt to capture and comprehend the passage of Indian agriculture through the stresses and strains of the post-Green Revolution period and assess its preparedness to meet the impending opportunities and challenges.

The first task in the direction of preparing the manuscript was to mobilize a team of writers to deal with the different components of the whole story. Instead of approaching established senior scholars, we decided to explore relatively young authors who have made their marks in the respective sub-themes by publishing significant works in professional journals and volumes. Most of the people approached bought into the idea readily and enthusiastically agreed to join the team. The formation of the team actually reduced our task of compiling the volume by half. The rest of the work was the usual process of drafting of the chapters by the authors, peer review of drafts, revising and refining the drafts in light of reviewers' comments and finally arranging the chapters in a logical sequence.

Soon after independence from colonial rule in 1947, India adopted economic planning as the means of developing quickly through a programme of rapid industrialization. As the limited foreign exchange reserves had to be earmarked for procuring capital goods for the industrialization program, import of consumer goods was virtually prohibited, except for very basic goods, namely food grains. Though institutional reforms in the rural economy contributed to some agricultural growth through area expansion, India remained a chronically food-shortage economy until the Green Revolution changed it all. When the opportunity to break the productivity barrier arrived in the mid-1960s in the form of the technological breakthrough of high-yielding variety seeds, India went all out to turn the opportunity into a revolution in agricultural production. In no time the chronically food-shortage country was turned into one that was not only self-sufficient but also producing a surplus of wheat and rice. This remarkable achievement of independent India of course came with some undesirable consequences. Environmentally, the price came in the forms of degradation of agro-ecology and depletion of soil and water reserves, stoppage of which required corrective measures. Socio-politically, the Green Revolution created a rich and powerful farmer class that would not let such measures to go through. Finally, when India had to virtually abandon the state-controlled economic regime and adopt a market-oriented, liberalized and globalized economic system, the ballooning subsidies inherited from the previous regime were rendered unsustainable. Hard steps followed. As the negative externalities of the input overuse got internalized, the resulting escalation of the private costs of cultivation had telling effects on farmers' incomes. Farmers' woes were further compounded by decay in the state-provided extension service and by exposure to greater international competition following activation of agreements on opening up trade in agricultural commodities. The resulting tragedy of a large number of farmers resorting to suicides, especially during 1995 to 2004, has since been extensively studied and discussed. However, what has escaped the attention of most discussants is the resilience of the farming community and the endogenous innovation of institutions in the rural and agrarian economy that have not only helped the community to survive through the deep crisis but have enabled it to recover the lost ground almost on its own. The time is now right for nursing these positive elements with enabling institutions and environments in order to make Indian agriculture robust and sturdy enough to stand up to the challenges of the twenty-first century and to secure for Indian farmers a dignified living out of farming.

This, in short, is the underlying theme that weaves through the chapters of the book. Individual authors, being specialists in the sub-theme they have written on, have often gone beyond this broad strand into many finer details and implications thereof. We as editors have refrained from over-using our discretion to curb such details. Such details, we feel, have enriched the book with added content without seriously digressing from the flow of the basic narrative. However, conclusions and opinions documented in the individual chapters are, in the strict sense, those of the respective authors and not necessarily of the editors.

It was pleasure working with this relatively young group of chapter writers. We appreciate their contribution, and we thank each one of them for their active support and full cooperation. We are grateful to the publisher for having faith in us to come up with the manuscript in the agreed-on time frame. We would like to put on the record our special appreciation for the support and encouragement of Samantha Phua and Yongling Lam in carrying out and completing the work.

We dedicate the book to the reading public with the expectation that researchers, policy makers and others interested in Indian agriculture will find it useful and worthwhile reading.

Editors

1 Introduction

Binoy Goswami

Indian agriculture has traversed a long distance since the time the country became independent. The agriculture sector at the time of independence was characterized by acute food shortages resulting at times in crippling famines. To feed her people, India had to depend overwhelming on imports of food grains during that time. Thanks to the Green Revolution (GR) introduced in the mid-1960s, India became food self-sufficient in the mid-'70s and reached a stage by the mid-'90s when it had an unmanageable stock of food grains. The coming of age of Indian agriculture in terms of food grains production is reflected in the increase of its production over the past few decades. The production of food grains increased from a mere 51 million tonnes in 1950–51 to a mammoth 264 million tonnes in 2014–15. Similar trends could be observed in the cases of many non-food grain crops also (Narayanamoorthy, 2017). Today, India is not only self-sufficient in food grains, it is an exporter of food grains to many countries as well.

Notwithstanding the occasional hiccups, the increase in agricultural production has been largely steady. The sector itself, however, has undergone many changes over time. For instance, yield-improving technology was the primary contributor to agricultural growth in 1980s. In the 1990s, however, diversification from low to high-value crops (resulting in considerable changes in the cropping pattern) was as important a contributor to growth of the sector as technology was. In fact, the importance of technology as a determinant of growth in 1990s declined relative to the 1980s. In the subsequent decade from 2000–01 to 2009–10, the relative importance of area, yield, price and crop diversification as determinants of agricultural production and growth were further altered (Birthal et al., 2013). Meanwhile, formal and informal institutions governing agricultural production, especially factor markets such as the water market and rental markets for land and agricultural capital goods, have evolved considerably, arguably to the benefit of small and marginal farmers.

Significant changes have occurred in the sphere of infrastructure as well, especially in the cases of agricultural markets and irrigation. The unfolding of globalization, changes in the consumption basket due to increases in income and growing urbanization, speedy improvement and diffusion of information and communication technology, and changing roles of the state and private sector have altered the landscape of agricultural marketing in recent time in India

(Rao et al., 2017). Irrigation, which is a crucial component of infrastructure, has undergone changes as well. Not only the nature and forms of irrigation, but also its management have changed over the years (Mukherji, 2016).

Not all the changes, however, have been positive. The agriculture sector itself and the people engaged therein have confronted certain challenges. Though the GR helped the country to overcome shortages of food, it also created income disparities between large and small farmers and production imbalances between regions and among crops. However, by the time the benefits of green revolution became more widespread, the unintended consequences of the technology, including falling groundwater table and increasing salinity of soil, among other effects, became perceptible. Moreover, the technology that had driven the growth of the sector in the 1980s started showing signs of fatigue by the early 1990s, and productivity of the GR crops, especially rice, stagnated. Meanwhile, the Government of India adopted a structural reform programme in 1991 which forced the government to exercise fiscal restraints. Following these economic and financial reforms, the state's support of agriculture was also reoriented and indeed reduced in some areas. Subsidies on several inputs were withdrawn, though gradually and partially. Falling yields, rising private costs of cultivation due to withdrawal of subsidies and some other factors reduced returns from cultivation. The financial condition of the farmers worsened and their indebtedness increased. A sizable number of them were even pushed to the edge and ended their lives by killing themselves (Reddy and Misra, 2009). Until the late 1990s, however, farmers' suicides did not receive adequate attention. Scholars and policy makers started taking note of the agrarian stress and farmers' distress only in recent years, when the suicides began again (Narayanamoorthy, 2017).

The stress on the farmers was compounded in the early 1990s due to the implementation of the Agreement on Agriculture (AoA) under the Uruguay round of General Agreement on Tariffs and Trade (GATT), which exposed the farmers to global competition. Among Indian farmers, oil seed and spice growers have been the hardest hit by globalization. Preparing farmers to adjust to the World Trade Organization (WTO) regime will continue to be a challenge for Indian policy makers. In the meantime, agriculture in India, as in the rest of the world, will have to deal with uncertainties accentuated by climate change. Scholars have already warned that a warmer India with erratic rainfall does not auger well for the yield of rice, which is the leading food grain in terms of area sown and output (Gupta et al., 2014). New technological breakthroughs may open up opportunities for the sector but are likely to pose new challenges too.

An in-depth analysis of the changes that Indian agriculture has undergone and the challenges the sector and the farmers have confronted since the introduction of GR, as well as a discussion of measures to be undertaken to overcome the challenges, are presented in this collection of 14 chapters.

Chapter 2 presents an overview of the performance of Indian agriculture in the post-GR period. The chapter covers six major aspects of the sector: (i) growth of agricultural gross domestic product (GDP) and changes in the share of agriculture in India's GDP and employment generation over time; (ii) changes in the composition of the agriculture sector; (iii) changes in cropping pattern and crop diversification; (iv) capital formation or investment in agriculture; (v) costs and profitability in crops cultivation; and (vi) terms of trade between agriculture and non-agriculture sectors.

One significant change that Indian agriculture has witnessed over the last five decades is a change in the ownership of land holdings. While the share of marginal-size land holdings increased from 52.98 per cent in 1971–72 to 75.41 per cent in 2013, the shares of all other size categories declined. The shares of small, semi-medium, medium and large classes fell from 15.49 per cent, 11.89 per cent, 7.88 per cent and 2.12 per cent in 1971–72 to 10 per cent, 5.01 per cent, 1.93 per cent and 0.24 per cent in 2013, respectively. In terms of area owned, however, while the marginal, small and semi-medium categories gained over time, the medium and large size classes lost. The marginal, small and semi-medium categories improved their shares in owned area from 9.76 per cent, 14.68 per cent and 21.92 per cent in 1971–72 to 29.75 per cent, 23.53 per cent and 22.07 per cent in 2013 respectively. On the other hand, the share of medium size class declined from 30.73 per cent in 1971–72 to 18.83 per cent in 2013, and that of the large size class fell from 22.91 per cent to 5.81 per cent during the same time (Government of India, 2013). The improvement in the shares of the marginal and small size classes and the fall in the share of the large size class is noteworthy. Though farmers even within the same size class of operational holding across states may not be exactly comparable, Das (2015) has shown that the top 15 percentiles of holdings have lost shares and the bottom 50 percentiles have gained shares in operational landholdings over time. These developments suggest that despite all the land reforms measures not being implemented fully and effectively, there may not be enough land to redistribute and bring all units to a minimum threshold size. Redistribution may thus result in pulling down all rather than pulling up the marginal size class. Therefore, rather than redistribution, what assumes more significance in today's context is improving farmers' access to land through an efficiently functioning land rental market. Chapter 3, in this context, explores certain aspects of the agricultural land rental market in India. The chapter analyzes changes in the extent and pattern of the agricultural land lease market over time, determinants of leasing decisions of rural households and their implications for rural development. Some major changes in the extent and pattern of the leasing arrangements which took place in recent time have been reported. An analysis in this chapter, based on the 70th round of NSSO data, suggests that there will be more supply of land in the rental market in the future. Consequently, certain reforms in the existing tenancy laws have been suggested in order to ensure efficient and equitable use of these lands.

Besides the land rental market, two other emerging agricultural factor markets in the country are water market and rental market of capital goods. These factor markets are important mainly because they correct imbalances in resource endowments across rural households. Besides, factors of agricultural production being complementary, it is necessary that these markets develop simultaneously (Goswami, 2012). Chapter 4 discusses various issues related to the functioning of the water market and the rental market of capital goods. The discussion in the chapter shows that these markets, besides preforming the usual function of correcting imbalances in factor endowments, enhance the extent of mechanization of agriculture and encourage adoption of production- and productivity-enhancing practices. Further, it appears that by benefitting small and marginal farmers the most, these markets have replaced India's long-pending agrarian reform in terms of consolidation of holdings. These markets are, however, not free from imperfection, and hence intervention for their regulation is desired.

While land, water, machinery and so on are important factors in agricultural production, credit and insurance play enabling roles. Agriculture being susceptible to the vagaries of nature in India, insurance is absolutely crucial. In fact, the importance of insurance may be even higher in the future than it is now as uncertainties stemming from climate change are expected to increase. Moreover, eliminating the credit constraint may not be sufficient to induce a farmer to make an appropriate amount of investment if the risks are not insured. Instead, the right mix of credit and insurance can result in an efficient level of investment by a farmer. Chapter 5 develops a conceptual framework to establish this point. The analysis in this chapter suggests that interlinked credit and insurance contracts not only incentivize the farmers to make an efficient amount of investment, but also improve contract enforcement and facilitate development of markets for credit and insurance by mutually reinforcing each other. The chapter also traces the evolution of crop insurance schemes in India. Special emphasis is given to the critical evaluation of the National Agricultural Insurance Scheme in light of the conceptual framework developed in the chapter.

The importance of such infrastructure as markets and irrigation for agricultural growth requires no explanation. The deployment and diffusion of GR technology and the subsequent tremendous growth in agricultural production and productivity were enabled to a large extent by irrigation infrastructure. The market plays a crucial role in the post-harvest season. One of the factors that determines returns on investment in agriculture is the price received for produce, which in turn is related to, among others, available marketing opportunities. As discussed above, these two components of infrastructure in India have undergone remarkable changes over the past few decades. Chapter 6 captures the changes in the sphere of agricultural marketing, and chapter 7 analyzes the evolution of the irrigation sector. Chapter 6 briefly reviews policies related to and performances of agricultural markets in the pre-reform period and focuses in greater detail on agricultural marketing policies in the post-reform period. In particular, it focuses on the implications for smallholders of the rapid diffusion of supermarkets. The chapter concludes with policy recommendations that draw upon lessons from other countries that share similar characteristics, particularly China and Indonesia, to prepare a roadmap for a more inclusive and competitive agricultural marketing system in India. Chapter 7 examines the trend of growth in irrigated area across sources and across states, as well as issues in the management of irrigation infrastructure. It has been found that while there has been tremendous growth in irrigated area in the country following the Green Revolution, significant spatial variations exist in this regard. The chapter also outlines various challenges, both technical and institutional, which have been confronted while developing and managing the irrigation infrastructure. Some such challenges include underutilization of created irrigation potential, reduced public investment in recent decades and participation of stakeholders in irrigation management.

Once enabling institutions and adequate infrastructure are in place, technological development can take the growth of agriculture to the next level. Given the stagnating yields of some of the major crops, a technological breakthrough in Indian agriculture is extremely desirable. However, a mere breakthrough will not suffice if the technology does not get diffused through its adoption by the farmers. Chapter 8 asks (i) who uses technology in Indian agriculture, (ii) what are the determinants of technology use in agriculture, (iii) how do farmers obtain information on modern technology and (iv) is technology use limited to specific crops. The chapter uses the National Sample Survey 70th-round data to answer these questions.

While appropriate domestic institutions and good infrastructure are of utmost importance for the growth and development of the agriculture sector, in today's globalized world, the performance of the sector and of the people engaged therein also depends on the extent to which the sector is exposed to global competition through international trade. As discussed above, implementation of the AoA under the Uruguay round of GATT in the mid-1990s did cause some turbulence in Indian agriculture, though it created some opportunities as well. Chapter 9 attempts to understand the linkage between trade liberalization and agricultural production through the mediating impacts of trade composition changes and price movements. It presents evidence of the shifts in the crop mix in Indian agriculture along with the aggregate trade patterns pertaining to agricultural commodities. While there is evidence of increased production in the case of the major export crops, it is found that domestic prices for the majority of India's top agricultural exports remain lower than their export prices. Thus farmers may not gain substantially, even for export crops with thriving international demand. It is therefore suggested that the institutional arrangements in the Indian agricultural marketing system that prevent farmers from obtaining remunerative prices need a long-overdue restructuring.

Chapters 10–13 discuss the challenges confronting Indian agriculture and farmers. Since the early 1990s, Indian agriculture has been in a crisis for the better part of the time, a symptom of which is the high rate of farmers' suicide. Chapter 10 recounts the factors that went into brewing this agrarian crisis. Discussion in the chapter argues that the seeds of the crisis were in the very policy measures that earlier made the GR a resounding success. As far as farmers' suicides are concerned, a closer examination of the data, however, reveals that the suicide rate among farmers has generally been lower than that among non-farmers, notwithstanding the fact that the suicide rate was unusually high among farmers during 1995–2004. The chapter suggests policy options for strengthening farmers' natural resilience in order to enable them to cope better with the uncertainties they typically encounter.

Given the agrarian crisis, it is not surprising that between 2001 and 2011, 8.9 million cultivators left cultivation (Venkatanarayana and Naik, 2013). Chapter 11, using nationally representative data for the years 1993–94 and 2011–12, analyzes the age profile of working individuals and examines whether they are more or less likely to be engaged in agriculture and allied areas now as compared to the period when the Indian economy underwent the first round of economic reforms. It has been found that the likelihood of younger people being engaged in agriculture than that of older ones declined over the time period considered in the study.

One unintended outcome of the GR that became discernible as early as in the 1980s is the environmental consequences of the HYV seeds and agro-chemical–based production package. The environmental challenges have in fact assumed alarming proportions, especially in the locations where the GR was first introduced. Chapter 12 analyzes the nature and magnitude of the environmental consequences of the GR in terms of soil degradation, depletion in the ground-water table and impacts of pesticides use on human health. The chapter stresses that more calibrated policy responses are required to avoid these problems.

In the future, as in other parts of the globe, climate change is going to pose serious challenges to agriculture in India. Chapter 13 is devoted to a discussion of the impacts of climate variables on agriculture. The chapter reviews the extant literature on the impacts of climate changes on agriculture, focusing on studies that have been conducted in India. Applying non-parametric median regression technique to state-level time series data on average yield of rice and wheat, and on temperature and rainfall from 1968 to 2001, the chapter investigates the impacts of changes in these climate variables on rice and wheat yields. The results indicate that rising temperature has a significant negative impact and rising rainfall variability has a significant positive impact on the average rice yield. Furthermore, an increase in temperature variability over the crop year appears to have a significant positive impact on wheat yield.

Given the changes that Indian agriculture has undergone and the challenges the sector has faced over the past few decades as discussed in chapters 2–13, chapter 14 discusses what the way forward ought to be. Multifaceted policy interventions required to make Indian agriculture strong enough to stand up to the impending challenges of the 21st century are discussed in this chapter. The discussion suggests that policy interventions should aim at creating an enabling environment by supporting the relevant infrastructure and institutions. However, honouring farmers by ensuring a decent and dignified living out of farming should be the end goal of any policy intervention. Fortunately, in the policy discourses now, there is a discernible shift of emphasis from increasing production at any cost, for which the country has had to pay dearly in the past, to raising farmers' income and welfare. The change is opportune and welcome.

The mandate of this book is to document the changes and challenges that Indian agriculture have confronted since the introduction of the GR. Without a claim of being exhaustive, an attempt has been made to cover most of the major issues. While writing the essays, the contributors have utilized their research experience of many years in their respective areas. More importantly, findings from aggregate data have been complemented by insights from the field wherever possible. Thus, the policy suggestions provided in the book are rooted in the agro-economic realities of the countryside. It is expected that the book will be a useful reference for anybody with an interest in Indian agriculture.

References

Birthal, P. S., Joshi, P. K., Negi, D. S. and Agarwal, S., 2013. *Changing Sources of Growth in Indian Agriculture: Implications for Regional Priorities for Accelerating Agricultural Growth*. IFPRI Discussion Paper.

Das, D., 2015. Changing Distribution of Land and Assets in Indian Agriculture. *Review of Radical Political Economics*, 47(3), pp. 412–423.

Goswami, B., 2012. *Economic Implications of Tenancy: A Study in Assam's Agrarian Set-Up*. Unpublished PhD Thesis submitted to Gauhati University, Guwahati, Assam.

Government of India, 2013. *Household Ownership and Operational Holdings in India*. NSS Report No. 571, 70th Round, National Sample Survey Organization, Ministry of Statistics.

Gupta, S., Sen, P. and Srinivasan, S., 2014. Impact of Climate Change on Indian Economy: Evidence From Food Grain Yield. *Climate Change Economics*, 5(2), pp. 1–29.

Mukherji, A., 2016. Evolution of Irrigation Sector. *Economic and Political Weekly*, LI(52), pp. 44–47.

Narayanamoorthy, A., 2017. Farm Income in India: Myths and Realities. *Indian Journal of Agricultural Economics*, 72(1), pp. 48–75.

Rao, N. C., Sutradhar, R. and Reardon, T., 2017. Disruptive Innovations in Food Value Chains and Small Farmers in India. *Indian Journal of Agricultural Economics*, 72(1), pp. 24–47.

Reddy, D. N. and Misra, S., 2009. Agriculture in the Reforms Regime. In Reddy, D. N. and Misra, S. (eds.), *Agrarian Crisis in India*, Oxford University Press, New Delhi, Ch. 1.

Venkatanarayana, M. and Naik, V. S., 2013. *Growth and Structure of Workforce in India: An Analysis of Census 2011 Data*. MPRA Paper No. 48003, available at https://mpra.ub.uni-muenchen.de/48003/, accessed 23/03/2017.

2 Indian agriculture after the Green Revolution

An overview

Kirtti Ranjan Paltasingh, Phanindra Goyari and Kiril Tochkov

1 Introduction

After independence in 1947, Indian agriculture experienced two phases – the successful Green Revolution, which made the nation food grain self-sufficient during 1968–1978, and more significantly, the agrarian crisis after economic liberalization. On the eve of independence, the country was suffering from food shortages, particularly due to poor productivity. The Green Revolution initiated in India in 1964–65 aimed mainly at achieving self-sufficiency in food grains. Initially, the success of the Green Revolution was observed most noticeably in the highly irrigated areas of India, especially in Punjab and Haryana in the northwestern region. The success of the Green Revolution was made possible by the introduction of high-yielding varieties of seeds, increased use of chemical fertilizers, irrigation and other modern farming methods. This crop revolution[1] spread to other regions of the country over time and resulted in a spectacular growth of major cereals like wheat and rice at the expense of coarse grain and pulse crops during the late 1960s and early 1970s (Gulati and Kelley, 1999). However, Indian agriculture faced several problems starting from 1980s in the form of degradation of natural and environmental resources like soil and water, rising cost of cultivation and declining profitability, dwindling of farm productivity and so on. The extreme manifestation of the crisis was a spate of farmers' suicides (Bezbaruah, 2014). Neo-liberal economic reforms which India initiated in 1991 and the new environment after the establishment of the World Trade Organization (WTO) in 1994 brought both new challenges and opportunities for the agriculture sector. While adjusting to such changing circumstances, Indian agriculture has experienced changes in many dimensions.

This chapter gives an overview of the performance of the agriculture sector in India after the Green Revolution. The chapter is organized into eight sections. Section 2 describes the growth performance of the agriculture sector in comparison to the overall economic growth of the country. A discussion on variations in agricultural growth across regions and states is also presented in this section. Section 3 deals with compositional changes within agriculture which have occurred over time. Changes in cropping patterns and the extent of crop diversification across regions are discussed in section 4. The changes in investment in the agriculture sector over time are described in section 5. Section 6 discusses the cost of cultivation and income from farming. Section 7 analyzes the trend in terms of trade between the agriculture and non-agriculture sectors since the 1950s. The conclusion is in the last section.

2 Growth trends in Indian agriculture

2.1 The trend in overall growth of GDP and agricultural GDP

The Indian economy was growing at around 2 per cent annually immediately after partition. However, after 1950 with the adoption of economic planning, the growth rate of the Indian economy has risen significantly, as shown in Figure 2.1. India's average annual real GDP growth rate was 6.52 per cent during the post-liberalization period (1991–92 to 2013–14), compared to 4.06 per cent during the pre-liberalization time (1951–52 to 1990–91). During the early phase of the Green Revolution (1967–68 to 1980–81), the average annual growth rate of real GDP was 3.9 per cent, which increased to 5.4 per cent during the period of wider dissemination of the modern agricultural technology (1981–82 to 1990–91). It further rose to 5.7 per cent during the first decade of economic reforms and reached 7.7 per cent during the second decade of reforms. The period 2011–2014 showed a decline in the growth rate compared to previous sub-periods.

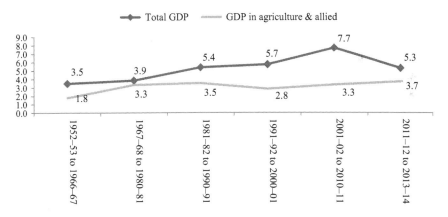

Figure 2.1 Annual growth rate of India's GDP and GDP from agriculture and allied sectors during 1952–53 to 2013–14 (in %)

Notes: (i) GDP data at factor cost at constant prices of 2004–05. (ii) Growth rate is average of annual growth rates in each sub-period.

Sources: Compiled from the CSO database, October 31, 2014, and Planning Commission, Govt. of India (Databook for PC: 22 December 2014, pp. 10–11).

While the overall growth of the Indian economy has been remarkable, all the sectors did not grow impressively. The growth rate of agriculture was lower than the overall growth rate in every sub-period, as shown in Figure 2.1. Agricultural GDP growth did increase from around 2 per cent in the 1950s to 3.33 per cent during the Green Revolution period (1967–68 to 1980–81) and to an even higher level (3.52 per cent) during the later sub-period. However, since the beginning of economic reforms until 2010–11, the growth rate of agricultural GDP slowed down. The recent sub-period, 2011–2014, showed marginal revival as compared to previous sub-periods, but the rate is still lower than the overall GDP growth rate.

As a consequence of slower growth in agriculture compared to the economy as a whole, the share of agriculture in the country's total GDP has been declining sharply in the post-reform period. At current prices, the share of agriculture and allied sectors in overall GDP was 51.81 per cent in 1950–51 (compared to 14.16 per cent for industry and 33.25 per cent for the services sector). It declined to 29 per cent in 1991–92, and then further to 22 per cent in 2000–01. At 2011–12 prices, composition shares of agriculture and allied sectors, industry and services were 16.11 per cent, 31.37 per cent, and 52.52 per cent, respectively, for the year 2014–15. The fall in the contribution of the agriculture sector to the total GDP of the country would not be a problem had the proportion of people engaged in this sector also declined.[2] In fact, the decline in the share of workforce engaged in the agriculture sector (cultivators and agricultural labourers) has been much slower than the decline in the sector's contribution to the country's total GDP over time. For example, from 1980–81 to 2010–11, the share of the agricultural sector in the overall GDP declined by 17 percentage points (from 35.39 per cent in 1980–81 to 18.21 per cent in 2010–11); however, the share of the workforce engaged in agriculture as a part of the total main workforce declined by only 13.7 percentage points (from 68.1 per cent in 1981 to 54.6 per cent in 2011). This implies that the average labour productivity in agriculture has remained at a low level, and other sectors of the economy have not been able to absorb labour from agriculture. As per the countrywide "Situation Assessment Survey of Agricultural Households" conducted by the National Sample Survey Office (NSSO) for the 2012–13 crop year, about 58 per cent of rural households in India were engaged in farming activity, which, in turn, contributed only about 60 per cent to their average total monthly incomes (Damodaran, 2014).

2.2 *Agricultural growth across regions and states*

Agricultural growth performance has varied across different regions of the country over time due to differences in agro-climatic conditions, levels of adoption of modern technology, procurement policies and market conditions. Birthal et al. (2013) analyzed the performance of the crop sector across four regions of the country for the period 1980–2010. They found that while the western and southern regions performed consistently well throughout the period of study, the northern and eastern regions did well during the 1980s and 1990s but poorly during 2000–01 and 2009–10. In the northern region, the annual compound growth rate of the real value of crop output increased from 3 per cent in the

1980s to 3.5 per cent in the 1990s, but then fell to only 1.8 per cent during 2009–10. The corresponding figures for the eastern region are 3.7 per cent in the 1980s, 3.3 per cent in the 1990s and 1.8 per cent during 2000–01 and 2009–10. On the other hand, the annual compound growth rate in real value of crop output in the western region increased from 2.6 per cent in 1980s to 4.4 per cent in 1990s and then further to 5.7 per cent in the subsequent decade, and the corresponding growth rate has been slightly above 3 per cent in the southern region throughout the period of the study. The study further shows that while growth in crop output in the rice-wheat dominated regions, particularly in the northern region, has been technology led, the western and the southern regions depended more on crop diversification as a growth strategy. Price effect also played an important role in the northern and eastern regions.

Sawant and Achuthan (1995) examined the growth trend of agricultural GDP for 15 major states. They found that all states (except Andhra Pradesh, Maharashtra and Gujarat) exhibited an acceleration of agricultural GSDP from period I (1968–69 to 1981–82) to period II (1981–82 to 1990–91). In terms of food grain production, three southern states (Andhra Pradesh, Karnataka and Kerala) and two western states (Gujarat and Maharashtra) recorded a deceleration in growth rate of food grain production from period I to period II. For the post-reform period, Mathur et al. (2006) estimated the growth rate of the value of food grain production instead of quantity of production at 1993–94 prices. They found that many states performed well, but states like Madhya Pradesh, Tamil Nadu, Gujarat, Karnataka and Maharashtra recorded negative growth during the study period. Chand and Parappurathu (2012) compared the growth rate of agricultural net state domestic product from 1999–2000 to 2008–09 at 2004–05 prices. They found that Gujarat made remarkable progress in the 10-year period, particularly after 2002–03. Other states that registered more than 4 per cent growth rates are Chhattisgarh, Andhra Pradesh, Maharashtra, Rajasthan and Madhya Pradesh. States like Gujarat, Maharashtra and Andhra Pradesh, which recorded a deceleration in food grain output and in the share of agriculture in net state domestic product, performed really well, particularly after 2003–04.

An important feature of the post-2000 growth pattern in the agricultural sector is that the growth of production has been faster in moderately and even in relatively low-irrigated states such as Madhya Pradesh, Bihar, Odisha, Andhra Pradesh, Maharashtra, Gujarat and Assam than in the highly irrigated states of Punjab, Uttar Pradesh and West Bengal. As a result, there has been a regional diversification of total agricultural production in the country (Bezbaruah, 2014 and 12th Five Year Plan document, vol. 2, Government of India, 2013).

3 Compositional change in agriculture

3.1 Performance of the constituting sub-sectors of agriculture

Broadly, the agriculture sector includes sub-sectors of crops, livestock, forestry and fisheries. In Indian agriculture sector, crops have dominated in terms of the income share as compared to other sub-sectors. However, the share of crops in agricultural income has been declining over the period, particularly after 1990-91 (Figure 2.2). On the other hand, the combined share of incomes from livestock, forestry and fisheries has been increasing. For example, the share of income from crops in total income from the agriculture sector was 75 per cent during the triennium ending (TE) 1990–91 but declined to 65 per cent during the TE 2002–03. On the other hand, the share of income from livestock increased from 17 per cent to 25 per cent, an increase of 8 percentage points during the same period. Such a change in composition has implications for patterns of resource requirements in future growth. These sub-sectors are complementary to each other; the growth of one may help the other and vice versa. For example, growth in the livestock sector may require less land and irrigation directly per unit of GDP contribution as compared to conventional crops. But, growth in the live-stock sector will require the cultivation of more fodder crops.

Livestock and fishing also recorded higher growth rates over time since the Green Revolution period as compared to all crops in terms of value of out-put (Table 2.1). For example, the values of output of livestock and fishing increased from 3.3 per cent and 3.1 per cent during the Green Revolution to 4.8 per cent and 3.6 per cent respectively during the 11th plan period. The value of all crops together grew from 3 per cent to 3.4 per cent during the same period. Within all crops, the output value of horticulture crops has been growing at a faster rate than non-horticulture crops after the liberalization period.

3.2 Changes within the crop sector: food grains vs. non-food grain

Crops can be classified broadly into food grains (like rice, maize, bajra and other cereal crops, and pulses) and non-food grains (like oil seeds, fibre crops of cotton

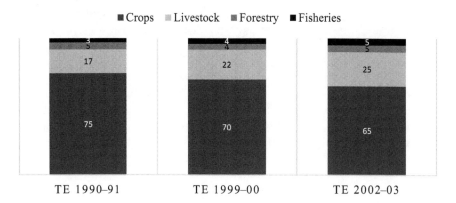

Figure 2.2 Shares of different sub-sectors in total income from agriculture in India (at current prices)

Source: Compiled from Singh et al. (2006)

Table 2.1 Growth of values of outputs of different sub-sectors within agriculture in India (at 2004–05 prices)

Sub-sectors	Pre-Green Revolution	Green Revolution	Wider coverage	Early Liberalization	9th Plan	10th Plan	11th Plan
	1951–52 to 1967–68	1968–69 to 1980–81	1981–82 to 1990–91	1991–92 to 2001–02	1997–98 to 2001–02	2002–03 to 2006–07	2007–08 to 2011–12
Non-horticulture crops	3.2	2.7	3.0	2.1	1.7	2.1	2.8
Horticulture crops	2.6	4.2	3.1	5.7	3.8	2.6	4.7
All Crops	**3.0**	**3.0**	**3.0**	**3.1**	**2.3**	**2.1**	**3.4**
Livestock	1.0	3.3	4.8	4.0	3.6	3.6	4.8
Fishing	4.7	3.1	5.7	7.1	2.7	3.3	3.6
Forestry	1.7	-0.2	0.3	0.3	2.7	1.3	2.3

Note: Growth rates are averages of annual growth rates in respective periods

Source: Compiled from the 12th Five Year Plan (2012–17), Economic Sectors, vol. 2. Planning Commission, Government of India, 2013.

and jute, plantation crops of tea and rubber, etc.). Several studies have examined the growth of the crop sector in India. Sawant and Achuthan (1995) found that growth in production of non-food grains (2.41 per cent) was marginally higher than that of food grains (2.21 per cent) during 1967–68 to 1981–82. Further, the output growth in non-food grain (4.30 per cent) was higher than that of food grain (2.92 per cent) during the second phase of the Green Revolution period (i.e., 1981–82 to 1991–92). Mathur et al. (2006) estimated that the growth rate of the real value of food grains was negative at –3 per cent during the 1990s and –5 per cent during 1999 to 2002–03. Deokar and Shetty (2014) also estimated that during the post-reform period of 1995–96 to 2004–05, the production of total food grain grew at a low rate of 0.92 per cent and area under food grains production experienced a negative growth rate (–0.24 per cent). Balakrishnan (2000) found that growth rates of both food grains and non-food grains came down from 3.54 per cent and 4.84 per cent, respectively, during the 1980s to 1.66 per cent and 2.36 per cent, respectively, during the 1990s. Studies (Bhalla and Singh, 2009; Vaidyanathan, 2010) attributed the slowdown in the 1990s and early 2000s to a number of factors, such as technology fatigue, low public investment in research and developmental activities, gradual breakdown of extension networks and so on.

Since 2004–05 onwards, however, the growth rate of food grain production experienced a slight acceleration. During the eight-year period from 2004–05 to 2013–14, the growth rate of total food grain output was 3.43 per cent, which was mainly contributed by yield growth. The revival in food grain production from 2005–06 onwards is due to the high growth in low-irrigation areas rather than in high-irrigation and high-productivity areas (Deokar and Shetty, 2014). The recovery after 2004–05 onwards is also attributed to new initiatives by the government in the form of Rashtriya Krishi Vikas Yojana (2007), National Food Security Mission (2007) and a special emphasis on certified seed production.

It may be mentioned in this context that the importance of various sources of growth in the crop sector has changed over time. Improvement in yield was the main source of growth in the crop sector in the 1980s. In the 1990s, the importance of yield fell, and diversification towards high-value crops became as important a source of growth as yield. Price also became an important source of growth. In the subsequent decade, notwithstanding a marginal decline in its contribution to the growth of crop output, diversification continued to be an important source. The contribution of yield, however, improved. Interestingly, area expansion also appeared to be an important source of growth in the crop output in this period (Birthal et al., 2013).

4 Changes in cropping pattern and crop diversification

The term 'cropping pattern' is generally defined as the share of various crops in the gross cropped area of a region at a particular point of time, usually one year. Table 2.2 shows the cropping pattern of India for the triennium ending (TE) average figures of areas under various crops during 1960–2013.

Table 2.2 Cropping pattern in India during 1960–2013 (% of gross cropped area)

Crop/Groups	TE 1960–61	TE 1970–71	TE 1980–81	TE 1990–91	TE 2000–01	TE 2007–08	TE 2012–13
Rice	22.33	23.02	23.18	23.00	23.82	22.57	21.99
Wheat	8.50	10.42	12.98	13.04	14.28	14.18	15.69
Coarse cereals	26.35	28.48	25.25	20.48	16.17	15.14	13.00
Total cereals	61.10	61.93	60.41	56.53	54.27	51.88	50.62
Total pulses	15.60	13.50	13.23	12.94	11.49	11.93	11.30
Total food grains	76.70	75.54	73.67	69.47	65.32	63.52	61.91
Total oil seeds	8.30	9.85	10.11	12.51	12.96	13.93	14.97
Groundnut	3.30	4.42	4.14	4.64	3.68	3.20	2.71
Cotton	4.30	4.70	4.27	4.08	4.70	4.68	6.11
Jute	0.40	0.42	0.51	0.39	0.45	0.41	0.40
Total fibres	5.10	5.41	5.08	4.64	5.27	5.18	6.58
Sugarcane	1.30	1.62	1.62	1.90	2.23	2.47	2.80
Tobacco	0.30	0.27	0.25	0.22	0.21	0.19	0.22
Condiments/Spices	0.90	1.04	1.23	1.32	1.52	1.55	1.70
Potatoes	–	0.31	0.43	0.51	0.69	0.76	0.85
Onions	–	–	0.14	0.17	0.24	0.36	0.28
Total fruits	2.12	2.24	2.77	3.57	4.35	5.10	5.05
Fodder crops	4.11	4.15	4.50	4.59	4.55	4.26	4.73
Total non-food grains	19.19	19.39	20.13	23.60	25.44	26.41	28.41
Gross cropped area	100	100	100	100	100	100	100

Notes: Figures are calculated by taking triennium ending (TE) average and gross cropped area.

Source: Compiled from Singh et al. (2006) and Ministry of Agriculture and Farmers Welfare, and Directorate of Economics and Statistics, Government of India (*https://data.gov.in*)

The cropping pattern in the post-Green Revolution period in India witnessed two significant changes. First, the cropping pattern changed in favour of non-food grains at the cost of food grain crops. The acreage share of non-food grains has been continuously increasing, from about 19 per cent of gross cropped area (GCA) during the 1960s to about 28 per cent during TE 2012–13. But total food grain has been witnessing a declining share of acreage over the years, from about 77 per cent of the GCA during the pre-Green Revolution period to about 62 per cent in the recent period. Second, rice, the dominant crop in India, has had almost constant acreage share at around 22 per cent of GCA. But, high-value non-food grain crops like oil seeds, spices and fruits showed increasing acreage shares, particularly in the period after 1990–91. The increase in area shares of non-food grains came mainly from the decline in area shares of coarse cereals and total pulses.

Demand side factors played an important role in the observed changes in crop mix. The change in the production mix is consistent with the change in the consumption basket. The per person consumption of food grains fell from 179 kg/year in 1983 to 141 kg/year in 2009–10. During the same period, the per capita consumption of fruits and vegetables increased from 51 kg/year to 62 kg/year. The consumption of edible oils also increased significantly during this time. Supply-side factors such as improvements in roads, modes of transportation, communication, and electricity complemented the demand-driven growth in the horticultural crops sector (Birthal et al., 2013).

Among food grains, wheat is the only crop which showed a consistently increasing area share over the years, from 10.42 per cent in TE 1970–71 to about 13 per cent in 1990–91 and further to about 16 per cent in 2012–13. The increase in area under wheat can be attributed to (i) area expansion in the 1990s in states like Madhya Pradesh, which is not traditionally a wheat growing state, (ii) assured procurement through a public distribution system and (iii) increase in the minimum support price (Birthal et al., 2013).

Among non-food grains, the increase in acreage share has been more noticeable in total oil seeds than in other crop groups, like total fibres, total fruits, total fodder and vegetables. The increase in the acreage share of oil seeds is due to the conscious efforts of the government to increase their production by providing favourable incentive and protection structures. The government of India launched the Technology Mission on Oilseeds in 1986 to increase the production of oilseeds. In 2004, another programme, the Integrated Scheme of Oilseeds, Pulses, Oil palm and Maize, was introduced in order to increase production further. At the same time, the area shares under total fruits increased consistently, from around 2 per cent in TE 1970–71 to 5 per cent in TE 2012–13. Both domestic and export demand contributed to the increase in area under fruits.

The regional variations in the cropping patterns in India are shown in Table 2.3. As evident from Table 2.3, the acreage share of non-food grains has increased over the years in all the regions. The cropping pattern is still dominated by cereals and food grains throughout the country. Given this broad national trend, the experiences in different parts of the country show some variations in

Table 2.3 Changes in cropping patterns across India: regional variations (1968–2005)

Region	Year	Cereals	Pulses	Food grains	Oil seeds	Fibres	Condiments and Spices	Others	Non-food grains
Eastern	1968	78.72	12.59	91.30	3.23	2.51	0.34	2.61	8.70
	1980	75.05	12.83	87.89	5.07	3.73	0.71	2.60	12.11
	1990	73.98	11.95	85.83	7.33	2.95	0.88	3.01	14.17
	2000	79.65	6.90	86.55	5.38	3.84	0.85	3.38	13.45
	2005	79.01	7.07	86.08	5.54	3.60	1.06	3.72	13.92
Northern	1968	68.26	15.19	83.46	4.94	7.31	0.26	4.02	16.54
	1980	72.37	10.75	83.12	5.26	9.13	0.22	2.27	16.88
	1990	74.87	7.45	82.32	5.09	10.07	0.08	2.44	17.68
	2000	83.12	1.76	84.87	4.03	8.22	0.05	2.82	15.13
	2005	80.41	1.73	82.14	6.33	8.85	0.14	2.55	17.86
Western	1968	59.98	9.72	74.64	12.03	11.94	0.53	0.86	25.36
	1980	58.14	11.02	73.64	13.13	11.20	0.73	1.30	26.36
	1990	52.17	12.88	69.42	18.94	9.12	0.78	1.75	30.58
	2000	50.07	15.47	65.54	18.75	12.35	0.78	2.58	34.46
	2005	44.93	15.99	60.92	24.94	11.03	0.66	2.45	39.08
Central	1968	63.82	18.29	82.10	12.41	1.92	0.13	3.44	17.90
	1980	66.07	15.94	82.00	12.36	1.55	0.27	3.82	18.00
	1990	63.59	16.82	80.41	12.88	1.38	0.38	4.94	19.59
	2000	60.15	15.13	75.28	16.85	1.26	0.47	6.13	24.72
	2005	58.18	16.86	75.03	16.15	1.52	0.60	6.70	24.97
South	1968	66.16	9.58	75.77	13.11	6.08	1.65	3.39	24.23
	1980	60.31	12.54	72.85	14.21	6.23	2.93	3.78	27.15
	1990	50.95	13.93	64.88	22.75	5.41	2.82	4.14	35.12
	2000	50.08	15.87	65.96	18.60	6.29	3.45	5.71	34.04
	2005	48.76	14.89	63.65	22.50	5.70	2.83	5.32	36.35

Source: Calculated from state-level data compiled by the Directorate of Economics and Statistics, Department of Agriculture and Cooperation, Ministry of Agriculture, Government of India.

the rates and patterns of crop composition changes. The eastern and northern regions still have around four-fifths of their total cropped area under cereals. In fact, there has been a 12 per cent increase in the acreage share of cereals in the northern zone, from around 68 per cent in 1968 to 80 per cent in 2005. This region comprises the two major beneficiaries of the Green Revolution, namely Punjab and Haryana. Likewise, the share of cereals in the eastern zone decreased from around 79 per cent in 1968 to 74 per cent in 1990 before rising to 79.65 per cent in 2000 and eventually falling slightly to 79.01 per cent in 2005. In the rest of the regions there has been a significant shift in the cropping patterns from cereals to non-cereals.

The changes in the cropping pattern in a particular region over time may lead to either concentration around a few crops or diversification across a larger number of crops, depending on the nature of such changes. The two major sources of growth in agriculture, area expansion and productivity growth, which served well in the past, are now plagued with some limitations. Therefore, a third alternative which may prove to be very useful in this context, at least in the short run, is to move towards diversification, particularly into high-value crops (Mandal, 2011). Moreover, Indian agriculture is characterized by risk and uncertainty, as more than two-thirds of the cultivable land is dependent on monsoon rains (Gopalappa, 1996). The farmers are often the victims of natural and market-induced risk. A diversified cropping pattern can be a useful strategy for the farmers to cope with the risk and uncertainty associated with agriculture (Shiyani and Pandya, 1998; Kumar et al., 2002). In fact, as held by Mandal (2014), farmers on

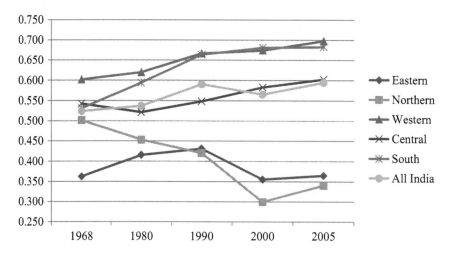

Figure 2.3 Cropping pattern diversification in India: regional variations

Note: Herfindahl index has been used. The index is computed as the sum of the squares of acreage shares of different crops in the total cropped area. The Herfindahl index is, in fact, a measure of concentration. Hence it is transformed into a diversification index by subtracting it from 1.

Source: Table 2.3.

many occasions try to cope with price and production risks in their own capacities by making adjustments in the cropping patterns across crops as well as seasons, especially when they do not have any other ex-ante coping mechanisms, like crop insurance and contract farming.

The broad cropping patterns, along with changes in and across the country (as shown in Table 2.3), have been summarized in an index of crop diversification. Figure 2.3 shows the dynamics of cropping pattern diversification in India along with its regional patterns. It is interesting to note that the northern region, which includes Punjab and Haryana, the major beneficiaries of Green Revolution, has experienced a sharp increase in concentration in their cropping pattern towards cereals (see Table 2.3). The eastern zone diversified its cropping pattern until 1990 and thereafter has concentrated towards cereals. This concentration may be attributable to the government policy of intensifying application of Green Revolution technology in the eastern region to enhance production of rice. In sharp contrast, all other regions and India as a whole have diversified their cropping pattern away from cereals toward high-value commodities.

5 Trends in agricultural investment

Investment is a key driver of growth in any sector or in the whole economy. The fixed capital formation in agriculture is considered to be more effective in enhancing agricultural output than subsidies because investment has a longer term and sustained impact on agricultural growth rate while subsidies are effective only in the short run (Mathur et al., 2006). The gross capital formation (GCF) broadly includes spending on land improvements (like fences, ditches, drains, and so on); plant, machinery, and equipment purchases; and the construction of roads, canals, railways, private residential dwellings, and commercial and industrial buildings.[3]

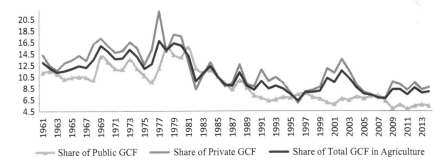

Figure 2.4 Gross capital formation (GCF) in agriculture (both public and private) as a percentage of total GCF in the Indian economy

Sources: Compiled from Ministry of Agriculture and Farmers Welfare, and Directorate of Economics and Statistics, Government of India (https://data.gov.in)

Figure 2.4 shows the trend of GCF in agriculture as a percentage of total GCF in the economy at current prices. Two important trends can be observed in the GCF in Indian agriculture: (i) an increasing trend in the share during the Green Revolution period and up to 1980, and (ii) a declining trend in share after 1980.

On the average, GCF in agriculture was about 13 per cent of total GCF in the Indian economy during the 1960s. While the share of private GCF was 14 per cent, that of public GCF was 11 per cent. During the 1970s, the GCF in agriculture (public and private) as a percentage of total GCF increased to 14.5 per cent, with private investment (16 per cent) having a larger contribution than public investment (12.4 per cent). During the 1980s, the share of overall GCF in agriculture declined to 11.2 per cent of total GCF in the economy. The decline was marked in the share of both private and public investment. Thereafter, it persistently declined in the 1990s as well as in the 2000s to 8 per cent. Although the share of both components declined, it was more noticeable in public GCF than in private GCF in recent years.

Many studies have analyzed the trend of investment in Indian agriculture.[4] Shetty (1990) examined the trend in public and private investment from 1960–61 to 1987–88 at 1980–81 prices as well as at current prices. The growth of the GCF at 1980–81 prices during the decade 1960–61 to 1970–71 was 5.2 per cent. It rose to 5.3 per cent during 1970–71 to 1980–81. But over the seven-year period from 1980–81 to 1987–88, it declined at a rate of –1.5 per cent. Singh (2014) estimated that during 1980–81 to 1989–90 the growth rate of public GCF at 1994–95 prices was negative (–4.18 per cent), while private GCF grew at a positive rate of 2.23 per cent per annum. In the subsequent decade public GCF declined (–1.85 per cent) and private GCF grew at a positive rate of 1.52 per cent. During the next decade, 2000–01 to 2009–10, total investment went up and private investment grew at a higher rate (11.55 per cent) than public investment (7.56 per cent). Thus, the hypothesis of the crowding-in effect of public investment in agriculture in India was quite apparent.[5] The deceleration of public investment in the 1980s was mainly due to large resources flowing in terms of subsidies for various inputs rather than actual investment (Singh, 2014).

Figure 2.5 shows the trend in GCF in agriculture as a percentage of agricultural GDP. Notwithstanding some fluctuations, the overall GCF in agriculture as a percentage of agricultural GDP has shown an increasing trend over the years (Figure 2.5). Between 1961 and 1976, the share of public GCF in agricultural GDP was a little above 2 per cent and increased to about 4–5 per cent during 1977–1988. Thereafter, however, it fell to slightly above 2 per cent throughout the period from 1989 to 2004. Though public GCF grew after 2005, it increased only by a percentage point until 2010. In 2014, public GCF as a percentage of agricultural GDP was only 5.40 per cent. Private investment as a percentage of GDP from agriculture stagnated at around 5–6 per cent during the 1980s and the 1990s. But after 2000 private investment as a percentage of agricultural GDP experienced a substantial jump, and the gap between private and public investments has been widening since then. Many studies

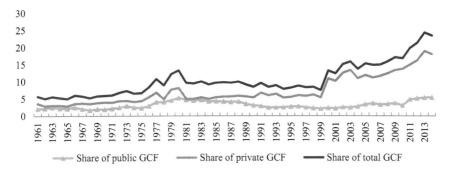

Figure 2.5 Gross capital formation (GCF) in agriculture (both public and private) as a percentage of agricultural GDP in India

Sources: Compiled from Ministry of Agriculture and Farmers Welfare, and Directorate of Economics and Statistics, Government of India (https://data.gov.in)

attribute this gap to the adoption of neo-liberal economic reforms in India which emphasized the reduction and/or withdrawal of input subsidies, reduction in public employment leading to the decline of extension services and privatization/marketization of economic activities (Patnaik, 2006; Vaidyanathan, 2006; Srinivasalu, 2015; Siddiqui, 2015).

6 Cost of cultivation and farm income

One of the important reasons behind the recent agrarian crisis in India, as argued by researchers, is the rising costs of cultivation and a declining net returns from many crops. Empirical studies on the topic include Sen and Bhatia (2004), Raghavan (2008), Dev and Rao (2010), and Narayanamoorthy (2013, 2017). Crop-specific and time-series studies show that the overall costs of cultivation, in terms of both per unit of land and output, has been rising because of the rise in input costs due to reduction/withdrawal of input subsidies after the liberalization policy. Raghavan (2008) examined the cost of cultivation of wheat in five major states of India – Haryana, Madhya Pradesh, Punjab, Rajasthan and Uttar Pradesh. He found that costs increased moderately during the 1970s and further picked up in 1980s before recording dramatic increases in the 1990s and in the first half of the 2000s. He found that the major drivers of increase in costs of cultivation are costs on inputs like fertilizer, irrigation, machine, labour and seeds.

Narayanamoorthy (2013) showed that cost C2 and cost C3 items,[6] on an average, have increased from 1975–76 to 2006–07 (post-Green Revolution period) for six crops – rice, wheat, gram, groundnut, sugarcane and cotton. In the case of paddy, the cost C2 was Rs 2193 per ha in 1975–76 and increased to Rs 10,258 per ha in 1991–92, which is a 368 per cent increase in cost. Then, in subsequent years, it rose to even higher levels, such as Rs 17,980 per ha in 1995–96,

Rs 27,043 per ha in 2001–02 and Rs 30,492 per ha in 2006–07. The cost C3 followed an almost identical pattern. At the same time, profitability of many crops has been declining because of several reasons, such as failure of the increase in the minimum support price (MSP) to keep pace with the rise in the cost of cultivation, insignificant increases in value of output due to market failure, poor infrastructure, low productivity and so on. It can be observed from Narayanamoorthy (2013) that in many years net returns for many crops were negative. Paddy, the dominant crop in India, witnessed negative profit in all years from 1975–76 to 2006–07 when cost C3 is considered, and the negative return has been rising at a faster rate since 1985–86. Cotton farmers faced huge losses in 2001–02 and 2006–07. Wheat is the only crop that can earn good net returns even though this crop also experienced negative profit in some years during the 1970s and 1980s. Wheat farmers were able to reap profits in four out of seven time points, and net returns were very high during 2001–02 and 2006–07. Overall good returns of wheat in the post-reform period occurred because of a steep increase in MSP announced by the government (Dev and Rao, 2010). Using Agricultural Costs and Prices Commission (CACP) data, Narayanamoorthy (2017) updated the same analysis for the above-mentioned six crops. Except for sugarcane, profits in relation to cost A2 were found to be very low in the triennium ending 2003–04 and in 2013–14 in both high and low productivity states. In fact, in relation to cost C2, profits were negative for paddy and groundnut and very low for the other crops considered except sugarcane.

Narayanamoorthy (2017) examined various issues related to farm income in India using both the Cost of Cultivation Survey (CCS) data from 1971–72 to 2013–14 and the Situation Assessment Survey (SAS) data for the periods 2002–03 and 2012–13. He observed that the income realized by the farmers from various crop cultivation has been very low over the years, and the year-on-year fluctuation was very high. According to SAS data at the national level, the average annual income from crop cultivation increased from Rs. 3645 in 2002–03 to Rs. 5502 in 2012–13 (at constant prices of 1986–87) per farmer household. The increase in income from crop cultivation was not very significant as compared to the income realized through the farming of animals. This implies that the farmers who are relying purely on cultivation not only earned less income but their growth of income was also lower than those who did animal husbandry. The study further found that the annual income from cultivation per farmer household varied substantially across the states in India. During 2012–13, it varied from Rs. 19,396 per household in Punjab to Rs. 1748 in West Bengal. Besides substantial variations in farm income among states, many predominantly paddy-cultivating states had much lower income than the national average.

Contrary to what usually is believed, estimates by Narayanamoorthy (2017) show that the average incomes from cultivation for the 'States Having Above National Level Irrigation' (SHANLI) are not substantially different from those of the 'States Having Below National Level Irrigation' (SHBNLI) during 2002–03 and 2012–13. During 2012–13, the average annual income from cultivation for states in the SHANLI category was Rs. 7796 per household, whereas it was

Rs. 5641 per household for states in the SHBNLI category, a difference of only about Rs. 2155. In fact, a good number of states belonging to SHBNLI category were able to earn higher income from cultivation than a few states under SHANLI category. The reason for this has been explained in Narayanamoorthy (2017, p. 55): 'Although the gross income from the crops cultivated under irrigated condition is higher because of higher productivity, increased cost of cultivation might have counterbalanced the net returns from crops cultivation'.

7 Terms of trade

The domestic terms of trade is an index which helps to understand how people engaged in one sector have fared vis-à-vis another sector. This section discusses the movement in the index of terms of trade between agriculture and non-agriculture sectors in India since 1950. Usually two variants of terms of trade are used when analyzing the terms of trade between agriculture and non-agriculture sectors: barter terms of trade (BoT) and income terms of trade (IoT). The net BoT is the ratio of the index of prices received by the agriculture sector to the index of prices paid by the sector in its transactions with the non-agriculture sector. Dividing the agricultural GDP deflator by the same for the non-agriculture sector, the gross BoT is obtained. An increase in the BoT implies that a given quantity can be bought by the agriculture sector from the non-agriculture sector by selling a lesser amount to the later. However, if the relative price of agricultural commodities increases, the amount of commodities sold by the sector may fall, and the aggregate command over non-agricultural commodities may essentially decline. In order to capture these dynamics, the IoT has been developed. It is the net BoT weighted by the index of marketed surplus at constant prices.

The movement in the terms of trade between the agriculture and non-agriculture sectors may affect the welfare of the people engaged in these sectors through many channels. For example, favourable terms of trade to agriculture may in fact have an adverse effect, at least in the short run, on the rural poor. Since money wages do not increase immediately, a rise in agricultural prices means a fall in real wages. The rural poor being the net purchasers of cereals, a fall in real wages leads to less consumption. By contrast, Misra (2004) shows that a favourable terms of trade to agriculture while raising private investment in agriculture can increase aggregate crop output as well as productivity per hectare of net sown area.

The starting point of the discussion on terms of trade between agriculture and non-agriculture sectors in Indian context is the work by Thamarajakshi, which she has updated from time to time. Thamarajakshi (1990) computed the terms of trade for the period 1961–62 to 1987–88. She divided the entire period into two sub-periods, 1961–62 to 1973–74 and 1974–75 to 1987–88. She found that though the annual compound growth rates of BoT in both periods were positive, the rate was lower in the second period. Her estimation, however, showed that the agriculture sector gained more than it lost during both sub-periods. Kahlon and Tyagi (1980) criticized Thamarajakshi on many counts. However, the estimation of index of terms of trade by them revealed a similar trend to that of Thamarajakshi.

Raghavan (2004) presents the growth rate of BoT using estimates based on GDP deflators and those provided by the Commission for Agricultural Costs and Price (CACP) for four sub-periods spanning from 1950–51 to 2000–01. Both series have been found to have behaved in a similar manner for all the sub-periods. The compound growth rate of BoT was negative during the first sub-period, 1950–51 to 1963–64, which is attributed to a deliberate attempt to keep the terms of trade unfavourable to agriculture to serve the policy of industrialization. Further, substantial imports of food grains under PL-480 during that period also contributed towards preventing agricultural prices from rising. During 1963–64 to 1973–74, the BoT was favourable to agriculture for the following reasons: severe droughts in 1965 and 1966, which pushed the price of agricultural commodities up; subsidies provided to farmers on several inputs, which enabled them to make yield-improving investments, and no tax on agricultural income (Raghavan, 2004). In the subsequent period, 1973–74 to 1990–91, the growth rate of BoT was negative. There is, however, no unanimous explanation as to why the BoT became unfavourable to agriculture during this time. In the last sub-period (1990–91 to 2000–01), though the growth rate of BoT was positive, Raghavan (2004) estimated that the BoT based on CACP was 91.7 during this period, implying it was against the agriculture sector. During this period, private capital formation decelerated, and costs of production increased due to withdrawal of subsidies. Further, this period witnessed persistent price crashes and income losses, pushing farmers to commit suicide. The conditions have not changed much in recent time, and BoT tends to be against agriculture in most of the years during 2004–05 to 2014–15, as shown in Figure 2.6.

It is clear from Figure 2.6 that the terms of trade between the agriculture and non-agriculture sectors, and between farmers and non-farmers, have remained unfavourable to agriculture and farmers for most of the years from 2004–05 to 2014–15. In fact, during 2004–05 to 2007–08, the index of BoT was substantially

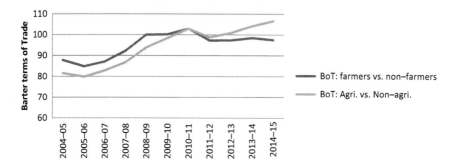

Figure 2.6 Barter terms of trade between agriculture vs. non-agriculture sectors and farmers vs. non-farmers during 2004–05 to 2014–15 in India

Source: Authors' construction based on data provided by Directorate of Economics and Statistics, Department of Agriculture, Cooperation & Farmers Welfare

unfavourable to the agriculture sector and the farmers. In other words, the agriculture sector and the farmers have lost more than what the sector and the people engaged therein have gained. Only in the last three years of the time period considered was BoT slightly in favour of agriculture. On the other hand, the BoT was marginally in favour of the farmers only in one year (2010–11) of one decade considered in Figure 2.6.

8 Concluding remarks

This chapter provides an overview of the performance of Indian agriculture since the introduction of Green Revolution. Over the years, the sector has undergone many changes. Within the sector, the combined income share from livestock, fisheries and forestry has been increasing, whereas that from conventional crops has been declining. Cropping patterns in the country have been changing in favour of non-food grain at the cost of food grain crops. Initially, Green Revolution technology was concentrated in highly irrigated regions like Punjab and Haryana. But the post-2000 growth pattern in the sector showed that growth of production has been faster first in the medium irrigation states of Madhya Pradesh, Bihar, Odisha and Andhra Pradesh, and later on even in the relatively low irrigation states of Maharashtra and Assam, than in the high irrigation states of Punjab, Uttar Pradesh and West Bengal.

One of the remarkable achievements of the Green Revolution technology was that it made India a food-grain self-sufficient nation. By the mid-1990s, India had a huge stock of food grains, which has been maintained since then. But, the sector suffered several problems from the mid-1990s onwards. While the contribution of the sector to overall GDP came down rapidly and substantially, the proportion of the workforce engaged in the sector did not decline as fast. Meanwhile, the growth of food grain production slowed down after 1991. Other challenges faced by the sector are rising costs of cultivation and poor rates of return from crops, declining investment and unfavourable terms of trade in recent years. As a result, the sector has been in a crisis since the early 1990s, the extreme manifestation of which is a series of farmer suicides in many states. Chapter 10 discusses the agrarian crisis and farmer suicides in detail.

While all problems associated with the agrarian crisis cannot be solved in a short span of time, they can be addressed or at least minimized with proper policies in the long run. A comprehensive set of policy interventions to overcome the agrarian crisis are discussed in the concluding chapter of the book.

Notes

1 In Indian agriculture, the terms Green Revolution and Yellow Revolution are used to denote mainly the successes achieved in the production of food grain and oil seeds, respectively. Initially a net importer, India became self-sufficient and turned into a net exporter of oil seeds during the early 1990s, thanks to the setting up of the Technology Mission on Oilseeds in 1986 (Rai, 1999). Another term, White Revolution, is used to denote the success in milk production due to Operation

Flood – the world's largest agricultural dairy development programme. This programme transformed India from a milk-deficient nation to the world's largest milk
producer, with about 17 per cent of global output in 2010–11 (www.drkurien.com
and The Hindustan Times, 2011).
2 In the United States, the proportion of employment in agriculture is very low and
has been declining over time (4.4 per cent in 1970, 2.7 per cent in 1990, 1.6 per
cent in 2011). In the world, the agriculture sector contributes merely 3 per cent of
the global GDP; while, more than 25 per cent of the GDP is derived from agriculture in many least-developed countries (FAO Statistical Yearbook, 2014).
3 www.economicshelp.org (accessed in March 2017)
4 See, for instance, Shetty (1990), Alag (1994), Mishra and Chand (1995), Mishra
(1996), Dhawan and Yadav (1997), Chand (2000), Gulati and Bathla (2001),
Mathur et al. (2006), Chand and Parappurathu (2012) and Singh (2014).
5 Studies like Shetty (1990), Mallik (1993) and Dhawan and Yadav (1997) concluded that there is a crowding in effect of public investment in Indian agriculture,
while studies like Mishra and Chand (1995) refuted the complementary hypothesis
both conceptually and factually.
6 The Commission for Agricultural Cost and Prices (CACP) uses different cost
concepts, like cost A1, cost A2, cost B1, cost B2, cost C1 and cost C2. Cost C1
and cost C2 are used for measuring profitability of crop cultivation because cost
C2 covers actual expenses in cash and kind incurred in production by the owner,
rent paid for leased-in land, imputed value of family labour and the interest on
value of own capital assets (excluding land). Cost C3 includes all the components
of cost C2 and adds 10 per cent in account of managerial functions performed by
the farmer. For details, see Sen and Bhatia (2004) and Narayanamoorthy (2013,
2017).

References

Alag, Y. K., 1994. Macro Policies for Indian Agriculture. In Bhalla, G. S. (ed.), *Eco-
nomic Liberalization and Indian Agriculture*, Institute for Studies in Industrial
Development, New Delhi.
Balakrishnan, P., 2000. Agriculture and Economic Reforms: Growth and Welfare.
Economic and Political Weekly, 35(12), pp. 999–1004.
Bezbaruah, M. P., 2014. Agricultural Development in India: Post-Reform Experi-
ence. *Arthabeekshan*, 22(4), pp. 159–172.
Bhalla, G. S. and Singh, G., 2009. Economic Liberalization and Indian Agriculture:
A State-Wise Analysis. *Economic and Political Weekly*, 44(52), pp. 34–44.
Birthal, P. S., Joshi, P. K., Negi, D. S. and Agarwal, S., 2013. *Changing Sources of
Growth in Indian Agriculture: Implications for Regional Priorities for Accelerating
Agricultural Growth*. IFPRI Discussion Paper.
Chand, R., 2000. *Emerging Trends and Regional Variations in Agricultural Invest-
ments and Their Implications for Growth and Equity*. Policy Paper 11, National
Centre for Agricultural Economics and Policy Research, New Delhi.
Chand, R. and Parappurathu, S., 2012. Temporal and Spatial Variations in Agri-
cultural Growth and Its Determinants. *Economic and Political Weekly*, 47(27),
pp. 55–64.
Damodaran, H., 2014. Only 40 Percent of the Rural Households Dependent on
Farming as Main Income Source: NSSO. *The Indian Express*, December 22.
Deokar, B. K. and Shetty, S. L., 2014. Growth in Indian Agriculture: Responding
to Policy Initiatives since 2004–05. *Economic and Political Weekly*, XLIX(26–27),
pp. 101–104.

Dev, S. M. and Rao, N. C., 2010. Agricultural Price Policy, Farm Profitability and Food Security. *Economic and Political Weekly*, 45(26–27), pp. 174–182.

Dhawan, B. D. and Yadav, S. S., 1997. Public Investment in Indian Agriculture: Trends and Determinants. *Economic and Political Weekly*, 32(14), pp. 710–714.

FAO, 2014. *FAO Statistical Yearbook, Asia and the Pacific Food and Agriculture*, Food and Agriculture Organization of the United Nations Regional Office for Asia and the Pacific, Bangkok, Thailand.

Gopalappa, D. V., 1996. Crop Diversification and Income Levels in Karimnagar District of Andhra Pradesh. *Indian Journal of Agricultural Economics*, 51(3), pp. 381–387.

Government of India, 2013. *Twelfth Five Year Plan (2012–2017) Economic Sectors*, Vol. II, Planning Commission, New Delhi.

Gulati, A. and Bathla, S., 2001. Capital Formation in Indian Agriculture: Revisiting the Debate. *Economic and Political Weekly*, 36(20), pp. 1697–1708.

Gulati, A. and Kelley, T., 1999. *Trade Liberalization and Indian Agriculture*, Oxford University Press, New York.

The Hindu, 2006. The Green Revolution Is Blamed for Farmers' Suicides. April 19.

The Hindustan Times, 2011. India Largest Milk Producing Nation in 2010–11: NDDB. December 20.

Internet Websites, available at www.planningcommission.nic.in, www.niti.gov.in, www.fao.org, www.data.gov.in, www.drkurien.com, www.economicshelp.org (accessed September 2016 to March 2017).

Kahlon, A. S. and Tyagi, D. S., 1980. Inter-Sectoral Terms of Trade in India. *Economic and Political Weekly*, 15(52), pp. A173–A184.

Kumar, A., Sharma, S. K. and Vashist, G. D., 2002. Profitability, Risk and Diversification in Mountain Agriculture: Some Policy Issues for Slow Growth Crops. *Indian Journal of Agricultural Economics*, 57(3), pp. 356–365.

Mallik, S. K., 1993. Capital Formation in Indian Agriculture: Recent Trends. *Indian Journal of Agricultural Economics*, 48(4), pp. 667–677.

Mandal, R., 2011. Cropping Pattern Diversification across Assam: Variations and Causes. *IUP Journal of Agricultural Economics*, VIII(1), pp. 7–17.

Mandal, R., 2014. Flood, Cropping Pattern Choice and Returns in Agriculture: A Study of Assam Plains, India. *Economic Analysis and Policy*, 44, pp. 333–344.

Mathur, S. A., Das, S. and Sircar, S., 2006. Status of Agriculture in India: Trends and Prospects. *Economic and Political Weekly*, 41(52), pp. 5327–5336.

Mishra, S. N., 1996. Capital Formation and Accumulation in Indian Agriculture Since Independence. *Indian Journal of Agricultural Economics*, 51(1–2), pp. 28–34.

Mishra, S. N. and Chand, R., 1995. Public and Private Capital Formation in Indian Agriculture: Comments on Complementarity Hypothesis and Others. *Economic and Political Weekly*, 30(25), pp. A64–A79.

Misra, V. N., 2004. *State of the Indian Farmer: Terms of Trade*, Academic Foundation, New Delhi.

Narayanamoorthy, A., 2013. Profitability in Crops Cultivation in India: Some Evidence from Cost of Cultivation Survey Data. *Indian Journal of Agricultural Economics*, 68(1), pp. 104–121.

Narayanamoorthy, A., 2017. Farm Income in India: Myths and Realities. *Indian Journal of Agricultural Economics*, 72(1), pp. 49–75.

Patnaik, U., 2006. Unleashing the Market: Global Capitalism, Deflation and Agrarian Crisis in Developing Countries. In John, M., et al. (eds.), *Contested Transformations: Changing Economies and Identities in Contemporary India*, Tulika Books, New Delhi.

Raghavan, M., 2004. Terms of Trade between Agriculture and Non-Agriculture in India, 1950–51 to 2000–01. *Social Scientist*, 32(3/4), pp. 16–29.

Raghavan, M., 2008. Changing Pattern of Input Use and Cost of Cultivation. *Economic and Political Weekly*, 43(26–27), pp. 123–129.

Rai, M., 1999. *Oilseeds in India: A Success Story in a Mission Mode*, APAARI Publication 1999/1, Asia-Pacific Association of Agricultural Research Institutions, Bangkok.

Sawant, S. D. and Achuthan, C. V., 1995. Agricultural Growth across Crops and Regions: Emerging Trends and Patterns. *Economic and Political Weekly*, 30(12), pp. A2–A13.

Sen, A. and Bhatia, M. S., 2004. *Cost of Cultivation and Farm Income in India*, Academic Foundation, New Delhi.

Shetty, S. L., 1990. Investment in Agriculture: Brief Review of Recent Trends. *Economic and Political Weekly*, 25(7–8), pp. 17–24.

Shiyani, R. L. and Pandya, H. R., 1998. Diversification of Agriculture in Gujarat: A Spatio-Temporal Analysis. *Indian Journal of Agricultural Economics*, 53(4). pp. 627–639.

Siddiqui, K., 2015. Agrarian Crisis and Transformation in India. *Journal of Economics and Political Economy*, 2(1), pp. 3–22.

Singh, N. P., Kumar, R. and Singh, R. P., 2006. Diversification of Indian Agriculture: Composition, Determinants and Trade Implications. *Agricultural Economics Research Review*, 19(CN), pp. 23–36.

Singh, P., 2014. Declining Public Investment in Indian Agriculture After Economic Reform: An Inter-State Analysis. *Journal of Management and Public Policy*, 6(1), pp. 21–33.

Srinivasalu, K., 2015. *Agrarian Crisis and Farmers' Suicides: Reflection on the Green Revolution Model*. Monograph 75, CMDR, Dharwad.

Thamarajakshi, R., 1990. Inter-Sectoral Terms of Trade Revisited. *Economic and Political Weekly*, 25(13), pp. A48–A52.

Vaidyanathan, A., 2006. Farmers' Suicides and the Agrarian Crisis. *Economic and Political Weekly*, 41(38), pp. 4009–4013.

Vaidyanathan, A., 2010. *Agricultural Growth in India: Role of Technology, Incentives and Institutions*, Oxford University Press, New Delhi.

3 Rental market of agricultural land

Changing context and need for tenancy reform

Binoy Goswami

1 Introduction

As discussed in chapter 1, one of the important changes that Indian agriculture has witnessed is the loss of land shares by higher size classes and gain by lower size classes over time. This change is discernible in terms of both areas owned and operated. Such a development suggests that there may not be enough land now to redistribute and to bring all units to a minimum threshold size. Redistribution may result in pulling down all rather than pulling up the marginal ones. Therefore, rather than redistribution, what assumes more significance in today's context is improving the access of the needy farmers to land to operate on. It is in this context that the land rental market may play an important role.

The important function of the land rental market is to bring about a better matching of land and labour endowments across rural households. Rural households rarely own land and labour, which are the two important factors of agricultural production, in right proportion. While some households may own more land relative to labour, some others may have more labour compared to land owned. The land rental or lease market, in the form of tenancy contracts, facilitates transfer of land for use from land-abundant households to labour-abundant households.

The functioning of the land lease market has important implications for better and equitable utilization of land. Leasing arrangements ensure better utilization of land resources by bringing in such land under cultivation which otherwise would have remained unutilized by labour-scarce households. Such arrangement also results in more egalitarian use of land by improving the access of land-scarce households to cultivable land. Thus, by ensuring better utilization of land and labour resources of households, the lease market can potentially increase agricultural output.

While leasing arrangements can increase agricultural production, the implications of various forms of lease contract for production of agricultural output may vary. Between sharecropping and fixed rent, the two major forms of lease arrangements, the former is usually considered to be inefficient compared to the later (Marshall, 1920). Under sharecropping, since the tenant gets to retain only half (usually) of the produce, he/she does not have an incentive to supply an adequate amount of effort, resulting in a less than economically efficient level of output. The fixed-rent tenant, on the other hand, does not suffer from this incentive problem since he/she can retain the entire output after paying the rent. Consequently, an economically efficient level of output gets produced under fixed rent. However, the view that sharecropping is relatively inefficient was challenged by Johnson (1950), who suggested that sharecropping could be as efficient as fixed rent provided certain conditions are fulfilled. Empirical evidence has failed to settle the debate on this issue conclusively.

Another related issue discussed in the literature and still unsettled is whether a tenancy arrangement, especially sharecropping, could prevent the adoption of better technology and hence agricultural growth. While Bhaduri (1973) argued that sharecropping could be inimical to agricultural development, Byres (1972) and Newbery (1975) suggested otherwise. Nevertheless, the impression that one gets after reviewing the vast body of literature is that sharecropping is generally viewed as inefficient.

In spite of being considered inefficient, sharecropping, is widespread in the real world. There are several rationales provided in the literature for the existence of sharecropping. The predominant explanation is that sharecropping is not only an output contract but also an insurance contract. Under sharecropping, not only the output but the risk associated with it also gets shared between the tenant and the landlord. On the other hand, under fixed rent, the risk of crop failure is entirely borne by the tenant. Consequently, a tenant may prefer sharecropping to fixed rent. Even the landlord, especially an absentee landlord, may prefer sharecropping under certain circumstances (Ray, 1998).[1]

Besides the equity and efficiency implications of leasing arrangements as discussed above, a lease market can also contribute to occupational diversification and rapid rural transformation (Government of India, 2016). In the absence of a lease market, a rural household owning some cultivable land for which agriculture is not viable and hence wanting to move to the non-farm sector would either remain stuck in agriculture or would keep the land idle. By allowing the land to be leased out, the lease market will release the labour of such households to be employed in the non-farm sector. This, in turn, can contribute to the growth of the non-farm sector and thereby to the overall development of the rural economy.

Against this backdrop, this chapter analyzes the extent and pattern of leasing arrangements in the rural land lease market in India (section 2), and it identifies some determinants of leasing decisions of rural households (section 3). Further, the chapter provides a discussion of the implications of its analysis in the context of the legal framework that exists to manage the land lease market (section 4) and ends with a few concluding remarks (section 5).

2 Extent and pattern of land leasing

As per the 70th round of the National Sample Survey Organization (NSSO) report, the number of households reporting leasing out and leasing in of land in rural India were 5.09 million and 21.29 million, respectively, during the period of January–June 2013 (no. 571, p. 29). In terms of area coverage, the leased-out and leased-in area were 3.92 million hectares and 10.66 million hectares, respectively, during the same period. These numbers suggest that the incidence or extent of rural tenancy in India is sizable.

Table 3.1 shows the percentage distribution of tenant holdings and leased-in area across size classes of operational holdings over time.

Tenant holdings as a percentage of operational holdings declined from 25.70 per cent in 1970–71 to 9.90 per cent in 2002–03, and this decline was continuous. However, as per the 70th round of the NSSO report (the latest one on this subject), tenant holdings increased to 13.70 per cent in 2012–13.

In terms of leased-in area, the overall pattern is the same as it is in case of tenant holdings, although leased-in area in 1991–92 was slightly higher than it was in 1981–82. Area under lease fell from 10.60 per cent in 1970–71 to 6.50 per cent in 2012–13 and then increased to 11.30 per cent in 2012–13 (see Table 3.1). The recent increase in tenant holdings and leased-in area can be attributed to exodus of cultivators from the agriculture sector. As per the Census of India, between 2001 and 2011, the number of cultivators declined by 8.9 million (Venkatanarayana and Naik, 2013). Decrease in the number of cultivators increased the supply of land for lease.

Figures in Table 3.1 reveal that while in 1970–71 and 1980–81 the percentages of tenant holdings were higher in marginal and small size classes relative to the large size class of operational holdings, the opposite is the case since 1991–92. In the case of leased-in area, the pattern is the same as in the case of tenant holdings until 1991–92. However, in 2002–03, the percentage of leased-in area by the large size class was less than that by the marginal and small size classes of operational holding. Moving on to 2012–13, the proportion of area leased in by the large size class was slightly higher than that by small and marginal size classes, though the percentage of leased-in area was the highest for the semi-medium size class of operational holding in that year. Thus, the pattern is not very clear for the leased-in area.

Table 3.2 shows variations in the extent of tenancy across the states of India during January–June 2013. Among the major Indian states, Andhra Pradesh has the highest incidence of tenancy in terms of percentage of households leasing in land. While the percentage of households leasing in land in Andhra Pradesh was 37.21 per cent, leased-in area as a percentage of owned area was 59.03 per cent during the same time in the state. Some other states with a higher incidence of tenancy (both in terms of percentage of households leasing in land and that of leased-in area in owned land) are Kerala, Tamil Nadu and Telangana in the southern region; Bihar, Haryana, Punjab and Uttar Pradesh in the northern region; Chhattisgarh in the central region; and Odisha and West Bengal in the eastern region. On other hand, while the percentage of households leasing in land in Himachal Pradesh is relatively higher, the percentage of leased-in land in owned land is less. The reason for lower incidence of tenancy in terms of leased-in area in Himachal Pradesh is the small size of tenant holdings, as reflected in the lower value of the average leased-in area.

Table 3.1 Percentage of tenant holdings in total holdings and leased-in area in total operated area across land-size classes over time

Size classes*	Tenant holdings					Leased-in area				
	1970–71	1981–82	1991–92	2002–03	2012–13**	1970–71	1981–82	1991–92	2002–03	2012–13**
Landless	–	–	–	–	2.60	–	–	–	–	1.37
Marginal	27.00	14.40	9.30	9.80	13.20	18.90	9.70	8.70	8.60	11.30
Small	27.80	17.90	14.90	10.70	13.60	14.60	8.50	8.50	6.80	11.25
Semi-Medium	24.80	15.90	12.20	10.30	18.00	11.70	7.30	7.40	6.30	13.14
Medium	20.0	14.50	13.10	7.80	14.80	8.70	6.60	6.90	4.20	8.64
Large	15.90	11.50	16.70	13.80	21.80	5.90	5.30	11.40	6.10	12.59
Overall	**25.7**	**15.20**	**11.00**	**9.90**	**13.70**	**10.60**	**7.20**	**8.30**	**6.50**	**11.30**

Notes: *Landless < =0.002 ha, Marginal = 0.002–1 ha, Small = 1–2 ha, Semi-medium = 2–4 ha, Medium = 4–10 ha, and Large > 10 ha.

**Corresponds to the period of January–June 2013

Source: Adapted from NSSO 2012–13, statements 5.7 and 5.8, report no. 571, p. 43.

Table 3.2 Extent of tenancy across major states of India during January–June 2013

State	Households leasing in land (%)	Households leasing out land (%)	Leased-in land as a % of owned land	Average leased-in area (in ha)
Andhra Pradesh	37.21	4.64	59.03	0.779
Karnataka	8.64	6.02	6.99	0.687
Kerala	14.29	2.01	10.26	0.148
Tamil Nadu	13.16	1.91	15.03	0.400
Telangana	16.45	1.20	18.59	0.793
Gujarat	6.15	2.10	6.38	0.833
Maharashtra	8.41	0.90	3.60	0.383
Rajasthan	7.56	5.22	6.36	1.242
Bihar	18.72	3.11	30.71	0.395
Haryana	12.94	5.48	16.38	0.963
Himachal Pradesh	21.17	4.91	5.47	0.102
Jammu & Kashmir	3.03	0.52	0.24	0.034
Jharkhand	5.90	2.64	2.18	0.178
Punjab	15.77	5.25	29.10	1.157
Uttar Pradesh	10.64	3.90	8.61	0.394
Madhya Pradesh	5.61	2.14	5.41	1.081
Chhattisgarh	13.66	3.46	9.30	0.537
Assam	7.04	1.78	4.50	0.397
Odisha	19.28	4.82	20.47	0.403
West Bengal	17.80	3.57	17.29	0.167

Source: Adapted from NSSO 2012–13, statement S4.7, report no. 571, p. 30.

The explanation for the state-wise variations in the incidence of tenancy can be sought in terms of the average size of area owned per household in the states. Except for Telangana, the average area owned in all the states mentioned above from the southern region is smaller than the national average of area owned. While the average area owned for all India is 0.592 hectare, the average areas owned in Andhra Pradesh, Kerala and Tamil Nadu in 2012–13 are 0.491 hectare, 0.209 hectare and 0.348 hectare, respectively. Karnataka in the southern region, which has a lower incidence of tenancy also has higher average size of land owned (0.851 hectare). The same explanation applies in the cases of Bihar and Uttar Pradesh in the northern region.

By contrast, Punjab and Haryana, in the northern region, have higher incidences of tenancy and also have comparatively higher size of average area owned. However, these two states have a relatively higher share of people engaged in agriculture (cultivators and agricultural labourers) in the total rural working population, resulting in more demand for land under lease. The shares of rural working population engaged in agriculture in Punjab and Haryana are 53.64 per cent and 63.38 per cent, respectively, as per the 2011 census (Government of India, 2015). The lower incidence of tenancy in Madhya Pradesh from the central region and Assam from the eastern region also can be explained in terms of higher average size of land owned. The opposite is the case for Odisha and West

Bengal from the eastern region, though. It may be noted here that all the states in the western region of the country show relatively lower incidence of tenancy. As in the cases of other states having lower incidence of tenancy, the reason for lower incidence of tenancy in these states could be the higher amount of area owned by an average household. The sizes of average area owned in Gujarat, Maharashtra and Rajasthan in 2012–13 are 0.804 hectare, 0.903 hectare and 1.483 hectare, respectively, as opposed to the national average of 0.592 hectare in that year.

Figure 3.1 shows the percentage distribution of area under lease by major forms of tenancy contracts. It is clear from Figure 3.1 that since 1991–92 the area under fixed rent (cash + kind) has been increasing and that under sharecropping has been declining. In fact, in 2002–03 and 2012–13, fixed rent had clearly emerged as the dominant form of tenancy contract. The area under fixed rent increased from 27 per cent in 1971–72 to 58.10 per cent in 2012–13. On the other hand, area under sharecropping declined from 47.90 per cent in 1971–72 to 28.70 per cent in 2012–13.

The increase in the area under fixed rent and the decline in that under sharecropping can be explained in terms of the change in cropping pattern over time. As shown in chapter 2 (see Table 2.2), a major change has happened in the cropping pattern in India over the last four decades. While area under food grain (except for wheat) has declined, that under non-food grain has increased continuously. In particular, areas under oil seeds and vegetables have increased continuously. In other words, there has been shift in the cropping pattern from coarse cereals and pulses to high-value crops like oil seeds and fruits. This shift in the cropping pattern has been accompanied by a shift in the importance of the forms of tenancy contract from sharecropping to fixed rent. This change in the cropping pattern has become more visible since 1991–92, and this is also the

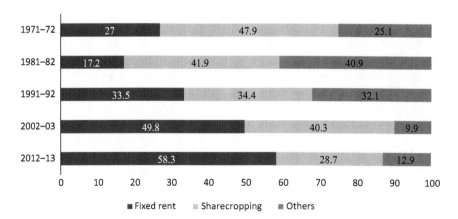

Figure 3.1 Percentage distribution of area under lease by major forms of tenancy contracts in India over time

Source: Adapted from NSSO 2012–13, statement 5.9, report no. 571, p. 44.

period when areas under fixed rent and sharecropping were almost equal. Since 1991–92, fixed rent has remained as the dominant form of tenancy contract, and areas under high-value crops have been increasing consistently.

Goswami and Bezbaruah (2013) in the context of Assam explained that farmers preferred fixed rent to sharecropping while cultivating high-value crops. These crops are usually cultivated on a commercial basis; hence while cultivating these crops, the tenants use better quality seeds and other expensive inputs like chemical fertilizers, irrigation and so on, resulting in higher production. Use of these inputs also reduces production risk. Thus, due to lower risk and higher production when cultivating these crops, the tenants prefer fixed rent, which allows them to retain the entire produce after paying the rent to the land owners. Besides, in case of high-value crops like fruits and vegetables, the natural choice of tenancy contract for lessors will be fixed rent since these crops are perishable and hence cannot be stored for a long time. This explanation may be consistent at the national level too, as is evident from the simultaneous shift in the cropping pattern from coarse cereals and pulses to high-value oil seeds and fruits, on the one hand, and the shift from sharecropping to fixed rent, on the other.

Table 3.3 shows percentage distribution of leased-in area by terms of lease across the major states of India. While sharecropping is predominant in Karnataka,

Table 3.3 Percentage distribution of area under lease by terms of lease across major states during January–June 2013

States	Fixed rent			Sharecropping	Relatives under no specific terms	Other
	Cash	Kind	Total			
Andhra Pradesh	51.9	20.9	72.8	21.2	4.4	1.4
Karnataka	34.4	8.4	42.8	50.3	2.7	3.9
Kerala	39.4	9.7	49.1	8.7	30.0	6.2
Tamil Nadu	72.3	6.6	78.9	5.7	13.3	2.1
Telangana	55.8	5.9	61.7	35.1	0.3	1.1
Gujarat	12.0	0.0	12	57.6	29.3	1.0
Maharashtra	43.6	3.5	47.1	29.0	8.4	4.2
Rajasthan	52.8	5.9	58.7	25.0	9.9	3.7
Bihar	17.3	10.9	28.2	55.8	6.0	2.6
Haryana	75.8	8.7	84.5	1.9	10.7	1.2
Himachal Pradesh	31.4	1.0	32.4	7.0	46.2	12.4
Jharkhand	17.4	7.0	24.4	72.2	0.0	0.0
Punjab	93.7	1.4	95.1	1.9	1.2	1.3
Uttar Pradesh	24.2	9.5	33.7	35.6	5.2	21.2
Madhya Pradesh	16.8	10.4	27.2	35.8	15.7	20.0
Chhattisgarh	5.3	61.6	66.9	21.3	8.2	0.4
Assam	17.3	10.9	28.2	55.8	6.0	2.6
Odisha	9.5	27.6	37.1	58.3	1.1	2.9
West Bengal	39.3	15.8	55.1	34.6	2.2	5.5
India	41.9	15.1	57.0	28.4	6.2	5.5

Source: Adapted from NSSO 2012–13, statement 5.9, report 571, p. 46.

Gujarat, Bihar, Jharkhand, Assam and Odisha, fixed rent is the major form of tenancy contract in the other states. In fact, in states like Punjab and Haryana, the proportion of leased-in area under fixed rent is very high.[2] In Punjab, 95.10 per cent of the leased-in area is under fixed rent. Haryana, Andhra Pradesh, Tamil Nadu, Telengana and Chhattisgarh are some other states where the leased-in areas under fixed rent are very high.

3 Determinants of leasing decision

Having examined the extent and pattern of leasing in the rural land lease market in India, this section now aims at understanding the factors contributing towards leasing decisions. Existing literature suggests that some of the factors which may affect the leasing decision of a household are availability of farm workers, inequality of land holding, age, sex and education level of the head of the farm household, primary occupation of the farm household, proportion of operational holding under irrigation, access to credit and ownership of bullock and machinery for tilling (Goswami and Bezbaruah, 2013; Laha and Kuri, 2011; Kuri, 2003).

Accordingly, a regression model has been constructed wherein the leasing decision of the households is regressed on some of the above-mentioned variables. The choice of the explanatory variables included in the model is guided by availability of data. The unit-level data from the 70th round of the NSSO has been used for the regression analysis.[3] In addition to the above mentioned explanatory variables, three dummies for social groups and four regional dummies have also been incorporated in the regression analysis.

The dependent variable (Y), that is, the leasing decision, is constructed as:

Y = {(operational holding – land owned)/(operational holding + land owned)}. In this formulation, Y will range between –1 and 1.
Y = –1, if a farmer is a pure lessor
Y = 0 if a farmer is an owner operator
Y = 1 if a farmer is a pure tenant.

Construction of Y in this manner helps to capture the intensity of leasing as explained in Goswami and Bezbaruah (2013).

The definitions and notations of the explanatory variables along with their expected impacts on leasing decisions are shown in Table 3.4.

Since the dependent variable is bounded by –1 and 1, a both-side censored Tobit model has been applied instead of a linear regression model. The Tobit model is constructed by using a latent variable Y_i^*, which may not always be observable. The final model estimated is given by equation 1.

$$Yi^* = \beta_0 + \beta_1 FW_i + \beta_2 AGE_i + \beta_3 EDU_i + \beta_4 SEX_i + \beta_5 GINI_i \\ + \beta_6 S_{1i} + \beta_7 S_{2i} + \beta_8 S_{3i} + \lambda_1 R_{1i} + \lambda_2 R_{2i} + \lambda_3 R_{3i} + \lambda_4 R_{4i} + U_i$$

– – – – – (1), where U_i is the random disturbance term.

Table 3.4 Definitions of the explanatory variables and their expected impact on leasing decisions

Variables	Definitions	Expected impact
Farm worker (FW)	Number of farm workers per hectare of operational holding	+
Age (AGE)	Age of the head of the household	−
Education (EDU)	Education of the head of the household in years	−
Sex (SEX)	$D_1 = 1$ if the head of the household is male and 0 otherwise	+
Inequality of land holding (GINI)	Gini coefficient for land holding at the level of NSS region within a state	+
Social groups	$S_1 = 1$ for ST household and 0 otherwise; $S_2 = 1$ for SC household and 0 otherwise; $S_3 = 1$ for OBC household and 0 otherwise (General is the reference category)	+/−
Regional characteristics	Four regional dummies have been used: R_1, R_2, R_3, and R_4 where $R_1 = 1$ for North and 0 otherwise; $R_2 = 1$ for South and 0 otherwise; $R_3 = 1$ for West and 0 otherwise, $R_4 = 1$ for Central and 0 otherwise (Eastern region is the reference category)	+/−

The observed dependent variable Y_i is linked to the latent variable Y_i^* as per the following configuration:

$$Y_i = -1 \; for \; Y_i^* < -1$$
$$= Y_i^* \; for \; -1 \le Y_i^* \le 1$$
$$= 1 \; for \; Y_i^* > 1$$

The maximum likelihood estimates of the parameters have been estimated by using STATA 11.0. The results of the regression analysis are presented in Table 3.5.

The results presented in Table 3.5 are in the expected line. The F statistic is statistically significant at the 1 per cent level and hence the model is accepted as a good fit. The coefficients of all the variables except SEX are statistically significant and have expected signs. Moreover, the coefficients of all the statistically significant variables except the social group dummy S_3 are significant at the 1 per cent level. The coefficient of the variable FW is positive, implying that the households with more farm workers are more likely to lease in land. The negative coefficient of AGE suggests that a household with an older head is less likely to lease in land. The coefficient of the variable EDU is negative, which implies that education creates an aversion towards agriculture. A household headed by a person having a higher level of education is more likely to lease

Table 3.5 Results of the both-side censored Tobit regression

Breusch-Pagan test for heteroskedasticity	
Chi² [11] = 18.62*	
Prob. = 0.0981	
Result: presence of heteroskedasticity	

Variables/Constant	Estimates of the Coefficients/Values
FW	0.0013***
	(0.00015)
AGE	−0.0027***
	(0.0002)
EDU	−0.008***
	(0.0008)
SEX	0.004
	(0.011)
GINI	0.483***
	(0.05)
S_1	−0.023***
	(0.009)
S_2	0.076***
	(0.01)
S_3	0.014**
	(0.006)
R_1	−0.07***
	(0.009)
R_2	0.04***
	(0.009)
R_3	−0.068***
	(0.008)
R_4	−0.08***
	(0.009)
Constant	0.11***
	(0.029)
Pseudo R^2	0.1172
F[12, 14519]	68.60***

Figures within ( ) and [ ] are robust standard errors and degrees of freedom, respectively.
***, ** indicate significant at 1 and 5 per cent, respectively.

out land. These results are consistent with Goswami and Bezbaruah (2013) and Kuri (2003). The positive coefficient of GINI implies that the higher the level of inequality in land holding in the location of a household, the higher the possibility of leasing in land by a household is. Among the social groups, while the ST households are more likely to lease out land, SC and OBC households are more likely to lease in land relative to the general category households. Furthermore, while a household in the southern region is more likely to lease in land, households in the northern, western and central regions of the country are more likely to lease out land relative to a household in the eastern region of the country.

4 Discussion of the results

4.1 Implications of the changing scenario of the land lease market

The analysis in section 2 highlights two significant changes that have happened in the land lease market in recent time. These changes are (i) an increase in the incidence of tenancy, as revealed from the latest NSSO survey on ownership and operational holdings, and (ii) the emergence of fixed rent as the dominant form of tenancy contract. The increase in the incidence of tenancy in recent time, as discussed in section 2, may be due to the exodus of cultivators from agriculture, which made more land available for lease. While the cultivators may leave agriculture for several reasons, such as increasing costs of cultivation and falling income resulting in a distress-like situation (Varmal, 2015), a part of such exodus may be natural.

The results of empirical analysis presented in section 3 suggest that a household headed by an individual having a higher level of education tends to lease out land. Education creates an aversion towards agriculture and induces people to look for employment in the non-farm sector. This implies that with the improvement in education, there will be a greater supply of land in the lease market. Thus, the increase in the incidence of tenancy in recent time may, at least partly, be attributed to the improvement in the literacy rate in India. One would, in fact, expect that as the level of literacy improves further, more land will be available for lease in the future. Implementation of the rural development schemes initiated by the Government of India and a consequent expansion in non-farm employment may speed up the process of migration of the educated working population from the farm sector to the non-farm sector, and such a development may result in an even larger supply of land in the lease market.

Given the inefficiency associated with sharecropping, one may consider the emergence of fixed rent as the dominant form of tenancy contract as good for Indian agriculture. While fixed rent may contribute to increased agricultural production, in the light of what Goswami and Bezbaruah (2015) have reported, it is not necessary that fixed rent be the most desired form of tenancy arrangement. In a two-period optimization framework, Goswami and Bezbaruah (2015) have shown that while sharecroppers undersupply effort, fixed-rent tenants in fact oversupply efforts. The oversupply of efforts in the form of excessive use of inputs, such as chemical fertilizers, is not desirable given their implications for soil health. Overuse of chemical fertilizers may degrade the natural soil fertility, which has adverse implications for sustainable agriculture. In fact, Goswami and Bezbaruah (2015), using primary data from the plains of Assam, have shown that fixed-rent tenants have the tendency to apply chemical fertilizers in excessive quantity, especially when the duration of the contract is short, because their objective is to maximize returns from leased-in land within the stipulated period of the contract. Further, they apply more chemical fertilizers than even the owner operators, who do not suffer from any incentive problem. Figure 3.2 drives home this point clearly.

As shown in Figure 3.2, the amount of chemical fertilizers applied by fixed-rent tenants is much higher than that used by the owner operators. In fact, it is higher than the recommended level in case of both summer paddy and cabbage.

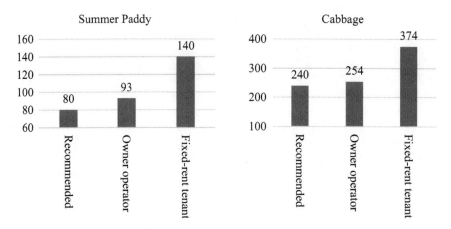

Figure 3.2 Application of NPK by fixed-rent tenants relative to that by owner operators and the recommended level (in kg/ha.)

Source: Adapted from Goswami and Bezbaruah (2015).

4.2 *Policy recommendations*

Given these changes in the land lease market, the challenge for policy makers is to ensure that the land that will be available for lease is efficiently utilized. There is, however, a concern that given the prevailing tenancy laws in the states, ensuring efficient utilization of such lands will not be possible. This concern has been expressed by many scholars and even at the policy-making level, such as Goswami (2012), Sharma (2006), and Government of India (2016).

The existing tenancy laws enacted by the states in the 1960s and 1970s aimed at dislodging a feudal agrarian structure inherited from the colonial rule, which was characterized by high levels of inefficiency and inequality. The tenants received only subsistence wages and had no right or security of tenure. Consequently, the tenants did not have any incentive to supply sufficient effort in cultivation. Moreover, the landlords did not invest in the development of land. These factors contributed to lower levels of productivity and efficiency in agriculture. In order to displace this unequal and inefficient agrarian structure, all the states passed land and tenancy reforms laws. As far as the tenancy reforms are concerned, though there are variations in provisions of the tenancy laws across states, the common features of the tenancy laws are (i) giving security of tenure to tenants who cultivate land continuously for a certain span of time; ii) regulating rent at a judicious level, usually 20 to 25 per cent of gross produce; and iii) conferring ownership rights to the tenants, subject to certain restrictions. The basic objective of these provisions was to improve the incentive of the tenants to supply adequate efforts in cultivation by protecting their interest, which ultimately would bring about efficiency in production.

While the tenancy laws were passed, they were, however, never implemented properly, except for in a few states, such as Kerala and West Bengal. The political class lacked the willingness to implement the tenancy laws. Thus, while the benefits of the tenancy laws have been realized only marginally, many unanticipated outcomes surfaced due to restrictions on either leasing of land itself or on leasing arrangements.[4] As a result of these restrictive provisions, tenancy became informal (Murty and Reddy, 2017). Informal tenancy hurts the tenants since they cannot take advantage of the law to protect their interests. The other outcome is the shortening of duration of contract. Goswami and Bezbaruah (2013), in the context of Assam, reported that due to the restrictive provision in the tenancy law that a tenant can potentially become the owner of land if he/she cultivates the land continuously for three years, the land owners did not want recording of tenancy and would not lease out land for more than two years even when the contracts were informal. Short duration of tenancy reduces the incentive of the tenants to care for the development of the land. In fact, they (especially fixed-rent tenants) may use inputs like chemical fertilizers excessively during the short duration of contract to maximize return without caring for natural fertility of land, as shown by Goswami and Bezbaruah (2015). While this finding was in the context of Assam, one may expect to observe the same phenomenon in other states as well, given the restrictive provisions in the tenancy laws.

Another adverse outcome of the restrictions on leasing is the reduction in occupational mobility in rural areas (Government of India, 2016). In fear of losing ownership of land on account of being an absentee landlord, many land owners do not want to lease out their land. In spite of having the options of migration and taking up employment in the non-farm sector, many land owners are forced to be in agriculture even if they lack the skill and motivation to be in agriculture, resulting in lower production efficiency.

Given these undesired outcomes of the tenancy laws, the time is appropriate now to have a fresh look at the existing legal provisions regulating tenancy relations. In fact, many of the provisions in the tenancy laws have become redundant today due to the changing realities of the countryside. The restrictive provisions aimed at protecting the interests of the tenants were justifiable when these laws were enacted, given the characteristics of the landlords of that time. Today, however, the characteristics of land owners are different from those of the landlords at the time of independence (Goswami, 2012). Most of the land owners are now small and marginal farmers like the tenants, and unlike the landlords of the pre-independence period. As per the NSSO report number 571, while 85.41 per cent of households belonged to the marginal and small size categories in 2012–13, only 0.24 per cent of households were in the large category. Further, the average size of land holdings declined from 1.01 hectare in 1992 to 0.592 hectare in 2012–13. Transferring the titles of lands from the land owners to the tenants will only create another class of landless people. In other words, it is equally important that the interests of these marginal and small land owners are also protected. It may be mentioned in this context that Kerala was the only state where there was an absolute transfer of ownership right from the landlords to the tenants and tenancy was completely banned. Studies, however, have shown that tenancy resurfaced in Kerala in informal form (Nair and Menon, 2006). Moreover, the transfer of property rights to the tenants did not yield the expected results as far as agricultural production was concerned. The growth rate of food grains in the aftermath of the tenancy reform in Kerala in fact worsened (Mahendradev, 1987). Even a programme like Operation Barga, which did not endorse outright transfer of ownership rights to tenant but sought to improve the security of tenure, cannot be an ideal intervention. Such an intervention, by giving hereditary occupancy right on land, makes it difficult for future generations to access land for cultivation. The impact of Operation Barga on production efficiency was also mixed (Goswami, 2012). Further, in West Bengal, where this programme was implemented, exploitative sub-tenancies emerged (Rudra, 1981).

Keeping in view the unintended outcomes of the existing tenancy laws and the changing realities of the countryside, this chapter suggests that the restrictive provisions in the tenancy laws should be scrapped. The leasing in and out of land should be made legal and hassle free. Land owners should be able to lease out land without the fear of losing it, even if they are absentee owners. If the land owners can lease out land without the fear of losing the ownership, they may not prevent recording of tenancy and will also make land available for lease under long-duration contracts. Recording of the tenancy contract is the first step towards improving the welfare of the tenants. If tenancy could be recorded, the tenants would be able to avail themselves of credit, insurance and other opportunities. Further, recording of tenancy should reduce the exploitation of the tenants by the lessors. The lessors can potentially exploit the tenants not only by charging higher rent but also through interlinked markets. The lessors may extract exorbitant interest rates on credit offered to the tenants. Recoding of tenancy should bring respite, at least to some extent, for the tenants from such exploitation by facilitating their access to credit and other opportunities.[5]

Moreover, long-duration contracts will improve the incentive of the tenants to invest in the land and to take care of the natural fertility of land through judicious use of inputs like chemical fertilizers. Moreover, if the land owners do not hesitate to lease out land, more land will be available in the lease market, which will improve access to land for tenant households with scarcity of land. Further, by enabling the land owners to lease out land, the occupational mobility of the land owners shall also be improved, which will in turn contribute to overall growth of the economy, especially of the rural economy. Tenancy, being an institution that facilitates mobility of labour, should not be impinged upon (Khusro, 1973). A hassle-free land lease market is further justified given the findings of this chapter that participants in the lease market are likely to be those who are relatively poor or have benefited less from the growth process (while ST households are more likely to lease out, SC and OBC households are more likely to lease in compared to the general category households; see Table 3.5).

5 Conclusion

Two major changes have unfolded in the rural land lease market over the last few decades. First, the incidence of tenancy has increased. Second, fixed rent has emerged as the dominant form of tenancy contract. The increase in the incidence of tenancy is attributed, at least partly, to the exodus of farmers from agriculture in the last decade. The other reason seems to be the increase in the level of education of the rural population. This argument is based on the finding of this chapter that with an increase in level of education, people tend to lease out land. In fact, it is expected that with further increases in the level of education, there may be more supply of land in the land lease market.

With respect to the emergence of fixed rent as the dominant form of tenancy, one may believe that it is a desirable change since this form of tenancy contract is usually considered to be more efficient. However, as Goswami and Bezbaruah (2015) showed in the context of Assam, fixed rent is not necessarily the most desired form of tenancy. If the duration of the contract is short, fixed-rent tenants may apply excessive amounts of inputs like chemical fertilizers, which has adverse implication for sustainable agriculture.

In view of these changes, the challenge before the policy maker is to ensure efficient utilization of the land that will be supplied in the lease market. The existing legal framework, however, is not conducive for efficient utilization of such land. In fact, the prevailing tenancy laws, which were enacted in the 1960s and 1970s, have resulted in many unintended outcomes owing to some restrictive provisions – even though these laws were never implemented properly, except for in a few states. Consequently, it is important that these restrictive provisions are scrapped and tenancy is legalized. Given the mismatch in the endowments of land and labour across rural households, banning or restricting tenancy is neither feasible nor desirable. The recent increase in the incidence of tenancy in spite of bans in some states and restrictions in most states confirms this. Therefore, it is important that reforms are undertaken in the tenancy law which will facilitate hassle-free leasing arrangements. Notwithstanding certain imitations, the Model Agricultural Land Leasing Act of 2016, proposed by the expert group appointed by the Government of India, which advocates for legalizing tenancy, can pave the direction in this regard. Given the fact that relatively less-advantaged groups of people are more likely to participate in the lease market, making the leasing arrangement tenant friendly will be a socially desired outcome.

Notes

1 See Goswami (2012) for a detailed discussion on (i) efficiency/inefficiency implications of tenancy contracts, (ii) various explanations for the existence of sharecropping contracts and (iii) whether sharecropping is inimical to agricultural development.
2 Cultivation in these states is done in a condition supported by assured irrigation, which reduces the production risk. Hence, it is not surprising that fixed rent is the dominant form of tenancy in spite of paddy and wheat, that is, food grains being the main crops cultivated therein.
3 States included in the regression analysis are Andhra Pradesh, Karnataka, Kerala, Tamil Nadu and Telangana in the southern region; Gujarat, Maharashtra and Rajasthan in the western region; Bihar, Haryana, Himachal Pradesh, Jharkhand, Punjab and Uttar Pradesh in the northern region; Madhya Pradesh and Chhattisgarh in the central region; and Assam, Odisha and West Bengal in the eastern region.

4 Please see the "Report of the Expert Committee on Land Leasing" by Niti Aayog of Government of India (2016) for a discussion on the restrictive provisions with regard to land leasing in the states.
5 Any effort to only record the tenancy without making it legal and taking care of the fear of lessors of losing the ownership right will not yield desired results. The experience of the Andhra Pradesh (composite) Land Licensed Act of 2011 can be cited in this context. This act seeks to register the tenants and issue them loan eligibility cards, which allow them to access credit, insurance, input subsidies and disaster relief. However, Murty and Reddy (2017) have reported that the coverage of the act has remained very limited. The reason suggested by them is the restrictive provisions in the Telangana and Andhra tenancy acts which make it difficult for land owners to get the lands back from tenants. In fear of losing their ownership right, the lessors prevent the registering of their tenants.

References

Bhaduri, A., 1973. Agricultural Backwardness Under Semi-Feudalism. *Economic Journal*, LXXXIII(1), pp. 120–137.

Byres, T. J., 1972. The Dialectic of India's Green Revolution. *South Asian Review*, 5(2), pp. 99–116.

Goswami, B., 2012. *Economic Implications of Tenancy: A Study in Assam's Agrarian Set-Up*. Unpublished PhD Thesis submitted to Gauhati University, Guwahati, Assam.

Goswami, B. and Bezbaruah, M. P., 2013. Incidence, Forms and Determinants of Tenancy in the Agrarian Set-Up of the Assam Plains. *Economic and Political Weekly*, 48(42), pp. 60–68.

Goswami, B. and Bezbaruah, M. P., 2015. *Revisiting the Tenancy-Inefficiency Question With an Inter-Temporal Optimisation Framework: Insights From the Agrarian Set-Up of Assam Plains in Eastern India*. Faculty of Economics, South Asian University Working Paper No. SAUFE-WP-2015-001.

Government of India, 2015. *Agricultural Statistics at a Glance*, Directorate of Economics and Statistics, Ministry of Agriculture and Farmers Welfare.

Government of India, 2016. *Report of the Expert Committee on Land Leasing, NITI Aayog*, available at http://niti.gov.in/writereaddata/files/writereaddata/files/document_publication/Final_Report_Expert_Group_on_Land_Leasing.pdf, accessed 23/03/2017.

Johnson, D. G., 1950. Resource Allocation Under Share Contracts. *Journal of Political Economy*, 58(2), pp. 111–123.

Khusro, A. M., 1973. *The Economics of Land Reform and Farm Size in India*, Macmillan, Madras.

Kuri, P. K., 2003. Factor Market Imperfections and Explanation of Tenancy: Testing an Econometric Model Using Evidence From Assam of North East India. *Indian Journal of Agricultural Economics*, 58(2), pp. 234–245.

Laha, A. and Kuri, P. K., 2011. Rural Credit Market and the Extent of Tenancy: Micro Evidence From Rural West Bengal. *Indian Journal of Agricultural Economics*, 66(1), pp. 76–87.

Mahendradev, S., 1987. Growth and Instability in Food Grain Production. *Economic and Political Weekly*, 22(39), pp. A82–A92.

Marshall, A., 1920. *Principles of Economics*, Macmillan, London.

Murty, S. C. and Reddy, M. S., 2017. AP Land Licensed Cultivators Act in Retrospect and Prospect. *Journal of Land and Rural Studies*, 5(1), pp. 1–11.

Nair, K. N. and Menon, V., 2006. Lease Farming in Kerala: Findings From Micro Level Studies. *Economic and Political Weekly*, XLI(26), pp. 2732–2738.

Newbery, D. M. G., 1975. Tenurial Obstacles to Innovation. *Journal of Development Studies*, 11(4), pp. 263–277.

Ray, D., 1998. *Development Economics*, Oxford University Press, New Delhi.

Rudra, A., 1981. One Step Forward, Two Steps Backward. *Economic and Political Weekly*, 16(25–26), pp. A61–A68.

Sharma, H. R., 2006. Liberalising the Lease Market. *Economic and Political Weekly*, 41(8), pp. 696–698.

Varmal, S., 2015. Why It Does Not Pay to Be a Small Farmer. *The Times of India*, available at http://timesofindia.indiatimes.com/home/sunday-times/Why-it-doesnt-pay-to-be-a-small-farmer/articleshow/46893469.cms, accessed 25/12/2016.

Venkatanarayana, M. and Naik, V. S., 2013. *Growth and Structure of Workforce in India: An Analysis of Census 2011 Data*. MPRA Paper No. 48003, available at https://mpra.ub.uni-muenchen.de/48003/, accessed 23/03/2017.

4 Emerging factor markets in Indian agriculture

Water and rental of capital goods

Anup Kumar Das and Jitu Tamuli

1 Introduction

As discussed in chapter 3, the availability of factors of production, especially land and labour, with farm households is not always in right proportion. Such imbalances in factor endowments across farm households have been the root causes of the emergence of land lease and labour markets in agriculture (Ray, 2011). Such markets allow farm households with factor endowment imbalances to trade their surplus factor for the factor in which they are poorly endowed. Notwithstanding the factor-endowment imbalance correcting effects of such markets, a disproportionately large number of holdings in the small and marginal size classes has attracted the attention of researchers not just from equity concerns but also from efficiency considerations. It used to be argued that for adoption of productivity enhancing practices, a cultivation unit should be of a minimum viable land holding size. The case of relatively higher cost of construction of well and installation of pump-set than the returns from them when landholding is small and fragmented compared to large and consolidated holdings as explained by Vaidyanathan (1986) supports this view.

Dobbs and Foster (1972) and Dutta (2007) found evidence of an adverse impact of small and fragmented landholdings on incentive to investment in tube well technology for groundwater irrigation. Further, cultivation in small and fragmented landholdings were found to be inconvenient for use of heavy machinery, such as tractors, power tillers and pump-sets (Singh, 2011). In order to reorganize small and fragmented holdings into viable cultivation units from the point of view of various good practices, including farm mechanization, consolidation of holdings was conceived as an important component of India's land reform agenda in the post-independence period. In practice, however, this component has been executed in only a few pockets in the country (Misra and Puri, 2004).

Despite consolidation of landholdings remaining unimplemented in most parts of India and average size of individual holding going down over the years (Indian Journal of Agricultural Economics, 2014), mechanization of farm operation seems to be on the rise and has been adopted even by small and marginal size farms in recent times. This has been possible because of the strengthening of factor markets in agriculture, with the emergence of water markets and rental markets for agricultural capital goods complementing and in most cases supplementing the traditional factor markets of land lease, labour and credit. The emergence of well-functioning rental markets for agricultural capital goods can alter the limitation of small and fragmented holdings considerably. The possibility of renting out opens up another source of returns to an owner of agricultural capital goods. Thus, even if a farmer cannot extract an attractive rate of return from his own agricultural operation, still he/she may be able to get sufficiently good total return from his/her investment in such capital goods by both using it on his/her own farm and renting it out at other times. Further, with the possibility of renting agricultural capital goods, small farms need not be prevented from using agricultural machinery and other improved practices. Capital to these farmers is no longer lumpy indivisible capital goods, but divisible machine time which he/she can hire to the extent required for his/her farm. The present chapter discusses the role and impact of two emerging factor markets in Indian agriculture. The next two sections of the chapter look into the various aspects and issues related to the water markets and rental markets of agricultural capital goods, respectively. The discussions are combined again for the two markets in the concluding section.

2 Water markets

We all know that there has been increasing use of groundwater for domestic, industrial and agricultural purposes all over the world. Presently, India is the world's largest user of groundwater, where groundwater provides about 80 per cent of India's drinking water and nearly two-thirds of irrigation needs. Though the two main sources of irrigation are canals and groundwater, the relative contribution of canal irrigation has been steadily declining over the years, while groundwater, especially that extracted through tube wells (both deep and shallow), has rapidly grown in significance over the last 30 years. This growth in groundwater-based irrigation in the country was triggered mainly by India's Green Revolution. As a result, over the last four decades, around 84 per cent of the total addition to irrigation has come from groundwater. With rapid development in groundwater-based irrigation, such economic institutions as rental markets for irrigation assets, groundwater markets and community-level farmer/user associations have come into force to govern use of groundwater in agriculture and distribution of it among farmers. In this section, we will confine the discussion to the groundwater market, or water market as it is popularly called.

In the literature on the water market, we find two different types of r markets: formal and informal. The first one refers to water markets that involve the annual or permanent transfer of the water use rights between a willing buyer and a willing seller in exchange for compensation determined by supply and demand, the cost of mobility, the reliability of the supply and the cost of mitigating any environmental and third-party effects (Simpson, 1994). Easter et al. (1998) adds that in the formal water market, the water sale can be for a specified volume of water or share of water rights for a set period of time, or the sale can be for the transfer of permanent water rights. Formal water markets are mostly found in the western United States, Chile, Australia, Peru, Spain and Mexico, as well as in some parts of South Africa, North Africa, Brazil (Bjornlund and McKay, 1998,2002; Bate, 2002) and Georgia (Isley and Middleton, 2003). Another type of water market refers to localized, village-level informal arrangements for water transactions whereby owners of water extracting devices (WEDs) (e.g., pump sets, tube wells, etc.) sell water or irrigation services to neighbouring farmers for prices mostly determined by the incremental cost of pumping (Shah, 1991,1993). According to Pant (1992), water markets are likely to exist in a situation where the following four conditions are satisfied: (a) the buyers perceive irrigation through purchase of groundwater as the most agreeable alternative in comparison to other sources of irrigation; (b) the water supplier has pumping capacity in excess of his own requirements and perceives water sales as a profitable proposition;.(c) willing buyers are available within the command area of the suppliers' irrigation equipment in case the pump sets are fixed (in case of mobile pump sets, there is no fixed command area and the managerial control in that case is more important); and (d) buyers are able to physically gain access to the water. This village-level type of informal water market is found mostly in Mexico (Thobani, 1997; World Bank, 1999), Jordan (Meinzen-Dick and Mendoza, 1996) and in Asian countries such as Pakistan, Bangladesh, (Rinaudo and Strosser, 1997; Meinzen-Dick, 1998; Shah, 1991,1993; Saleth, 1996,1998), Indonesia, and China (Zhang et al., 2006).

The water market found in India is an informal institutional arrangement (Shah, 1991,1993), and its existence is not uniform throughout the country. In some states, such as Gujarat, Maharashtra, Haryana, Andhra Pradesh, Tamil Nadu, Western Uttar Pradesh, Punjab and West Bengal, the presence of such markets is more widespread (Saleth, 1996). Although occurrence of groundwater markets is more widespread in these states, development of the market is most pronounced in Gujarat (Narain, 1997; Dubash, 2000; Mohanty and Gupta, 2002). This uneven growth of water markets in India suggests that the size and rate of proliferation of the markets depend upon the status of agricultural development, agro-climatic conditions, cost and availability of electricity, and development of tube wells under private ownership (Shah, 1993; Saleth, 1994).

Although most of the studies point out that the general mechanism underpinning operation of the market is similar, there are significant differences in the mode of operation and in the nature and types of contracts, with serious implications for the functioning of the market. Based on different commercial and noncommercial aspects of water markets, Saleth (1998) notes that water markets in India display a wide variation in terms of organizational features and Behavioral patterns.[1] However, proponents of groundwater markets have concurred that these differences are obvious when groundwater markets are village-level, localized institutions (Pant, 1991; Shah, 1993; Joshi, 2005; Zhang et al., 2006) and highly dependent upon agro-climatic conditions, status of agricultural and economic development, farming practices or technology, and socio-economic conditions of the farmers. In the presence of such differences, Dubash (2000) notes that instead of looking at how the markets work or do not work, it is important to look at how and why they work differently in different locations, under different social and hydrological circumstances and with what effects. In this respect, Palanaizami and Easter (1991) have observed that even in the presence of a monopoly position on the part of the well owners, in a water-abundant region the best strategy is to encourage or legalize trading and increase competition either through community or private well development. Shah (1991) observed that a water-abundant region (Eastern India in his example) offers a major opportunity, where the development of water markets can transform stagnant agriculture into a booming economy. The question in an abundant region, as Shah has pointed out, is how to speed up the development of water markets and saturate the available potential. In the same context, Saleth (1994) also observed that the issue in groundwater development in the eastern part of India, which is marked by abundant groundwater supply, is different from the water-scarce southern region. The major issue in a water-abundant region, according to Saleth, is promotion of the groundwater, rather than regulation, and one has to focus on correction of institutional and technical bottlenecks for more development of groundwater for the promotion of agriculture.

In view of the fact that small and marginal farmers with limited capability for capital investment dominate the agricultural scenario of the country, the emergence of the water market has helped ensure equity of access to irrigation across farmers, besides ensuring efficient utilization of the irrigation assets. Studies have confirmed that with increased access to assured irrigation, participating farmers have been able to enhance production and productivity, and achieve higher technical efficiency in cultivation (Srivastava et al., 2009; Manjunatha et al., 2009, 2011a, 2011b; Tamuli, 2014).

However, there is an increasing concern related to the growth of the water market in India: that the penetration of informal water markets may lead to over-exploitation of the groundwater resources, with serious inter-temporal externalities in the form of declining water tables, higher pumping costs, lower well yield or even abandonment of wells, especially in the water-scare regions.[2] (Moench, 1992; Shah, 1993; Janakarajan, 1993; Saleth, 1994, 1996; Narain, 1997; Meinzen-Dick, 1998; Singh, 2002;Mondal and Majumdar, 2008). Since individual farmers are more concerned with their private gains and costs, and may completely ignore social costs (negative externality) of the over-exploitation of groundwater resources, growth of groundwater markets may aggravate aquifer depletion (Saleth, 1998). The striking implication of such apprehension is connected with the property rights of groundwater in India. The ownership of groundwater in India is attached to land, and landowners have the right to extract groundwater beyond any limit until it is available.[3] Under such a situation, pricing of water that fails to reflect its scarcity value may lead to over-exploitation. This ultimately may result in allocative inefficiency, inequity in resource use and ecological unsustainability (Saleth, 1996; Narain, 1997). This negative externality associated with the growth of water markets is already very intensive in water-scarce or dry regions in India (Moench, 1992, 2002; Chandrakanth et al., 2004;

Scott and Shah, 2004). There have emerged conflicts over the use of ground-water among the farmers (Cullet, 2012; Janakarajan and Moench, 2006; Foster and Gardunu, 2004). However, whether this issue is present in water-abundant regions needs to be established.

It is clear from the preceding discussion that most of the issues of groundwater markets are region specific. While a number of important studies on water markets from water-scarce regions have become available, studies from water abundant regions are relatively limited. Here a case study from the state of Assam, which lies in the eastern part of India with abundant groundwater reserves and heavy monsoon precipitation ensuring easy replenishment, is presented to examine the importance and practice of water markets in agriculture.

According to the data available (Govt. of Assam, 2015), out of the total geographical area of 78.44 lakh hectares, the gross cropped area (GCA) of Assam is 41.05 lakh hectares. Against this, the ultimate gross irrigation potential (annually irrigable area) has been estimated at 27 lakh hectares, which constitutes 65.80 per cent of the GCA. Irrigation development in the state has been undertaken under two broad schemes: major/medium irrigation and minor irrigation (uses basically surface lift and groundwater lift). One interesting fact related to irrigation development in the state is the rapid growth of a groundwater-based minor irrigation scheme in the late 1990s. For example, the compound annual growth rate (CAGR) of total minor irrigation structures in the state was 11.40 per cent during 1986–87 to 1993–94, and increased to 16.08 per cent during 1993–94 to 2000–2001, while the same for India was 6.99 per cent during 1993–94 to 2000–01 (MoWR, 2001, 2005). Among the groundwater structures, shallow tube wells (STWs) have recorded phenomenal growth, outstripping surface irrigation schemes (surface flow and surface lift) in the state. Compared to surface flow and surface lift, STWs constituted about 68.36 per cent of the groundwater structures in 1986–87, marginally increased to about 69.13 per cent in 2000–01 and further increased to 87.29 per cent in 2000–2001. Shallow tube wells, thus, are now the most important and fastest growing sources of irrigation in Assam. One of the striking features of shallow tube well–based irrigation development in the state is that these tube wells are installed under private ownership and usually owned by an individual farmer. As per the Minor Irrigation Census 2000–01 of the Government of India, in Assam about 98 per cent of the total STWs are under individual ownership. Along with the government-supported development of STWs, there has been unprecedented development of STWs at the private initiative of the farmers themselves (Dutta, 2011). Most of the owners of a water extracting mechanism (wem) with excess capacity of their tube wells engage in water transactions with their neighbouring farmers who do not own a WEM (on their own) for market and non-market reasons (Dutta, 2011). This has resulted in the emergence of groundwater markets in the state.

A survey of 198 farm households from the Central Brahmaputra Valley Zone (CBVZ) of the state conducted by the authors during agricultural year 2011–12 reveals that water markets refunctioning quite extensively in rural Assam. About 90.91 per cent of the sample farmers are engaged in water transactions. There are six alternative market arrangements[4] for water trade: self-users (SU); self-users and sellers (SU+S); self-users, sellers and buyers (SU+S+B); self-users and buyers (SU+B); buyers (B); and owners and sellers (OS). The distribution of the sample farmers under these six different structures of water markets shows that 'buyers' alone constitutes the largest segment (39.90 per cent), followed by 'self-users and sellers' (38.38 per cent). The majority of the sample buyers are found to be small (41.54 per cent) and marginal (56.82 per cent) farmers. Buyers in the semi-medium category constitute only 5.13 per cent, indicating that buyers in the water markets are usually small and marginal farmers. In case of sellers, out of the total sample in the category of 'self-users and sellers', about 65.78 per cent are small and marginal farmers. The numbers of 'self-user and sellers' in the semi-medium and medium categories of farm holdings constitute about 28.94 and 5.26 per cent, respectively. That the majority of the water sellers are concentrated in the category of small and marginal farmers is in contrast with the established theory in the existing literature on water markets, which reports that the water sellers are usually the large farmers, whereas the buyers are small farmers (Saleth, 1998). Further, a few members of the group 'owners and sellers' do not hold any cultivable land but are in possession of shallow tube wells and engage in water selling. On the seller's side, it shows that the market has helped some of the tube well owners to sell water, taking groundwater pumping as an additional source of income. It also suggests that the market is not residual[5] to the buyers in all cases, in contrast to the popular belief that water markets are residual. Thus, field-level evidence supports that the water market has helped small and marginal farmers to gain access to irrigation.

Water markets are closely linked with other rural markets, like informal credit markets and land tenancy markets (Meinzen-Dick, 1998; Fujita and Hossain, 1995; Palmer-Jones, 1993; Saleth, 1998; Jacoby et al., 2004; Kajisa and Sakurai, 2003,2005, etc.). In our survey, about 31.95 per cent of the total sample of water buyers have leased in land from the water sellers, and about 42.27 per cent of the total sellers have leased out land to the water buyers. The majority of the buyers are small and marginal farmers, and in most cases they are tenants, leasing in small plots of land from the water sellers/land owners. The water market thus has helped to grow the land tenancy market, thereby bringing more plots under cultivation in the state.

Relating to the size of the water market, there is no macro-level estimate in India. However, some empirical micro studies from different parts of the country have estimated the size of the market in the respective study areas, primarily using two indices: percentage of total water output traded and average number of buyers per water seller. For instance, Shah (1993) estimated that more than 50 per cent of the gross area irrigated by private modern WEDs in Gujarat was served by water markets. Saleth (1998), using a methodology based on pump sets rental data put the figure at 6 million hectares, or 15 per cent of the total area irrigated by groundwater. Mohanty and Gupta (2002), assuming a contribution of irrigated cultivation to total output at $230/ha/year, have estimated the total value of output due to water sales to be $1.38 billion/year.

The estimates provided by Saleth (1998) and Mohanty and Gupta (2002) are based on several micro-level studies conducted across states in India. There is a great degree of variation in the size of water markets among different states. In northern Gujarat, nearly 80 per cent of the total irrigated acreage is irrigated through water markets (Shah, 1993), while in the eastern region and the western part of Uttar Pradesh, it is 73 and79 per cent, respectively (Pant, 2004). Similarly, about 40 to 60 per cent of irrigated land is irrigated through water markets in the Allahabad district of Uttar Pradesh (Shankar, 1992), followed by 30 per cent in Vaigai Basin in Tamil Nadu (Janakarajan, 1993). Dubash (2000) has noted that in the Ratanpura village of the Mehsana district of Gujarat, between 61 per centand71 per cent of the water pumped is sold, and 90 per cent of landed households depend fully or partly on purchased groundwater; 44 per cent rely entirely on purchased groundwater for irrigation. About 53.19 per cent of the total irrigated area has been served by water selling. Looking at the size of the water market from the buyers' point of view, it has been found that out of all buyers, about 74.23 per cent have purchased water from one seller, followed by 18.56 per cent purchasing from two sellers and the rest (7.22 per cent) purchasing from three sellers.

As discussed above, groundwater drafting is associated with a negative externality. Market-induced groundwater depletion is extensively reported from the water-scare regions of the country, such as Tamilnadu, Andhra Pradesh, Gujarat and so on. In areas with abundant groundwater reserves and heavy monsoon precipitation ensuring easy replenishment, like Assam in eastern India, this problem may not appear to be so serious. However, the possibility that unregulated groundwater extraction can eventually lead to local problems of groundwater over-exploitation can't be ruled out. In the context of the state of Assam, no such dispute over the use of groundwater has been noticed. The possible reason for this may be that the state has sufficient groundwater reserves which get amply replenished through an abundance of monsoon and pre-monsoon precipitation, unlike other parts of the country. In Assam, out of the total annual replenishable amount of groundwater, only 22 per cent of it has so far been developed for agricultural, industrial and domestic purposes, leaving plenty of scope for development of groundwater-based irrigation in the state. Yet, most of the market participants surveyed during 2011–12 reported failure of the pump sets in delivering sufficient water when all the pump sets in the field are operated concurrently, indicating that there is relative scarcity of groundwater in a few locations. Owing to this, a few farmers have expressed their apprehension that unfettered penetration of pump sets may cause conflict over the use of groundwater. Thus, a need for suitable regulation of operations of water markets even in richly endowed locations cannot be ruled out. Interventions for inducing the regulations to emerge may be needed. If the regulations emerge locally from community action, the possibility of the norms getting tailored to local environment is likely. A standard set of regulations for all conditions may not be suitable.

3 Rental markets of capital goods in India's agriculture

The hiring and renting of farm capital goods is not an entirely new phenomenon. Relatively old studies by Jodha (1974), Roy and Blasé (1978) and Agarwal (1984) reported the existence of rental markets of agricultural capital goods in different parts of India. The study by Jodha (1974) revealed that in Rajasthan farmers hired tractors to use in their farm operation, and owner users of tractors having excess capacity rented them out. It was also stated that the spatial extent of such transactions was beyond the district level. There is also evidence of the use of tractors in agriculture through hiring in Punjab (Roy and Blasé, 1978; Agarwal, 1984). Recently, Rath (2015) mentioned the hiring use of tractors in India due to maintenance difficulty of bullocks resulting from declining farm size.

Despite not being a new phenomenon, we consider the rental market of agricultural capital goods as an emerging market because the incidence of hiring and renting such goods has become extensive and pervasive in recent years. The extensive practice of renting and hiring of agricultural capital goods in recent time in India can be seen from the data provided by the Input Survey, India, 2011–12. In India, farmers of all size groups have been using different agricultural capital goods (Input Survey, India, 2011–12). The data reveal that even expensive farm machinery is used by at least some proportion of farmers of all the size groups (refer Table 4.1). In the country as a whole, use of all such capital goods is the highest by marginal size group farmers, followed by small size group farmers. Small and fragmented land holdings is a predominant characteristic of Indian agriculture,[6] which normally discourages own use of heavy capital goods in agriculture due to efficiency loss. Moreover, for most Indian farmers, especially for small and marginal farmers, such expensive farm capital goods may not affordable. Apart from these, maintenance and operational difficulty of such capital goods due to manpower shortage, inadequate availability of repairing facility and so on also limit the ownership of them. Given these, own use of such capital goods is not likely to be extensive. Thus, taking into account these propositions, it can be argued that use of such capital goods, at least by some proportion of farmers, especially in the small and marginal size classes, is through hiring, as pointed out by Rath (2015).

The literature and data make it clear that rental markets of agricultural capital goods are functioning in India. However, certain aspects of the rental markets of agricultural capital goods, like the extent and nature of such markets, impact on agriculture, linkage with other factor markets such as the credit market, presence of imperfection and so on, are not clear from the available data and empirical works. The authors fall back upon a field study in the plains of Assam[7] from November 2013 to January 2014 to examine some of these issues. An investigation based on a survey of 232 farm households from three parts of the plains of Assam reveals that rental markets of agricultural capital goods are quite extensive in the state.[8] Farmers of various size classes have participated in these markets.

Table 4.1 Size group-wise use of some heavy farm machineries in India

Types of machinery	Marginal (Below 1.0)	Small (1.0–1.99)	Semi-medium (2.0–3.99)	Medium (4.0–9.99)	Large (10 And Above)	All groups
Diesel engine pumpset	21,736,459 (23.45)	4,462,645 (18.03)	2,596,819 (18.72)	1,107,661 (18.92)	178,273 (18.71)	30,081,857 (21.78)
Electric pumpset	11,745,137 (12.67)	5,339,823 (21.58)	3,609,617 (26.03)	1,785,400 (30.50)	280,765 (29.46)	22,760,742 (16.48)
Power tiller	4,801,341 (5.18)	1,703,980 (6.89)	956,320 (6.90)	427,717 (7.31)	64,503 (6.77)	7,953,861 (5.76)
Agricultural tractor	40,615,189 (43.82)	10,572,257 (42.72)	6,117,484 (44.11)	3,189,945 (54.49)	638,076 (66.95)	61,132,951 (44.26)
Tractor-drawn board plough	6,088,863 (6.57)	3,350,334 (13.54)	244,3681 (17.62)	143,9329 (24.59)	327,452 (34.36)	13,649,659 (9.88)
Tractor-drawn disc harrow	4,457,499 (4.81)	2,446,517 (9.89)	1,996,004 (14.39)	137,8174 (23.54)	351,751 (36.91)	10,629,945 (7.70)
Tractor-drawn seed-cum-fertilizer drill	3,209,655 (3.46)	2,289,752 (9.25)	2,025,924 (14.61)	1,477,035 (25.23)	372,816 (39.12)	9,375,182 (6.79)
Tractor-drawn planter	872,975 (0.94)	518,610 (2.10)	375,557 (2.71)	245,374 (4.19)	56,306 (5.91)	2,068,822 (1.50)
Tractor-drawn leveler	4,857,044 (5.24)	2,398,702 (9.69)	1,776,488 (12.81)	1,120,216 (19.14)	272,906 (28.64)	10,425,356 (7.55)
Tractor-drawn potato digger	422,278 (0.46)	284,402 (1.15)	221,441 (1.60)	125,840 (2.15)	28,348 (2.97)	1,082,309 (0.78)
Combine harvester (tractor powered)	1,567,985 (1.69)	577,441 (2.33)	377,135 (2.72)	215,851 (3.69)	57,445 (6.03)	2,795,857 (2.02)

Note: Figures in parentheses indicate percentage of operational holdings using capital goods to the total operational holdings of the size group.

Source: Adapted from Input Survey, India, 2011–12

However, it has been found the lessors in such markets are relatively large farmers and more educated than the lessees. The rental markets of agricultural capital goods are found to be informal in nature.

Our field investigation reveals that rental markets of farm machinery contribute significantly to extending farm mechanization. A large proportion of users of both tilling and irrigation machinery have been found to be hirer. In fact, rental markets of capital goods facilitate mechanization of tilling and irrigation by hiring users as intensively as by owner users.[9] Further, it is understandable that the own use of those capital goods has been increased at least to some extent due to the possibility of renting out the excess capacity of such capital goods. Most of the owner users of tilling and irrigation machinery have been found to have rented out their machinery.[10]This implies that their cultivable land is not sufficient to utilize the capacity of their capital goods fully. Through renting out, such owner users can earn some income. In the absence of rental markets, fuller utilization of capital goods and earning of additional income would have not been possible for these owner users. In such situation, incentives to invest in such capital goods and also to use these machineries by themselves are likely to be less. Thus, rental markets of agricultural capital goods enhance farm mechanization not only by facilitating hiring use but also by encouraging own use of such machinery.

These markets are also found to have contributed, directly or indirectly, to intensive and diversified cultivation, and to yield realization of rice.[11] It has been found that users of irrigation machinery, either own or hiring, have been able to realize significantly higher cropping intensity, crop diversification and yield of rice as compared to non-users of such capital goods. However, there is no significant difference in the values of these indicators of production and productivity enhancing practices between users, either owner or hiring users, of tilling machinery and the non-users of it. Even though the positive impact of the rental market of tilling machinery on cropping intensity, crop diversification and rice yield is not visible directly, such markets contribute indirectly to them by enhancing the extent of mechanization of tilling which has significant bearing on adoption of improved farm practices.

In terms of size classes, the small and marginal farmers are the major participant group in rental markets of both tilling and irrigation machinery.[12] In the context of the present case study, a total of 86 per cent and 88 per cent of hiring users of tilling machinery and irrigation machinery, respectively, have been found to be small and marginal farmers. Area-wise too, 68 per cent of gross area tilled through hired machinery and 71 per cent of gross area irrigated through hired machinery belong to the small and marginal size classes. Given the fact that large-scale participation in rental markets of capital goods and their use through hiring are by small and marginal farmers who would not otherwise have been able to use such machinery in the absence of rental markets, it is clear that small and marginal farmers benefited immensely from the functioning of tilling and irrigation machinery rental markets. It may be mentioned at this juncture that by way of enabling the adoption of production and productivity enhancing practices by farmers of all size classes, and extending mechanization of farm operation, especially in small and marginal holdings, rental markets of capital goods have fulfilled the objective of the land reform measure of consolidation of holding.

In the functioning and spreading of rental markets of agricultural capital goods, access to credit has an important role (Das, 2016). However, the type of role played by credit is not the same across sources. By encouraging the ownership of farm capital goods, institutional credit increases the participation of farmers in rental markets of agricultural capital goods only as supplier. Procurement of capital goods, particularly the heavy ones such as tractor, power tiller, pump set, combine harvester and so on, requires a large amount of capital, and the interest burden is less in case of institutional credit. Hence, institutional credit is generally used for purchasing capital goods rather than for hiring of such capital goods. On the other hand, non-institutional credit encourages farmers' participation in such markets both as suppliers and as demanders. The impact of non-institutional credit on demanders in such markets can be attributed to the fact that decision making for hiring the agricultural capital goods is instant and requires less capital. These make non-institutional credit preferable over institutional credit for hiring agricultural capital goods.

While rental markets of agricultural capital goods have several positive impacts on agriculture, the equity and efficiency implications of the functioning of such markets depend on the absence of major imperfections. Presence of market power (monopoly/monopsony) is one source of welfare loss. Presence of market power may affect the equity and efficiency of these markets on two counts. First, as it is evident from the present field study, the suppliers of the rental markets of agricultural capital goods are predominantly large land holders. Under such circumstances, the possibility that the suppliers of capital goods exercise greater influence in a rural economy, by virtue of their greater control over land, cannot be ruled out. However, the presence of several competing suppliers can moderate such influence, provided there is absence of collusion among them. Second, most of the suppliers of capital goods are also users of them. Such suppliers will rent out their machinery only after completing the operation in their own fields. Hence, it is understandable that machinery is not available for hiring when they are being used by the owners. So, hiring users will have to wait their turn for the machinery to be available. Therefore, to the extent cultivation is weather and season dependent, the hiring users may not be able to get the machinery for use at the most opportune time for cultivation. While the first possible type of imperfection may result in a rental rate higher than the competitive market, some productivity losses may arise for the hiring users due to the second type of imperfection.

The market power–related imperfection in rental markets of agricultural capital goods can be reduced by enhancing competition among the suppliers by raising their volume. Greater penetration and deployment of institutional credit in the agriculture sector can help in this matter. This will help not only in neutralizing the impact of market power but also in extending the size of these markets.

4 Conclusion

The discussion in the chapter depicts that the emerging agricultural factor markets – rental markets of capital goods and water markets – are quite active and extensive in rural India. These two markets play a major role in better utilization of land and mechanization of agriculture. More importantly, small and marginal farmers, which constitute a large majority of Indian farmers, have gained immensely from the functioning of such markets. In the absence of these markets, a large section of farmers of the country would have remained outside the ambit of mechanized cultivation. Apart from facilitating farm mechanization and adoption and use of good farm practices, rental markets of farm capital goods also make cultivation in adverse situations possible. By making possible the adoption of production and productivity enhancing practices such as intensive and diversified cultivation, the realization of better yield and the extension of farm mechanization, especially by small and marginal farmers, rental markets of farm capital goods and water markets have substituted for the long-pending consolidation of landholding programme part of the India's agrarian reform.

Having noted the positive and prospective roles of these emerging factor markets in Indian agriculture, it is also necessary to be aware of the hazards of failures of these markets, especially of water markets in relatively drier parts of the country. Intervention for regulating market activities in the form of rules/norms set up by the state or the communities is desirable so that this priceless gift of nature is utilized efficiently and equitably for participative prosperity of the agriculture sector of the country.

Notes

1 Saleth (1998) notes, 'those in northern Gujarat operate almost like agribusiness with cash-based transactions complete with cash receipts and purchase records. In contrast, water markets in parts of Andhra Pradesh, Tamil Nadu, and southern Gujarat show shades of the feudal character involving 'water rent' and the provision for unpaid labour services. In between these two extreme fall those in the relatively water abundant Indo-Gangetic and deltaic regions that display a rather muted form of commercial character'.

2 Harmful effects of over-exploitation of groundwater in different states of the country have been recorded as follows: water logging and salinity in Punjab, Haryana and Western Rajasthan; fluoride contamination in north Gujarat and southern Rajasthan; and ingress of saline sea water into the aquifers in states like Gujarat and Maharashtra (Singh and Singh, 2003).

3 There are three laws that govern both ownership and use of groundwater in India. *Firstly,* The Easement Act, 1882 which allows usufructary rights in groundwater by viewing it as an easement connected to the land; *Secondly,* The Transfer of Property Act, 1882 (specially clause 6 (c)), which provides that an easement (groundwater in this case) can be given to one only if the dominant heritage (in this case land) is also transferred; *Thirdly,* Land Acquisition Act, 1889 which asserts that if someone is interested in getting rights over groundwater, he would have to be interested in the land (Narain, 1997). Thus, in the given circumstances defined by the three different laws, in India the land owners consider water beneath their land as private resource.

4 Self-users+sellers: Farmers with independent or joint ownership (or both) of tube wells use water for cultivating their own plots and sell water to needy farmers in the vicinity of the tube well, usually after meeting their own requirements.

   Buyers: Farmers buy water from the nearest single or multiple tube wells, usually adjacent to their agricultural plots. However, the possibility of water purchase from any distant source cannot be ruled out when there is suitable arrangement for water conveyance.

   Self-users+sellers+buyers: The owner of tube wells cultivate their agricultural plots with water from their own tube wells, sell water to willing buyers after meeting their own requirement, and buy water from other tube wells in another location, especially when their cultivable land is fragmented into two or more than two plots.

   Self-users+buyers: Farmers with independent ownership or joint ownership of a tube well or tube wells use water from their own tube wells for own use in one plot and buy water from other tube wells for other plots.

   Owner+sellers: Farmers have invested in tube wells not to meet their own irrigation requirements but primarily to sell water to other farmers.

   Self-users: Farmers with individual or joint ownership of tube wells use it for cultivation on their own plots

5 Water markets are residual in nature; that is, water sellers usually sell water after meeting their own requirements.

6 The average size of operational holdings in India is 1.15 hectare as per the Agriculture Census, Government of India, 2010–11.

7 One of the agro-based and small and marginal farmer preponderant states of northeast India. As per the Agriculture Census, Assam, 2010–11, a total of 67.31 and 18.26 per cent of the operational holdings in the state are marginal and small, respectively, and the average size of such holdings is 1.10 hectare.

8 The study covered rental markets of tilling and irrigation machinery. It has been found that the percentage of participation of sample farmers in rental markets of tilling machinery and irrigation machinery are 78.02 per cent and 34.91 per cent, respectively. Among the sample users of tilling machinery and irrigation machinery, the percentage of participations are 99.45 per cent and 77.14 per cent, respectively.

9 Refer to Table 6.1 in Das (2015).

10 A total of 94 per cent of tilling machinery and 29 per cent of irrigation machinery have been found to be rent out.

11 Refer to Tables 6.2, 6.3 and 6.4 in Das (2015).

12 As per data collected from field, in terms of operational holding, small and marginal farmers comprise around 82 per cent and 85 per cent, respectively, of participants in rental markets of tilling and irrigation machinery. By ownership holding of cultivable land, small and marginal farmers constitute around 87 per cent and 94 per cent, respectively, of the participants in tilling and irrigation machinery rental markets.

References

Agarwal, B., 1984. Tractors, Tube Wells and Cropping Intensity in the Indian Punjab. *The Journal of Development Studies*, 20(4), pp. 290–302.

Bate, R., 2002. Water – Can Property Rights and Markets Replace Conflict? In Morris, J. (ed.), *Sustainable Development: Promoting Progress or Perpetuating Poverty?* Profile Books, London.

Bjornlund, H. and McKay, J., 1998. Factors Affecting Water Prices in a Rural Water Market: A South Australian Experience. *Water Resources Research*, 34(6), pp. 1563–1570.

Bjornlund, H. and McKay, J., 2002. Aspects of Water Markets for Developing Countries: Experiences From Australia, Chile and the US. *Environmental and Development Economics*, 7(4), pp. 769–795.

Chandrakanth, M. G., Alemu, B. and Bhat, M. G., 2004. Combating Negative Externalities of Drought: A Study of Groundwater Recharge Through Watershed. *Economic and Political Weekly*, 39(11), pp. 1164–1170.

Cullet, P., 2012. Groundwater: Towards a New Legal and Institutional Framework In Cullet, P., Paranjape, S., Thakkar, H., Vani, M. S., Joy, K. J. and Ramesh, M. K. (eds.), *Water Conflicts in India: Towards a New Legal and Institutional Framework.* Forum for Policy Dialogue on Water Conflicts in India, Pune, International Environmental Law Research Centre, Geneva.

Das, A. K., 2015. *Functioning and Impact of Rental Markets of Agricultural Capital Goods in Assam*, available at http://hdl.handle.net/10603/94654, accessed 07/04/2017.

Das, A. K., 2016. Impact of Access to Credit on Rental Markets of Agricultural Capital Goods: Evidence from Assam of North-East India. *Bangladesh Development Studies*, XXXIX(1&2), pp. 83–101.

Dobbs, T. and Foster, P., 1972. Incentives to Invest in New Agricultural Inputs in North India. *Economic Development and Cultural Change*, 21(1), pp. 101–117.

Dubash, N. K., 2000. Ecologically and Socially Embedded Exchange: 'Gujarat Model' of Water Markets. *Economic and Political Weekly*, 35(16), pp. 1376–1385.

Dutta, M. K., 2007. Management of Groundwater Irrigation in Assam Through Water Markets. *Icfai Journal of Environmental Economics*, V(4), pp. 28–43.

Dutta, M. K., 2011. *Irrigation Potential in Agriculture of Assam*, Concept Publishing House Pvt. Ltd., New Delhi.

Easter, K. W., Dinar, A. and Rosegrant, M. W., 1998. Water Markets: Transaction Costs and Institutional Options. In Easter, K. W., Rosegrant, M. W. and Dinar, A. (eds.), *Markets for Water: Potential and Performance*, Kluwer Academic Publisher.

Foster, S and H. Gardunu (2004), *Tamil Nadu: Resolving the Conflict over Rural Groundwater Use Between Drinking Water and Irrigation Supply*, in GW MATE: Case Profile on Sustainable Groundwater Management Lessons from Practice, World Bank, Washington D.C., Retrieved from http://www.worldbank.org.gmate on 10/03/2012.

Fujita, K. and Hossain, F., 1995. Role of the Groundwater Market in Agricultural Development and Income Distribution: A Case Study in a North West Bangladesh Village. *The Developing Economics*, 33(4), pp. 442–463.

Government of Assam, 2010–11. *Agriculture Census*, Directorate of Economics and Statistics.

Government of Assam, 2015. *Economic Survey of Assam*, 2014–15, Directorate of Economics and Statistics.

Government of India, 2010–11. *Agriculture Census*, Available at http://agcensus.nic.in/document/ac1011/reports/air2010-11complete.pdf. Accessed 02/12/2016.

Government of India, 2011–12. *Input Survey*, available at http://inputsurvey.dac net.nic.in/RNL/nationaltable7.aspx, accessed 07/04/2017.

Indian Journal of Agricultural Economics, 2014. Inter-Conference Symposium of International Association of Agricultural Economists (IAAE) on Re-Visiting Agriculture Policies in the Light of Globalisation Experience: The Indian Context: A Brief Report. *Indian Journal of Agricultural Economics*, 69(4), pp. 501–503.

Isley, P. and Middleton Jr., R. J., 2003. *Water Markets in Georgia: An Overview of Ongoing Sales of Water.* Water Policy Working Paper, No. 2003-006.

Jacoby, H. G., Murgai, R. and Rehman, S. U., 2004. Monopoly Power and Distribution in Fragmented Markets: The Case of Groundwater. *The Review of Economic Studies*, 71(7), pp. 783–808.

Janakarajan, S., 1993. *Trading in Groundwater: A Source of Power and Accumulation*. In the Report, Costs and Productivity of Irrigation in Tamil Nadu, Planning Commission of India, Govt. of India.

Janakarajan, S. and Moench, M., 2006. Are Wells a Potential Threat to Farmers' Wellbeing? Case of Deteriorating Groundwater Irrigation in Tamil Nadu. *Economic and Political Weekly*, 41(37), pp. 3977–3978.

Jodha, N.S., 1974. A Case of the Process of Tractorisation. *Economic & Political Weekly*, 9(52), pp. A111+A113–A115+A117–A118.

Joshi, P. K., (2005). Ground Water Management: Problems and Opportunities. In Marothia, D. K. (ed.), *Institutionalising Common Pool Resources*, Concept Publishing Company, New Delhi.

Kajisa, K. and Sakurai, T., 2003. Determinants of Groundwater Price Under Bilateral Bargaining With Multiple Modes of Contracts: A Case From Madhya Pradesh, India. *Japanese Journal of Rural Economy*, 5, pp. 1–11.

Kajisa, K. and Sakurai, T., 2005. Efficiency and Equity in Groundwater Markets: The Case of Madhya Pradesh, India. *Environmental and Development Economics*,10(6), pp. 801–819.

Manjunatha, A.V., Speelman, S. M., Chandrakanth, G. and Huylenbroeck, V. G., 2009. *Efficiency of Water Use in Groundwater Markets: The Case of Peninsular India*. Paper presented in the Conference on International Research on Food Security, Natural Resource Management and Rural Development, University of Hamburg, October 6–8, available atwww.tropentag.de/2009/abstracts/full/47.pdf, accessed25/01/2011.

Manjunatha, A. V., Speelman, S. M., Chandrakanth, G. and Huylenbroeck, V. G., 2011a. *Can Groundwater Markets Promote Efficiency in Agricultural Production?* Paper presented in the 13th Biennial Conference of the International Association for the Study of the Commons (IASC), January 10–14, Hyderabad, India.

Manjunatha, A. V., Speelman, S. M., Chandrakanth, G. and Huylenbroeck, V. G., 2011b. Impact of Groundwater Markets in India on Water Use Efficiency: A Data Envelopment Analysis Approach. *Journal of Environmental Management*, 92(1), pp. 2924–2929.

Meinzen-Dick, R. S., 1998. Groundwater Markets in Pakistan: Institutional Development and Productivity Impacts. In Easter, K. W., Rosegrant, M. W. and Dinar, A. (eds.), *Markets for Water: Potential and Performance*, Kluwer Academic Publishers.

Meinzen-Dick, R. S. and Mendoza, M., 1996. Alternative to Water Allocation Mechanisms: Indian and International Experiences. *Economic and Political Weekly*, 31(13), pp. A25–A30.

Misra, S.K. and Puri, V. K., 2004. *Indian Economy*, Himalaya Publishing House, Mumbai.

Moench, M., 1992. Chasing the Water Table: Equity and Sustainability in Groundwater Management. *Economic and Political Weekly*, 27(51–52), pp. A171–A177.

Moench, M., 2002. When Management Fails: Evolutionary Perspectives and Adaptive Frameworks for Responding to Water Problems. Working Paper, Institute for Social and Environmental Transitions, Boulder, CO.

Mohanty, N. and Gupta, S., 2002. *Breaking the Gridlock in Water Reforms Through Water Markets: International Experience and Implementation Issues for India*. Working Paper Series, Julian L. Simon Centre for Policy Research, August.

Mondal, R. C. and Majumdar, D., 2008. Role of Water Markets in Groundwater Management in West Bengal. In Jharwal, S. M. (ed.), *Glimpses of Indian Agriculture: Macro and Micro Aspects*, Vol. 2: Micro Aspects, Academic Foundation, New Delhi.

MoWR, 2001. *Census of Minor Irrigation Schemes – 1993-94*, Minor Irrigation Division, Ministry of Water Resources, Govt. of India, New Delhi.

MoWR, 2005. *Third Census Minor Irrigation Schemes – 2000-01*, Minor Irrigation Division, Ministry of Water Resources, Govt. of India, New Delhi.

Narain, V.,1997. India's Water Crisis: Avenues for Policy and Institutional Reform. *TERI Information Monitor on Environmental Science*, 2(1), pp. 1–6.

Palanasami, K. and Easter, K. W., 1991. Hydro-Economic Interaction Between Tank Storage and Groundwater Recharge. *Indian Journal of Agricultural Economics*, 46(2), pp. 174–177.

Palmer-Jones, R., 1993. *Groundwater Market in South Asia: A Discussion of Theory and Evidence*. Paper Presented at the Workshop on Water Management: India's Groundwater Challenge at VIKSAT, Ahmadabad, December 1993.

Pant, N., 1991. Groundwater Resources Issues in Eastern India. In Meinzen-Dick, R. and Svendsen, M. (eds.), *Future Directions for Indian Agriculture – Research and Policy Issues*, International Food Policy Research Institute, Washington D.C., USA.

Pant, N., 1992. *New Trend in Indian Irrigation*, Ashish Publishing House, New Delhi.

Pant, N., 2004. Trends in Groundwater Irrigation in Eastern and Western UP. *Economic and Political Weekly*, 39(31), pp. 3463–3468.

Rath, N., 2015. Declining Cattle Population Will the Sacred Cow Finally Rest in the Temple? *Economic & Political Weekly*, 50(28), pp. 12–14.

Ray, D., 2011. *Development Economics*, Oxford University Press, New Delhi.

Rinaudo, J. D. and Strosser, P. R. T., 1997. Linking Water Market Functioning, Access to Water Resources and Farm Production Strategies: Example From Pakistan. *Irrigation Drainage System*, 11, pp. 261–280.

Roy, S. and Blasé, M. G., 1978. Farm Tractorisation, Productivity and Labour Employment: A Case Study in Punjab. *The Journal of Development Studies*, 14(2), pp. 193–209.

Saleth, M., 1994. Towards a New Water Institutions: Economics, Law and Policy. *Economic and Political Weekly*, 29(39), pp. A147–A155.

Saleth, M., 1996. *Water Institutions in India: Economics, Law and Policy*, Institute of Economic Growth, Common Wealth Publishers, New Delhi.

Saleth, M., 1998. Water Markets in India: Economic and Institutional Aspects'. In Easter, K. W., Rosegrant, M.W. and Dinar, A. (eds.), *Markets for Water: Potential and Performance*, Springer, Series: *Natural Resource Management and Policy*, Vol. 15, pp. 187–205, available at http://link.springer.com/chapter/10.1007%2F978-0-585-32088-5_12,accessed 29/11/2013.

Scott, C. E. and Shah, T., 2004. Groundwater Overdraft Reduction Through Agricultural Energy Policy: Insights From India and Mexico. *Water Resource Development*, 20(2), pp. 149–164.

Shah, T., 1991. Water Markets and Irrigation Development in India. *Indian Journal of Agricultural Economics*, 46(3), pp. 335–348.

Shah, T., 1993. *Groundwater Markets and Irrigation Development: Political Economy and Practical Policy*, Oxford University Press, Bombay.

Shankar, K., 1992. Water Markets in Eastern UP. *Economic and Political Weekly*, 27(18), pp. 931–933.

Simpson, L. D., 1994. Are 'Water Markets' a Viable Option? *Finance and Development*, 31(2), pp. 30–32.

Singh, D., 2002. Water Markets in Fragile Environments: Key Issues in Sustainability. *Indian Journal of Agricultural Economics*, 57(2), pp. 180–196.

Singh, D. R. and Singh, R. P., 2003. Groundwater Markets and the Issues of Equity and Reliability to Water Access: A Case of Western Uttar Pradesh. *Indian Journal of Agricultural Economics*, 58(1), pp 115–127.

Singh, J., 2011. *Scope, Progress and Constraints of Farm Mechanization in India*, available at http://agricoop.nic.in/Farm%20Mech.%20PDF/05024-03.pdf,accessed 30/04/2011.

Srivastava, S.K., Kumar, R. and Singh, R. P., 2009. Extent of Groundwater Extraction and Irrigation Efficiency of Farms Under Different Water-Market Regime in Central Uttar Pradesh. *Agricultural Economics Research Review*, 22(1), pp. 87–98.

Tamuli, J., 2014. *Institution for the Use of Groundwater in Assam: A Study of Groundwater Markets With Special Emphasis on Structure, Determinants, Reliability and Efficiency*. Ph.D. Thesis submitted to the Department of Humanities and Socials, Indian Institute of Technology Guwahati, available athttp://gyan.iitg.ernet.in/handle/123456789/493, accessed12/05/2017.

Thobani, M.,1997. Formal Water Markets: Why, When and How to Introduce Tradable Water Rights. *The World Bank Research Observer*, 12(2), pp. 164–179.

Vaidyanathan, A., 1986. *India's Agricultural Development in a Regional Perspective*, Centre for Studies in Social Sciences, Calcutta.

World Bank, 1999. *Mexico Policy Options for Aquifer Stabilizations*, The World Bank, Washington, DC.

Zhang, L., Wang, J. and Huang, J., 2006.*Groundwater Entrepreneurs in China: Selling Water to Meet the Demand for Water*. Contributed Paper prepared for presentation at the International Association of Agricultural Economists Conference, Gold Coast, Australia, August 12–18.

5 Implications of credit-insurance interlinked contracts

An evaluation of crop insurance schemes in India

Pravat Kumar Kuri and Arindam Laha

1 Introduction

In developing world, agriculture is exposed to several types of risks, such as production, ecological, market, institutional or regulatory, personal and financial. The production risk may have different dimensions: micro (or idiosyncratic) risk affecting an individual or household, meso or covariant risk affecting groups of households (e.g., rainfall), and macro or systematic risks affecting regions (e.g., droughts) (OECD, 2009). Due to the presence of different risks at the same time, farmers often face difficulty in making decisions about an optimal strategy to cope with such risks. Risk management strategies in agriculture can be grouped into three categories: prevention strategy, mitigation strategy and coping strategy. By using prevention and mitigation strategies, farmers can smooth out their income level, while coping strategy is intended to smooth out the level of consumption (Holzman and Jogersen, 2001). Against this backdrop, access to financial markets (e.g., savings, credit, insurance etc.) can be considered as a market-based solution to smoothing consumption overtime. On the other hand, through their participation in the insurance market (voluntary or compulsory), farmers can safeguard themselves from the impact of risk events (specifically meso or macro risk) once they have occurred.[1]

In spite of almost six and half decades of concerted efforts in agricultural development, Indian farmers are still highly dependent on rainfall and thus are susceptible to risks like droughts and floods. Their hardship due to weather-related uncertainties gets further accentuated due to the non-availability of sufficient credit and insurance. Credit and insurance, by eliminating the liquidity and risk constraints, allow farmers to make adequate investment in agricultural production and enable them to combat uncertainty resulting from natural calamities. Credit and insurance, however, work in a complementary manner. In other words, elimination of one constraint, while the other constraint is present, is not sufficient. A farm household may not make adequate investment to raise production and productivity even when there is access to credit if the risks are not insured.[2] Bundling of credit and insurance products together, however, may induce farmers to make optimal investment through elimination of both liquidity and risk constraints, and thereby can contribute to raising farm productivity, especially for small farms. Moreover, a credit-insurance mix can contribute to the deepening of rural financial markets. In other words, credit-insurance inter-linkage contracts can allow both the markets to develop by addressing the problems of poor contract enforcement mechanisms, information asymmetries and high transaction costs (Carter et al., 2011). The greatest advantage of the credit-insurance inter-linked contract is that the objectives of raising farm productivity and deepening of rural financial markets can be achieved simultaneously. Against this backdrop, this chapter tries to develop a conceptual framework of the rationale of credit-insurance mix in managing risk in agriculture. In addition, the chapter examines the outreach of insurance coverage in crop loans in India. A critical evaluation of the National Agricultural Insurance Scheme (NAIS) has been made in the light of the conceptual framework developed in the chapter.

2 Rationale of credit-insurance inter-linkage: a conceptual framework

In a simplified world of risk, farmer households often resort to self-insurance (precautionary savings via liquid assets) or participate in market-based intervention measures (e.g., crop insurance or weather insurance) for risk management and coping mechanisms (Clarke and Dercon, 2009). The agricultural cost of production is financed through their own capital (i.e., savings) or borrowing from financial institutions. Coverage of market-based insurance depends on whether the farm households are loanee farmers or non-loanee farmers. The strategy of compulsory coverage of loanee farmers in insurance (i.e., compulsory insurance) is often seen as a solution to mitigate the adverse selection problem[3] in rural financial markets. It has been seen that compulsory participation of loanee farmers would ensure participation of low-risk farmers and thereby cross-subsidize high-risk farmers for the sake of viability of the program (Mahul and Stutley, 2010). In other words, a risk-pooling strategy will be applied to ensure the viability of the agricultural insurance scheme by covering all categories of farmers (high risk as well as low risk). In addition, the strategy of risk pooling is expected to reduce the insurance premium and thereby provide disincentive to the borrowers in defaulting repayment of loan. Thus, the mixing of credit and insurance markets is observed to be a better strategy to mitigate risks as the markets mutually reinforce each other to combat risks. The development of credit and insurance markets in isolation does not guarantee the copping up of market risks (Carter et al., 2011). At the same time, voluntary insurance coverage to non-loanee farmers is aimed at increasing the outreach of insurance schemes to a large section of the population. Combining a compulsory insurance clause with voluntary insurance is often desirable to pool risks and cover fixed costs by ensuring at least minimum participation in the low-risk category. However, design of such insurance schemes may be socially suboptimal, 'because the basic concept of pooling relies on a group of homogeneous risks in which all participating agents will benefit from risk pooling' (Mahul and Stutley, 2010, p. 49).

Table 5.1 Linkages between credit and insurance markets

Credit / Insurance	Financing through own capital	Financing through informal borrowing	Financing through formal borrowing
Self-insured	Financial exclusion in credit and insurance	Financial exclusion in credit and insurance	–
Access to insurance	Financial exclusion in credit but financial inclusion in insurance (voluntary insurance for non-loanee farmers)	Financial exclusion in credit but financial inclusion in insurance (voluntary insurance for non-loanee farmers)	Financial inclusion in credit and insurance (compulsory insurance for loanee farmers)

Source: Authors' own compilation.

All five possible situations after combining credit and insurance markets is presented in Table 5.1.

2.1 Farmers' decision making in the context of risk in agriculture

Agriculture is subjected to different sources of uncertainty: production, price, technological and policy uncertainty (Moschini and Hennessy, 2001). Agricultural production is conditioned upon not only the production decisions of the farmers, but also the uncontrolled element of vagaries of weather, which can determine the amount and quality of output. The expected return of the farmers under conditions of risk depends on the following states of nature:

- Two possible states of nature are considered: high rainfall with probability p and low rainfall with probability $(1-p)$. Good monsoon rains result in a high value of output (i.e., Y_H); while low value of output (i.e., Y_L) appears in bad monsoon years. Hence the expected value of output is given by $E(Y) = (p)Y_H + (1-p)Y_L$
- Expected earning in insurance is also dependent on these two states of nature. In a bad state of nature with probability $(1-p)$, there is a provision of indemnity (I), which ultimately is determined by the amount of sum assured (S_A) or claim (C) made by the insured (i.e., $I \in \min (S_A, C)$). On the other hand, there will be a loss of insurance premium $(-\pi)$ in the event of a good state of nature. Total expected payoff of insurance is given by $E(I) = p(-\pi) + (1-p)I$
- In the absence of access to credit, farmers utilize accumulated savings to finance the cost of cultivation. The foregone rate of interest in the accumulated savings is considered as the opportunity cost of savings. The cost of financing agriculture is given by $(1+r)F$, where r is the opportunity cost of savings or rate of interest from financial institutions, and F is the cost of cultivation financed by accumulation of savings or borrowing from financial institutions.

2.2 Insured vs. non-insured farmers

Based on these assumptions, the problem of insured farmer versus non-insured farmer can be analyzed as follows. The farmer household decides to participate in an insurance program by comparing the following pay-offs of different situations:

> Insured farmer: $R_1 = p(Y_H - \pi) + (1-p)(Y_L + I) - (1+r)F$
> Non-insured farmer: $R_2 = pY_H + (1-p)Y_L - (1+r)F$

Now a farmer household will participate in an insurance program if $R_1 > R_2$, that is, if $p(-\pi) + (1-p)I > 0$, or $p\pi < (1-p)I$. The condition is binding only in a bad state of nature (i.e., p is low). In a bad state of nature, a farmer experiences downward risk in the loss of agricultural production (i.e., mean output is less than expected output). This downside risk is more relevant in agricultural production, where the risky outcome depends on non-linear interactions among several variables (Hardaker et al., 2004). Thus, the proposition that can be drawn from this conceptualization is that insurance is used by farmers as a coping strategy in mitigating the problems of downside risk.

2.3 Insured farmers: loanee vs. non-loanee

Let us now consider the problem of only insured farmers. Their choice of contract may be of two types: interlinked credit and insurance contract or non-interlinked contract (or compulsory vs. voluntary contract). Insurers consider non-loanee farmers as riskier than loanee farmers. Voluntary participation of non-loanee farmers provides no room to the insurer in diversifying risk, while compulsory participation of the loanee farmers facilitates risk pooling by the insurer. Thus, we can assume that farmers belong to two risk classes:[4] p^h denotes probability of crop success of high-risk non-loanee farmers, whereas p^l denotes the probability of crop success of low-risk loanee farmers. It is obvious to assume that $p^h < p^l$. Thus, we have the following pay-off functions of two groups of insured farmers (R_1): loanee (R_{11}) and non-loanee (R_{12}) farmers.

> Loanee farmer (interlinked contract): $R_{11} = p^l(Y_H - \pi) + (1-p^l)(Y_L + I) - (1+r)F$
> Non-loanee farmer (non-interlinked contract): $R_{12} = p^h(Y_H - \pi) + (1-p^h)(Y_L + I) - (1+r)F$
> In the extreme situation of crop success: $R_{11} = p^l(Y_H - \pi) - (1+r)F > R_{12} = p^h(Y_H - \pi) - (1+r)F$
> In the extreme situation of crop failure: $R_{11} = (1-p^l)(Y_L + I) - (1+r)F < R_{12} = (1-p^h)(Y_L + I) - (1+r)F$

In presenting these pay-off functions in Figure 5.1, the expected return value of each contract is measured along the vertical axis and probability of success along the horizontal axis. The difference in the probability of crop success is reflected in the difference in the slope of the pay-off functions. Non-interlinked

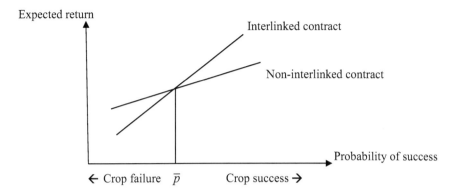

Figure 5.1 Expected return of interlinked and non-interlinked contracts
Source: Constructed by authors.

contracts are more profitable than interlinked contracts at low level of probability of success. The order is reversed when the probability of success is sufficiently high to allow the domination of interlinked contracts over non-interlinked contracts. Overall, the theoretical insights establish the proposition that non-loanee farmers participate in the insurance market (through non-interlinked contracts) to mitigate downside risk in agricultural production.

3 A critical assessment of crop insurance schemes in India

Since independence, the crop insurance policy in India has cantered around the choice of individual approach versus homogenous area approach, and interlinked credit-insurance product versus de-interlinked product (or compulsory versus voluntary contract). A special study commissioned in 1947–48 was in favour of the homogeneous area approach, which resulted in the implementation of the Pilot Crop Insurance Scheme (PICS) in 1979–1984. However, many small and marginal farmers (who were often excluded from institutional sources of credit) were excluded from participation in this crop insurance scheme as the area-based approach of this scheme was linked to crop loans. A similar comprehensive crop insurance scheme (1985–99) was linked to short-term credit and implemented based on the homogenous area approach. A compulsory arrangement of providing insurance coverage (rather than the voluntary arrangement in PICS) to only loanee farmers from institutional credit sources was the distinguishing characteristic of the comprehensive scheme. Subsequently in 1997, the Experimental Crop Insurance Scheme delinked insurance from credit product to ensure the participation of even those small and marginal farmers who do not borrow from institutional sources. The scheme was later modified in the framework of the

National Agricultural Insurance Scheme (NAIS) in 1999. After the formation of the Agricultural Insurance Company of India Ltd (AICI) in 2002, the government authorized the regulatory authority to monitor the implementation of NAIS. The newly designed scheme encompasses both the area approach (for widespread calamities), and individual approach (for localized calamities), and ensures participation of both borrowers and non-borrowers. The government later improved the features of NAIS and implemented the Modified National Agricultural Insurance Scheme (MNAIS) on a pilot basis in 50 districts from the rabi 2010–11 season. Meanwhile, a farm income insurance scheme (FIIS) was piloted during the rabi 2003–04 and kharif 2004 seasons to ensure farmers' income by providing a minimum guaranteed income. The scheme became infeasible for operation due to the presence of a minimum support price in covering price risk and the existence of NAIS in covering yield risks. In the same year, another rainfall insurance scheme was tested (known as the Weather Based Crop Insurance Scheme, WBCIS) to provide coverage against weather deviation from the notified standards. In recent times, the government has implemented a flagship insurance scheme, Pradhan Mantri Fasal Bima Yojana (PMFBY), with an aim of extending outreach of insurance coverage to 50 per cent of the country's farmers in three years. A notable success in the implementation of the scheme is recorded. The latest estimates on the coverage of the scheme suggest that 'about 3.15 crore farmers have been insured in this kharif 2015 season against 3.08 crore in the last year. The sum insured has also increased and nearly doubled for some states. The PMFBY has covered about 23 per cent of India's farmers in this kharif season against an initial target of 30 per cent' (Sen, 2016). Salient features of various crop insurance schemes in India are presented in Table 5.2.

Some of the operational guidelines, as discussed below, have been modified in PMFBY to address the problem of adverse selection in insurance contract:

- Unlike NAIS, the government has implemented a shorter duration of purchase deadline of 30 days before scheduled crop cycle under the PMFBY. While extension of the deadline to purchase insurance products may increase the reach of insurance coverage, it may also inadvertently welcome risky non-loanee farmers. Based on their expectation of yield, farmers may revise their insurance plan. It has a negative implication of an unduly burden of claim settlement on the part of the government.
- Provision of an area-based approach in PMFBY (like NAIS) not only reduces administrative cost in comparison to the individual-based approach, but also is expected to reduce moral hazard and adverse selection problem.
- To ensure the stability of the insurance coverage, theoretical insights suggest calculation of guaranteed yield based on long time series data. The shorter the time period, the higher the possibility of adversely selecting risky farmers in insurance coverage is. In NAIS, the three-year moving average for rice and wheat and a five-year average for all other crops, were considered in calculating area-average yield. On the other hand, PMFBY considers 10 similar crop cycles in estimating guaranteed yield to ensure efficiency in designing the policy for sorting out risky participants under its coverage.

Table 5.2 Salient features of various crop insurance schemes in India

Insurance scheme	Period	Approach	Crops covered	Farmers covered (lakh)	Salient features
Crop Insurance Scheme	1972–78	Individual	H-4cotton, groundnut, wheat, potato	0.03	Voluntary; implemented in six states
Pilot Crop Insurance Scheme	1979–84	Area	Cereals, millets, oilseeds, cotton, potato, chickpea	6.27	Voluntary for loanee farmers; 50 per cent subsidy on premium for small and marginal farmers
Comprehensive Crop Insurance Scheme	1985–99	Area	Food grains and oil seeds	763	Compulsory for loanee farmers
National Agricultural Insurance Scheme	1999	Area and individual	Food crops, annual commercial and horticultural crops	2402	Available to all farmers. Premium subsidy for small and marginal farmers to be phased out over a period of five years.
Farm Income Insurance Scheme	2003–04	Area	Wheat and rice	2.22	Insurance against to yield and price risks
Weather Based Crop Insurance Scheme	2003–04 continuing	Area	Groundnut, castor, paddy, wheat, oranges, grapes, vegetables, etc.	3	Voluntary; based on rainfall received at the IMD/mandal rain gauges
Pradhan Mantri Fasal Bima Yogana	2016 continuing	Area	Food crops, oil seeds, annual commercial and horticultural crops	315	Compulsory for loanee farmers and voluntary for non-loanee farmers

Source: Adapted from Raju and Chand (2007) with modification by the authors.

• A risk-pooling strategy can be effectively implemented by increasing the sum assured by the insurance scheme. In the PMFBY, there is no upper ceiling on the sum insured, and therefore, the entire loss of a farmer's crop can be covered. In practice, it has been reported that the sum insured has been increased significantly in the majority of the states. In about five or six states, the sum insured has actually been doubled (Sen, 2016).

However, it is too early to evaluate the relative merits or demerits of PMFBY over other insurance schemes.

3.1 Performance of NAIS

On the count of penetration of insurance coverage, NAIS set historic precedence in the coverage of loanee and non-loanee farmer households in India. Hence, this chapter examines the reach of NAIS among farmer households. Figure 5.2 presents the coverage of farmer households under NAIS for the whole time period of operation, from 1999 to 2015. More than 24 crore of farmers had been covered under this insurance scheme for the last 31 seasons, since rabi 1999–2000. In general, the number of farmers covered under this scheme in the kharif[5] season is comparatively higher that covered in the rabi season. Information on the number of farmers benefitted (i.e., claims considered) from the scheme is also recorded in Figure 5.2.

It becomes clear from Figure 5.2 that the trends for the number of farmers covered and farmers benefitted under the scheme are affected by the impact of climate change on agricultural production. The rising temperature in the Pacific Ocean (El Niño) and drought have significant implications for agricultural production (Brunner, 2000; Bhanumurthy et al., 2012; Saini and Gulati, 2014)[6] and

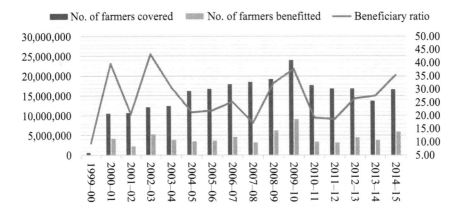

Figure 5.2 Number of farmers covered and benefitted under NAIS

Source: Authors presentation based on the data available in *Agricultural Statistics at a Glance*, 2015.

may determine the number of farmers seeking insurance and claims submitted to the insurance company. In the twenty first century, there were four El Niño years (2002, 2004, 2006 and 2009), and three of these (except 2006) resulted in drought years in India (Saini and Gulati, 2014). It is evident from Figure 5.2 that there was a sudden increase in the number of farmers covered under the insurance program in an El Niño and drought year, as well as in the immediate next year. The number of farmers under insurance coverage increased by 13 per cent, 30 per cent and 24 per cent in 2002–03, 2004–05 and 2009–10, respectively. Thus, this empirical evidence supports our theoretical proposition that non-insured farmers participate in an insurance program to mitigate downside risk in agricultural production.

As expected, the number of farmers benefitted from insurance coverage also increased in drought years (except in 2004), which is evident from the trend of beneficiary ratio (percentage of farmers benefited out of total number of farmers insured) in Figure 5.2.

The geographical outreach of insurance schemes in different states can be understood from Table 5.3. Though only nine states participated in the first year (i.e., rabi1999–2000) of the implementation of NAIS, almost all major states participated later on. It is to be noted that all the insurance schemes are not in operation in all Indian states. Interestingly, Punjab, Arunachal Pradesh and Nagaland have remained outside the reach of any insurance scheme (Table 5.3).

Table 5.3 Operation of agricultural insurance schemes in different states

Scheme (season)	States
PMFBY (since kkharif 2016)	Bihar, Chhattisgarh, Jharkhand, Odisha, West Bengal, Mizoram, Tripura, Himachal Pradesh, Haryana, Uttrakhand, Uttar Pradesh, Karnataka, Kerala, Andaman and Nicobar, Andhra Pradesh, Telangana, Tamil Nadu, Gujarat, Madhya Pradesh, Maharashtra, Rajasthan.
Modified NAIS (since rrabi 2013–14)	Andhra Pradesh (4 districts), Goa, Kerala, Rajasthan, Uttar Pradesh (65 districts) and Uttarakhand.
WBCIS (since rrabi 2013–14)	Assam, Andhra Pradesh (few districts), Himachal Pradesh, Kerala, Karnataka, Madhya Pradesh, Maharashtra, Rajasthan, Telangana, Uttarakhand, Uttar Pradesh (10 districts) and West Bengal.
NAIS (since rrabi 1999–2000)	Assam, Andhra Pradesh, Bihar, Chhattisgarh, Gujarat, Himachal Pradesh, Jharkhand, Karnataka, Maharashtra, Madhya Pradesh, Odisha, Tamil Nadu, Telangana and West Bengal.
No crop insurance	Punjab, Arunachal Pradesh and Nagaland

Note: Haryana, Manipur, Meghalaya, Sikkim and Tripura occasionally implemented insurance schemes.

Source: Adapted from Government of India (2016).

Table 5.4 shows the beneficiary ratio across states under NAIS for the entire period of operation of the scheme. As shown in Table 5.4, there is wide-spread variation in the beneficiary ratio across states. Assam, Chhattisgarh, Goa, Meghalaya, Sikkim and Jammu and Kashmir are some of the states which had a very low beneficiary ratio. By contrast, the states with relatively higher level of beneficiary ratio are Bihar, Gujarat, Himachal Pradesh, Jharkhand, Karnataka, Maharashtra, Manipur, Mizoram and Tamil Nadu. The beneficiary ratio in these states was above 30; that is, more than 30 per cent of the farmers covered under NAIS in those states were benefited (Table 5.4). There is, however, hardly any state

Table 5.4 State-wise distribution of coverage of farmers under NAIS (rabi 1999–2000 to rabi 2014–15)

State/UTs	No. of farmers covered	No. of farmers benefitted	Beneficiary ratio	Percentage of agricultural households to rural households
Andhra Pradesh	30,018,556	6,876,533	22.91	41.5
Assam	420,342	65,963	15.69	65.2
Bihar	7,616,212	3,269,864	42.93	50.5
Chhattisgarh	10,519,336	1,712,134	16.28	68.3
Goa	8,211	702	8.55	–
Gujarat	14,992,011	5,137,321	34.27	66.9
Haryana	635,778	129,424	20.36	60.7
Himachal Pradesh	346,302	108,562	31.35	66.5
Jharkhand	6,341,386	2,188,050	34.50	59.5
Karnataka	13,149,944	5,223,118	39.72	54.8
Kerala	461,282	85,470	18.53	27.3
Madhya Pradesh	38,247,033	7,476,038	19.55	70.8
Maharashtra	40,094,326	14,960,115	37.31	56.7
Manipur	28,131	22,418	79.69	68.2
Meghalaya	35,228	3,600	10.22	75.1
Mizoram	121	119	98.35	81
Odisha	17,716,672	3,233,123	18.25	57.5
Rajasthan	15,058,674	5,200,566	34.54	78.4
Sikkim	1913	86	4.50	58.6
Tamil Nadu	7,193,208	2,828,760	39.33	34.7
Telangana	266,043	53,591	20.14	51.5
Tripura	19,783	3,432	17.35	36.9
Uttar Pradesh	23,426,012	4,517,617	19.28	74.8
Uttarakhand	399,156	119,370	29.91	64.3
West Bengal	13,124,709	2,880,357	21.95	45
Jammu and Kashmir	49,065	4,492	9.16	82.1
Total	240,214,730	66,109,038	27.52	57.8

Note: The table presents the cumulative figure of the number of farmers covered and number of farmers benefitted starting from rrabi 1999–2000 to rrabi 2014–15

Source: Authors' calculation based on data taken from the Department of Agriculture, Cooperation and Farmers Welfare (Credit Division), and NSSO report on Situational Assessment Survey, July 2012–June 2013, as given in *Agricultural Statistics at a Glance, 2015.*

that experienced a continuous increase in coverage of the farmers. It is signifi-cant to note that in states (Madhya Pradesh, Megalaya, Rajasthan, Uttar Pradesh and Jammu and Kashmir) where more than 70 per cent of rural households are engaged in agriculture, a substantial proportion of insured farmers did not ben-efit from crop insurance under NAIS (except Rajasthan).

For further insights, this study considers the participation of loanee and non-loanee farmers under the NAIS within a relatively short period of time (i.e., rabi 1999–2000 to rabi 2004–05). Of the total 149.07 lakh farmers under NAIS dur-ing this period, nearly 80 per cent are loanee farmers and the rest are non-loanee farmers in the rabi season. On the other hand, 89.8 per cent of the total insured farmers were loanee farmers and the remaining 10.2 per cent were non-loanee farmers in the kharif season during the same time period (Table 5.5).

An analysis of the participation of loanee and non-loanee farmers in eleven seasons during rabi 1999–2000 to rabi 2004–05 (Figure 5.3) suggests that expe-riences of drought in July 2002[7] and 2004 resulted in greater participation of farmers in interlinked contracts of credit and insurance. There was an increase in the number of loanee farmers by 57.66 percentage during kharif 2003 to kharif 2004 (i.e., 70.13 lakh farmers in kharif 2003 to 110.57 lakh in kharif 2004). However, there was only a 5.59 percentage increase in loanee farmers during

Table 5.5 Distribution of loanee and non-loanee farmers under NAIS across landsize classes (rabi 1999–2000 to 2004–05 and kharif 2000–04)

Season	Total loanee farmers (in lakh)	Per cent share of total farmers	Total non-loanee farmers (in lakh)	Per cent share of total farmers	Total insured farmers (loanee and non-loanee; in lakh)
(1)	(2)	(3)=(2)/(6)*100	(4)	(5)=(4)/(6)*100	(6)
Overall Farmers					
Rabi	118.52	79.51	30.55	20.49	149.07
Kharif	426.81	89.8	48.5	10.2	475.31
Small/Marginal Farmers					
Rabi	85.63 [72.25]	88.15	11.51 [37.76]	11.85	97.14 [65.16]
Kharif	283.17 [66.34]	91.24	27.2 [56.08]	8.76	310.37 [65.30]
Medium/Large Farmers					
Rabi	32.89 [27.75]	63.48	18.92 [61.93]	36.52	51.81 [34.76]
Kharif	143.63 [33.65]	87.08	21.31 [43.93]	12.92	164.95 [34.70]

Note: Figures within [] in column (2) represent percentages of a particular group of farmers (small/marginal and medium/large farmers) in a season to total farmers in the same column in that season. So is the case for columns (4) and (6).

Source: Authors' modification of data from Vyas and Singh (2006).

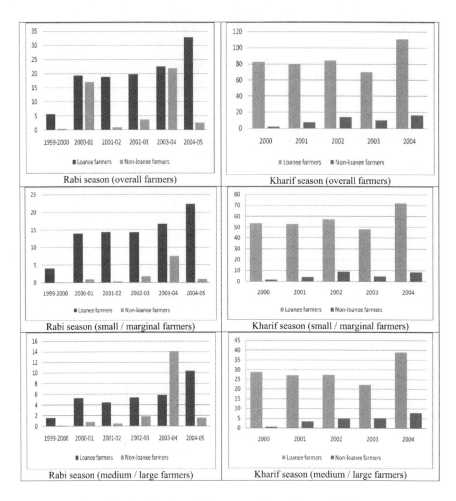

Figure 5.3 Year-wise distribution of loanee and non-loanee farmers under NAIS across landsize classes during 1999–2000 to 2004–05

Source: Authors' own presentation based on Agricultural Insurance Company data as reported in Vyas and Singh (2006).

kharif 2001 to kharif 2002. Also the trend suggests greater participation of non-loanee farmers after experiencing crop failure due to drought (Figure 5.3). Even though the participation of non-loanee farmers enhances the outreach of an insurance program, their 'selective' participation in drought years results in an adverse selection problem (Vyas and Singh, 2006).

Table 5.5 further shows the proportions of loanee and non-loanee farmers among the insured farmers belonging to two major landsize categories (small versus large farmers). The majority of insured farmers in the small and marginal categories are loanee farmers (91.24 per cent in kharif season and 88.15

per cent in rabi season). Similarly, loanee farmers constitute a predominant share in the category of large and medium farmers in both the kharif (87.08 per cent) and rabi season (63.48 per cent). Overall, the analysis suggests that small farmers participate in insurance coverage in greater numbers than large farmers. Small farmers constitute 65.16 per cent of total insured farmers in rabi season and 65.30 per cent in kharif season. Among loanee farmers, the share of small insured farmers is 72.25 per cent in rabi season and 66.35 per cent in kharif season. On the other hand, among non-loanee farmers, the participation of small farmers is 56.08 per cent in kharif season and 37.76 per cent in rabi season. The presence of a large number of small farmers in the group of loanee farmers suggests that the need for institutional finance probably draws the small farmer towards insurance (Ghosh and Yadav, 2008; Vyas and Singh, 2006). Thus, it implies that there is scope for increasing the reach of insurance programs through the expansion of credit supply to small farmers to satisfy their credit demand. In other words, as formulated in the conceptual model, an appropriate design of credit-insurance mix can facilitate the development of both credit and insurance markets in India.

4 Conclusion

Access to financial markets (e.g., savings, credit, insurance etc.) can be used as a coping strategy to safeguard against the impact of risky events in agriculture once they have occurred. The conceptual framework developed in this chapter suggests that insured farmers can manage downside risk in agriculture production in a more meaningful way than non-insured farmers.

The chapter also assesses the coverage of NAIS. It has been found that compulsory or voluntary participation of farmer households in the insurance market is influenced by the expectation of the occurrence of drought in India. It has further been observed that small farmers constitute an overwhelming share of loanee farmers under NAIS in comparison to non-loanee farmers. The predominance of the small farmers among the loanee farmers indicates that their credit need probably draws them to the insurance market. This implies that an effective implementation of credit-insurance mix policy can help both the markets to grow by mutually reinforcing each other.

Notes

1 In this context the work of Townsend (1994) is worth mentioning. Using data from three villages in the semi-arid tropics of southern India, Townsend made a critical evaluation of the 'full insurance model' in the presence of risk-sharing markets. Five such potential risk-bearing institutions were taken into account: diversification of agricultural production, storage of food grains, purchase and sales of assets such as bullocks and land, borrowing from village lenders, and gifts and transfers in family networks. Empirical results suggest that informal networks, gifts and transfers among family members and friends, and credit relations in the village economy were important institutional mechanisms in smoothing consumption overtime and thereby combating risk in agriculture.

2 In fact, insurance penetration (insurance premium as percentage of GDP) in India is significantly lower than it is in advanced economies, even though the penetration is relatively higher in comparison to several other emerging market economies. The insurance penetration ratio in India (3.15) is much lower than Japan (10.54), the United Kingdom (12.45), the Republic of Korea (10.25) and the United States (9.15). However, it is comparatively higher than China (2.70), Indonesia (1.52), the Philippines (1.48), Sri Lanka (1.46), Pakistan (0.67) and Bangladesh (0.61) (Asian Development Bank, 2007, as mentioned in Report of Currency and Finance, RBI, p. 335).

3 In a financial market with asymmetric information, an adverse selection problem often arises when 'hidden information' about the insured person results in increasing risk in the insurance contract. The insurance company is negatively affected by having different information on the risk characteristics of their customers. Moral hazard or 'hidden action' problems occur when one group of insured customers takes on more risk than others because someone else bears the cost of those risks.

4 The economic logic of segregating farmers into two different categories has been derived from Ahsan et al. (1982).

5 Kharif cropping season is from July to October during the southwest monsoon, and the rabi cropping season is from October to March (winter).

6 In India, the rising temperature in the Pacific Ocean (El Niño) is generally feared to cause a drought. It has been observed that since 1980 all Indian droughts happened in the years of El Niño, but all El Niño years did not result in droughts (Saini and Gulati, 2014).

7 A drought situation in 2002 was mainly caused by a dry spell in July, with the rainfall deficiency of 49 per cent during the month being 'the worst in the history of recorded observations' (Business Line, 2002).

References

Ahsan, S. M., Ali, A.G. and Kurian, N.J., 1982. Toward a Theory of Agricultural Insurance. *American Journal of Agricultural Economics*, 64(3), pp. 520–529.

Asian Development Bank, 2007. *Low Income Households' Access to Financial Services – International Experience, Measures for Improvement, and the Future*. EARD Special Studies, October.

Bhanumurthy, N.R., Dua, P. and Kumawat, L., 2012. *Weather Shocks, Spot and Futures Agricultural Commodity Prices: An Analysis for India*. Working Paper No. 219, Centre for Development Economics, Department of Economics, Delhi School of Economics.

Brunner, A.D., 2000. *El Nino and World Primary Commodity Prices: Warm Water or Hot Air?* IMF Working Paper, IMD Institute, December.

Business Line, 2002. *2002 Termed All India Drought Year*, available at www.thehin dubusinessline.com/2002/10/05/stories/2002100502840300.htm, accessed 20/01/2017.

Carter, M.R., Cheng, L. and Sarrist, A., 2011. *The Impact of Interlinked Index Insurance and Credit Contracts on Financial Market Deepening and Small Farm Productivity*, available at https://arefiles.ucdavis.edu/uploads/filer_pub-lic/2014/03/27/car_cheng_sarris_v11.pdf, accessed 20/01/2017.

Clarke, D. and Dercon, S., 2009. *Insurance, Credit and Safety Nets for the Poor in a World of Risk*. DESA Working Paper No. 81, October, available at www.un.org/esa/desa/papers/2009/wp81_2009.pdf, accessed 22/02/2017.

Ghosh, N. and Yadav, S.S., 2008. *Problems and Prospects of Crop Insurance: Reviewing Agricultural Risk and NAIS in India*. Final Report, Institute of Economic Growth, available at www.iegindia.org/ardl/2008_Crop%20Insurance%20Report_Nilabja.pdf,accessed 28/01/2017.

Government of India, 2016. *State of Indian Agriculture, 2015–16,* available at http://eands.dacnet.nic.in/PDF/State_of_Indian_Agriculture,2015-16.pdf, accessed 02/03/2017.

Hardaker, J.B., Huirne, R., Anderson, J.R. and Lien, G., 2004. *Coping With Risk in Agriculture,* 3rd ed., CABI Publishing, Oxfordshire.

Holzman, R. and Jorgensen, S., 2001. Social Risk Management: A New Conceptual Framework for Social Protection and Beyond. *International Tax and Public Finance,* 8(4), pp. 529–556.

Mahul, O. and Stutley, C.J., 2010. *Government Support to Agricultural Insurance: Challenges and Options for Developing Countries,* available at http://documents.worldbank.org/curated/en/698091468163160913/pdf/538810PUB0Gove101Official0Use0Only1.pdf, accessed 21/03/2017.

Moschini, G. and Hennessy, D.A., 2001. Uncertainty, Risk Aversion, and Risk Management for Agricultural Producers. In Gardner, B. and Rausser, G. (eds.), *Handbook of Agricultural Economics,* Vol. 1, Elsevier, Amsterdam, pp. 87–153.

OECD, 2009. *Managing Risk in Agriculture: A Holistic Approach,* available at www.oecd.org/tad/agricultural-policies/45558582.pdf, accessed 13/02/2017.

Raju, S.S. and Chand, R., 2007. Progress and Problems of Agricultural Insurance. *Economic and Political Weekly,* 42(21), May 26, pp. 1905–1908.

Reserve Bank of India, 2008. *Report on Currency and Finance, 2006-08,* vol. 1, available at https://rbi.org.in/Scripts/AnnualPublications.aspx?head=Report+on+Currency+and+Finance, accessed 12/12/2016.

Saini, S. and Gulati, A., 2014. *El Nino and Indian Droughts: A Scoping Exercise.* Working Paper 276, Indian Council for Research on International Economic Relations, June.

Sen, A. 2016. More farmers covered under crop insurance scheme. *Business Line,* September 27, available at http://www.thehindubusinessline.com/economy/agri-business/more-farmers-covered-under-crop-insurance-scheme/article9154666.ece, accessed 13/02/17

Townsend, R. M., 1994. Risk and Insurance in Village India. *Econometrica,* 62(3), pp. 539–591.

Vyas, V.S. and Singh, S., 2006. Crop Insurance in India-Scope for Improvement. *Economic and Political Weekly,* 41(43–44), November 4, pp. A61–A80.

6 Transition of agricultural marketing in India

Rajib Sutradhar

1 Introduction

A well-functioning agricultural market plays a critical role in a developing country like India. Broadly speaking, the functions performed by markets in such an economy include providing incentives to farmers to produce output at a desired rate, delivering the produce to consumers at reasonable prices, and providing the right signals to promote efficient use of resources in production and distribution of agricultural produce (Chand, 2012). More importantly, in an economy dominated by smallholders, who are numerous but have limited individual marketed surplus, agricultural markets as a platform for exchange of farm produce should be inclusive of smallholders. After 25 years of economic reforms, agricultural markets in India are now at a crossroad. The period since the beginning of the 2000s has seen evolving roles played by the public and private sectors. In the 1990s, it was expected that reforms in other macro sectors, such as industry and trade, would propel growth in the agriculture sector, but the period since early 2000s reflects a marked change in policies towards the sector, with the government at the centre circulating a model agricultural marketing act to bring changes to the marketing of farm produce. These policy changes have facilitated the entry of supermarket and other organized actors in the agri-food supply chain, which source produce from the farmer households, bypassing the traditional marketing system. To contextualize the changes in policies related to the agricultural markets, the present chapter briefly reviews policies and performances related to agricultural marketing in the pre-reform period. Given that there is already a plethora of literature that has dealt with policy changes in agricultural marketing in the pre-reform period (e.g., Chand, 2012; Acharya, 2004), this chapter largely focuses in greater detail on agricultural marketing policies in the post-reform period. In view of the rapid diffusion of supermarkets since 2000 and the concomitant changes in the agri-food supply chain, the chapter in particular focuses on the implications of the entry of supermarkets for smallholders in India. The chapter concludes with policy recommendations that draw upon lessons from other countries to prepare a roadmap for a more inclusive and competitive agricultural marketing system in India.

Throughout the chapter, we see the agri-food supply chain as consisting of two segments – upstream and downstream. Using the definition given in Reardon and Timmer 2005, we see the upstream segment as including only farmers and first-stage processors and the downstream segment as including wholesalers, second-stage processors, retailers and consumers. The upstream segment of the agri-food supply chain focuses more on the supply side, while the downstream segment is more concerned with the demand side of the agri-food chain. Until the late 1980s, that is, the pre-reform period, the actors in the upstream segment were more active, as the food chain was supply driven. This was a period when the agricultural market was largely a commodity market and produce was unbranded, non-standardized and unprocessed. In the post-reform period, with the entry of organized firms in the processing and distribution sector, actors in the down-stream segment have assumed an increasingly more active role as the agri-food supply chain has become demand driven. The growing presence of organized actors such as processing companies and supermarkets marks a transition of agri-cultural markets from commodity markets to product markets, where produce is differentiated by attributes such as variety, standards, quality, branding and processing. The present chapter focuses on the transition of agricultural markets over the last five decades and the implications for smallholders.

2 Agricultural marketing in the pre-reform period

In the period before independence, the marketed surplus was extremely limited and agricultural markets were largely unorganized and informal, with most pro-ducers resorting to direct sale to the rural markets or local brokers for the rural wholesale market. Farmers often failed to get appropriate prices as markets were underdeveloped, and unregulated traders and weight men resorted to several malpractices (Bhalla, 2007). Subsequently, based on the recommendation of the Report of Royal Commission on Agriculture in 1926, the Agriculture Produce and Marketing Commission Act (APMC) was passed in 1937. Almost all the states in India, with the exception of Kerala, Jammu and Kashmir and Manipur, adopted APMC, which mandated that the sale and/purchase of agricultural com-modities notified under the Act are to be carried out in 'regulated markets'. The act, implemented and enforced by the APMC committee set up under the act, aims to ensure that farmers aren't exploited by middle men and mercantile ele-ments. Among other things, the act has made provision for proper infrastructure in the regulated market and has mandated that prices of agricultural produce sold in the regulated market are to be determined in a transparent manner through auction in the presence of mandi officials. The act bestows upon the APMC committee the authority to fix commission charges and statutory charges, such as market fees and taxes, as well as produce handling charges, such as cleaning of produce and loading/unloading. The general consensus is that the Act was largely successful in establishing orderly and transparent markets, transforming agricultural markets in most states (Acharya, 2004).

However, the act over time led to some serious rigidity in the system as it discouraged development of a parallel marketing system as required by farmers and buyers. Farmers are required to go through a long chain of wholesalers, semi-wholesalers and commission agents to sell their produce. There are too many intermediaries who work on a small scale but on a high margin, adding little value to the produce (Chand, 2012). The traders charge commission rates arbitrarily, sometimes as high as 8 or 10 per cent, without offering any service such as grading and inspection. Marketing margin and marketing costs are often very high. In the case of fruits and vegetables, farmers receive only one-third to one-half of the final price paid by the consumers (Gandhi and Namboodiri, 2002). Moreover, the functioning of the wholesale market has come under criticism in recent times. Commission agents and wholesalers often work in collusion, at the expense of farmers' interests (Meenakshi and Banerji, 2005). Information on price is often secret and imperfectly available (Harriss-White, 1996, p. 525). In the post-liberalization period, the gaps created by the withdrawal of government in the provision of credit have yet to be filled by the private sector. The recent round of the All India Rural Debt and Investment Survey shows that the share of institutional sources in the total credit received by farmers declined from 66.30 per cent to 61.10 per cent in the post-reform period. Consequently, farmers are increasingly resorting to commission agents as a source of credit, which limits their freedom of whom they want to sell their produce (Chand, 2012). To resolve the problems that farmers face in the wholesale market system, the government took a number of initiatives in the 1960s and 1970s, which include setting up co-operative and direct marketing as alternative marketing channels.

2.1 Co-operatives

The history of the co-operative movement in India dates back to the pre-independence period when Amul was set up as milk co-operative in 1946. Over time, the milk co-operative evolved into a network of 2.12 million milk producers, organized in 10,441 independent milk collection co-operatives at the village level (Chandra and Tirupati, 2002). The main appeal of the co-operative lies in the removal of the perceived exploitation of farmers when they sell their produce to traders (Lele, 1981). The formation of a co-operative is also seen as an effective way to reduce the marketing margin and transaction costs that smallholders face in accessing services in both input and output markets. In fruits and vegetables, HOPCOMS and Mother Dairy serve as notable examples of successful co-operatives. Established in 1958, HOPCOMS presently has a membership of 15,000 farmers (Kolady et al., 2013). Initially set up in 1972 as a dairy co-operative, Mother Dairy diversified in 1980s into the sale of fruits and vegetables. The co-operative presently procures fruits and vegetables from 15 states through 110 associations run and managed by 10,000 farmers as members of its associations (Alam and Verma, 2013). Both HOPCOMS and Mother Dairy works through a network of decentralized collection centres, each centre procuring produce directly from farmers. Produce procured through the collection centre is sold through a network of retail booths run and managed by the co-operatives in major urban centres. These collective organizations have been largely successful in giving farmers more options to sell their produce near their farm lands, empowering them with greater bargaining power and reducing the transaction costs of selling their harvest. However, these successful co-operatives are exceptions rather than the norm.

Many of the co-operatives struggled because of the very nature and principle of co-operatives. These co-operatives face various constraints that include lack of financial, technical and managerial resources; lack of market orientation; absence of long-term vision; small size of operation; and a commitment to buy the entire produce of all members (Singh, 2008; Lele, 1981). If the members of co-operative include heterogenous groups, as is often the case, wealthier or more powerful farmers hijack the agenda of the co-operatives at the expense of the interests of the larger group, eventually diluting the very purpose for which the co-operative was formed. The sugar co-operative in Maharashtra is one such example (Banerjee et al., 2001).

2.2 Direct marketing

Some state governments have encouraged direct marketing by farmers outside the purview of the Agricultural Produce Marketing Act to help them overcome problems arising from the presence of middlemen in the regulated wholesale market. The rationale that guided direct marketing policies is to ensure that farmers get better price realization and consumers/buyers get better quality produce at reasonable prices (Ministry of Agriculture, 2013). The state government of Punjab and Haryana first started such an initiative as Apna Mandi in 1987. Towards the late 1990s or early 2000, a number of state governments adapted the model of Apna Mandi with certain improvements. These include Uzhavar Sandhai (Tamil Nadu), Rythu Bazar (Andhra Pradesh), Krushak Bazaar (Orissa), Shetkari Bazaar (Maharashtra) and Raita Santhe (Karnataka).

Typically, the state governments bear the expenses of maintaining these markets as policy initiatives to promote direct marketing by smallholders growing fruits and vegetables. The prices paid to the farmers in these markets are usually fixed at somewhere between the prevailing wholesale market prices and retail market prices so that both farmers and consumers stand to benefit from such interventions (Ministry of Agriculture, 2013). Typically, these prices are 20 to 30 per cent less than the retail prices and 30 to 50 per cent more than wholesale market prices. These markets have the potential to reduce margin and eliminate middlemen. However, such markets cannot be replicated at a wider scale, as they are largely concentrated in the big cities and can't cater to the farmers separated by geographical distance from the consumers (Chand, 2012). Moreover, most of these markets are devoid of basic infrastructure, such as grading facilities that are required to attract more demanding customers. Though these markets are only meant for smallholders, who come and sell their produce directly to the retailers or consumers, there are also reports that small traders/middlemen, without requisite identity cards, take over the places reserved for farmers. Thus, though initiatives such as co-operatives and direct marketing have been partly successful, they are at best piecemeal in nature.

2.3 Government as a purchaser of food grains

The government acts as a key actor in the food supply chain of cereals as the total volume of cereals procured by the government account for as much as 30 per cent of the total production in the country (Balani, 2013). The government's intervention in the food grain market can be traced back to the mid-1960s, at a time when the country was struggling with food shortage. In response to frequent food crises, in the mid-1960s the government launched the Green Revolution Package, which included the use of high-yielding varieties of seeds of wheat and paddy, supplemented with a package of chemical fertilizer and pesticides. To provide adequate policy support, the government intervened in the cereal market through price policy to ensure that farmers had adequate incentives to produce the crops, and at the same time, balance the interest of the consumers. The package of price policy measures included (1) protecting the producers through obligatory procurement at Minimum Support Prices (MSP); (2) maintaining a buffer stock of food grains; (3) ensuring price stability by sourcing additional produce at a procurement price for maintaining the buffer stock at FCI;[1] and (4) distributing food to consumers through fair price shops at reasonable prices.

While the price policy has attained reasonable success, in terms of securing food self-sufficiency, the policy instrument became a victim of its own success, as the farmer groups that benefitted from the Green Revolution lobbied the government to increase the MSP so much that over time the distinction between the MSP and the procurement price was lost. Moreover, such policy resulted in the shift of land away from the other crops, such as oil seeds, pulses and coarse cereals, leading to a serious imbalance in the demand and supply of different agricultural commodities in the country (Chand, 2012). Another consequence is over-exploitation of groundwater and other resources. Not surprisingly, the state government of Punjab has initiated several policy measures since 1990s to promote diversification of cropping pattern towards high-value crops (Singh, 2004).

3 Agricultural marketing in the post-reform period

In the post-reform period, the food basket of an average Indian, in response to higher growth in per capita income, has gradually diversified away from cereals towards high-value items that include vegetables, meat and fish. For example, the share of cereals in total food expenditure in urban areas declined from 36 per cent in 1972–73 to 24 per cent in 2005–06 (Kumar and Dey, 2007). The same trend is seen in rural areas, where the share of cereals in total food expenditure declined from 56 per cent to 32 per cent over the same period. However, the physical infrastructure in most wholesale markets, designed with a focus on handling cereals and pulses, has failed to respond to the changing diet composition in favour of non-cereal crops. The monopoly granted to the state by the act has been counter-productive, as the act discourages private investment in the marketing of agricultural produce. It is apparent that the marketing infrastructure has fallen short of the required demand at a time when the marketed surplus of agricultural produce has been increasing because of increased commercialization. The number of regulated wholesale markets increased from 6,217 in 1991 to 7.246 in 2008, only an increase of 22 per cent, as compared with a 70 per cent increase in volume of production over the same period (Chand, 2012).

Apart from quantity, the existing marketing infrastructure is also poor in quality, as is evident in the gaps in the infrastructure highlighted by the report of the Working Group on Agricultural Marketing appointed by the Planning Commission in 2011. For example, among 7,246 wholesale markets, there are only 1,637 grading units at the primary level in the country. Only 20 per cent of the markets have such facilities. There is also huge geographical variation in the spread of wholesale markets, which vary from 118 sq. kms in Punjab to 11,214 sq. kms in Meghalaya. A common auction platform is still not available in as much as one-third of the markets. The scientific storage capacity is only 30 per cent of what is required. Cold storage facilities are available for only 10 per cent of fresh produce. The revenues collected by the government through mandi taxes and other charges are not put into investment in upgrading infrastructure in the wholesale market (GOI, 2001). Over all, the mismatch in facility capacity has resulted in huge wastage of fruits and vegetables, with estimates varying from 15 to 20 per cent of the total value (Patnaik, 2011), or Rs 44,000 crore at 2009 wholesale prices (Ministry of Agriculture, 2013). Rural periodic markets that serve as substitutes for a regulated wholesale market also lack the basic infrastructure, resulting in huge losses at the village level. Some estimates show about 7 per cent of food grains, 30 per cent of fruits and vegetables and 10 per cent of spices are lost at the village level (Acharya, 2004). A recent study shows that small and marginal farmers suffer more from poor and congested infrastructure in the wholesale markets compared to large farmers (Shilpi and Umali-Deininger, 2008). The study finds that large farmers, with a relatively large marketed surplus, disproportionately appropriate the limited facilities available in the wholesale market.

3.1 Emergence of supermarkets in the Indian scenario

In the post-reform period, the downstream segment of the agri-food supply chain has undergone significant changes in response to changes in such macro trends as a rise in per capita income, growing urbanization and increased participation of women in the workforce, all of which have led to a rise in the demand for processed foods. Given the greater scope for economies of scale in processed foods, which is less perishable compared to fresh produce, processed food became the entry point for supermarkets (Reardon et al., 2003). Other concomitant changes, such as increased access to transportation, refrigeration and storage technology such as tetra packs, have created enabling conditions for the diffusion of supermarkets. Liberalization in FDI in retail first in single-brand and later in multi-brand retail has further facilitated this process. In a short span of a decade and a half, supermarkets have diffused in what is described as one of the fastest spreads of supermarkets (Reardon and Minten, 2011) to account for approximately

10 per cent of the total retail market (The Hindu, 2014). Perhaps in a reflection of diet preferences of a significant majority of the population, supermarkets made a relatively early entry into fresh fruits and vegetables.

A case study of Delhi shows that fresh produce already accounts for 20 per cent of the shelf space of supermarkets in the city (Minten et al., 2010). To differentiate itself from traditional markets, the procurement manager of a supermarket sources fresh produce that is uniform in quality and high in standards. Consequently, the downstream segment has assumed an increasingly more active part in the supply chain, as supermarkets dictate to farmers what they want to source from them based on the price signals received from consumers.

The institutional set up that exists in the regulated wholesale market is, however, incompatible with the requirements of supermarkets. The wholesale markets are integrated horizontally rather than vertically (Jha et al., 1997). Except for money and goods, little flows through these markets. The lack of co-ordination among different players in the supply chain leads to wastage of the produce. Evidence from field studies shows that there is little reward for quality of non-staple food in the traditional wholesale market (Fafchamps et al., 2008). The AGMARK facility, introduced to promote quality, has not yet become popular in the traditional wholesale market. The total value of AGMARK-certified output is estimated to be less than 1.5 per cent of the total value of crop produce in the country (Chand, 2012). From the perspective of a supermarket procurement manager, the transaction costs of sourcing the produce that he requires is very high in such a set up.

3.2 Reforms in the laws regulating marketing of agricultural produce

Over all, the feeling was that Agricultural Produce and Marketing Act had outlived its utility. Subsequently, the government constituted an Inter Ministerial Task force on Agricultural Marketing Reforms in 2002, and based on its recommendations, the working group drafted a model Agricultural Produce Marketing Act (2003).Among other things, the act provides for the transaction of agricultural produce outside the premises of regulated wholesale markets, establishment of direct-purchase centres and contract farming, and promotion of public/private partnerships in the management and development of agricultural markets. Agriculture being a state subject, the model act provides guidelines for the respective state governments to implement reforms in the marketing of agricultural produce. More than half the states have already implemented key reforms, such as direct sourcing and contract farming (for details, see Ministry of Agriculture, 2013).

3.3 Different models of sourcing fresh produce adopted by supermarket chains in India

Facilitated by reforms in laws regulating the marketing of agricultural produce, supermarket chains have started inserting their own supply chains, bringing changes in the organizations and institutions governing marketing of fresh produce. In New Institutional Economics terminology, 'organization' means the structure of relations among different agents of agricultural marketing, and 'institution' refers to the rules of the game (private standards) that govern transactions between various actors. Drawing on Williamson's (1979, 1993) theoretical insights on the relationship between transaction costs and structure of firms, we may conceptualize a supermarket chain as following a variety of procurement models to reduce transaction costs, which may include spot market, quasi market and hierarchical modes of contracting. We rely on case studies and interviews with the executives of supermarket chains in India to identify several procurement models followed by supermarkets in India. These models of procurement are, however, not competing or mutually exclusive, as a supermarket chain manager may opt for a mix of procurement models to meet its sourcing requirement.

a) Sourcing from commission agents (CA) in the mandi in spot transactions and via 'specialized/dedicated' intermediaries in the mandi

Sourcing from the wholesale market continues to be the most important channel for most supermarket chains in India. However, within the wholesale market, there are several variants of sourcing strategy adopted by the procurement manager of a supermarket chain. At an early stage, a supermarket chain most commonly procures fresh produce from mandi through auction just like any other buyer. However, they gradually move to form a relationship with commission agents or with wholesalers who buy from other CAs or from other wholesale markets (Singh, 2009). Some of these commission agents emerge as specialized wholesalers who supply only to the supermarket chains. The procurement agent of a supermarket sometimes acquires a APMC license to be able to buy from farmers in the mandi or elsewhere (Singh, 2016).

b) Procurement through consolidator

The supermarket procurement manager sometimes sources fresh produce from farmers through consolidators based in the villages. In such a set up, the procurement manager takes advantage of a network of village consolidators to procure produce of the required quality and standards. He pays a fixed commission to a consolidator who generally follows informal contracts with farmers. Typically, a consolidator sources and grades the produce, after which he sells the superior grade to the supermarket and the inferior product to the local wholesale market. ITC's e-choupal model is one of the most celebrated versions of this model of procurement (Singh and Singla, 2010).

c) Procurement from organized wholesalers

The supermarket chain also sources fresh produce by partnering with organized wholesalers, who follow a tightly controlled supply chain with the suppliers, using formal and informal contracts to meet the high quality standards demanded by the supermarket. For example, ABRL-owned More supermarket chain procures apples from Adani Agri-Fresh Ltd through a vendor (Pandey et al., 2013). To promote itself as a supplier of premium quality apples under the brand name of Farm Pick, Adani Agri-Fresh follows a tight co-ordination with apple growers through hub operators in Himachal Pradesh.

d) Sourcing from farmers directly via collection centre

Sourcing from farmers directly via a collection centre is a method commonly adopted by supermarket chains in India (Sutradhar, 2015; Singh and Singla, 2010; Bathla, 2016; Pritchard et al., 2010; Singh, 2009). This model of sourcing works through a hub-and-spoke format, with a number of collection centres linked to a distribution centre. Each collection centre, typically managed by a collection centre in-charge, procures fresh produce from farmers shortlisted by the in-charge in a catchment area, spread over several villages. The produce sourced through the collection centre is dispatched to a distribution centre where the it is graded and sorted again before dispatching it to retail outlets. Through such direct procurement, the supermarket chain dis-intermediates the supply chain of Fresh Fruits and Vegetables (FFV), gaining better control over the quality of produce sold in its retail outlets and saving significant costs by eliminating the margin paid to middlemen or vendors in the wholesale market.

e) Sourcing via contract farming

Supermarket chains occasionally source fresh produce through contract farming, which represents more active engagement with farmers. The listed farmers are provided a monitored contract with resource provisions, often involving provision of credit and technical assistance, to ensure availability of produce that is consistent in quality. Presently, few supermarket chains adopt contract farming as it entails high transaction costs of negotiation and enforcement of contract. For example, Namdhari Fresh follows contract farming with its listed suppliers, numbering 1,200 farmers, to source part of its fresh produce requirement (Dhananjaya and Rao, 2009).

f) Sourcing via lease land and hired labour

In a model of completely vertical integration, the procurement manager of a supermarket chain sometimes leases in land from farmers and uses hired labour for farming operations under close supervision of an agri-expert appointed by the company official. Unlike in contract farming, the owner of the land has no role in the production process in such models. Namdhari Fresh practices captive farming on 300 acres of land it leases in for a fixed period from farmers considered less skilful (Dhananjaya and Rao, 2009). However, few supermarket chains have used land leasing as a procurement strategy because of restrictive clauses in the land leasing laws.

g) Tie up with rural business hubs (RBH)

Supermarket chains sometimes build partnership with rural business hubs (RBH) to source fresh fruits and vegetables. Rural business hubs are 'combinations of small supermarkets and input stores with joint venture banks and even health units in rural areas' (Reardon et al., 2012, p. 12334). In a typical rural setting, an RBH offers a one-stop shop for farmers. Examples of RBHs include Choupal Saagar or Hariyali Kisaan Bazaar. The supermarket chain forms a partnership with the RBH to utilize the hub's already well-developed infrastructure to source the supermarket's fresh produce requirement. In one such example, Food Bazar and Godrej have recently formed a joint venture. Aadhar retailing, a rural business hub set up by Godrej, serves as a collection centre to procure fresh produce for Food Bazaar stores in western India (Krishnamacharyulu, 2011).

3.4 Implications for smallholders of emergence of supermarket chains

The case studies on procurement practices followed by supermarket chains in India show that sourcing via collection centre is the most common method adopted by supermarket chains in India (Sutradhar, 2015; Singh, 2012; Bathla, 2016; Pritchard et al., 2010; Mangala and Chengappa, 2008). The procurement manager of the supermarket chain banks on the local agent's knowledge to make a list of suppliers. In such a model, there is typically no binding agreement between two contracting parties as there is no commitment from either party to buy or sell the produce. A typical contract followed in this model has no provision of resources such as credit and extension services for the listed farmers, as the supermarket procurement manager seeks to take advantage of the resource position of smallholders. Higher standards and quality required by supermarkets in such situations translate into higher investment in the farm, raising the spectre of exclusion of resource-poor smallholders in more demanding agri-food system. Thus, the growing share of supermarkets in the retailing of fresh produce has significant implications for rural poverty in an agrarian setting dominated by smallholders.

Small and marginal farmers with land holdings less than 2 hectares account for as much as 85 per cent of land holdings in India. They figure prominently in the production of fruits and vegetables. In terms of numbers, small and marginal farmers together account for 83.50 per cent of vegetable growing households and 88.40 per cent of fruit growing households. They account for 61 per cent of vegetable production and 52 per cent of fruit production, both higher than their share in the arable land (41 per cent). However, smallholders face numerous constraints in the input and output markets. An NCEUS 2008 report documented poor resource endowment among smallholders. They have lower levels of education; only 56 per cent of small farmers and 48 per cent of marginal farmers report themselves as literate. They also lack access to formal credit compared to medium and large farmers, who are better endowed in terms of assets to offer as collateral. Only 25.90 per cent of small and marginal farmers report indebtedness to formal sources of credit, compared to 34.70 per cent of large farmers. Small-holders are also poor in social capital, with only 30 per cent of them reporting being members of co-operatives and only 20 per cent of them actually utilizing services of such co-operatives compared to as many as 50 per cent of the large farmer households reporting themselves as members of such collectivities. It is thus clear that most smallholders lack the required social, physical and human capital to meet the higher standards and quality demanded in a supermarket-driven agri-food system. Unsurprisingly, penetration of supermarkets into the rural landscape has raised the spectre of livelihood concerns in rural areas (Singh, 2012; Chandrasekhara, 2011; Shah, 2011; Singh, 2010).

Such concerns over the livelihood of smallholders in turn bring into question whether they have managed to participate in the supermarket-driven marketing system. The evidence emerging from India so far has been mixed. Two empirical studies in Karnataka indicate a trend towards supermarket chains working with larger and more capitalized farmers (Pritchard et al., 2010; Mangala and Chengappa, 2008). Other studies, however, show no bias against small farmers (Sutradhar, 2015; Bathla, 2016; Singh and Singla, 2010). Smallholders in Haryana have not only participated in the supermarket channel, but also have allocated a large proportion of their land to production of vegetables under contract (Bathla, 2016). A case study from Punjab also finds that as many as 52 per cent of farmers supplying vegetables to Reliance Fresh are small (Singh and Singla, 2010). In the outskirts of Jaipur, farmers supplying to supermarkets in the city do not differ from their traditional counterparts in terms of farm size; however, the supermarket farmers are better endowed with physical and human capital (Sutradhar, 2015).

3.5 Pattern of smallholder participation in other developing countries

The trend emerging from other parts of the developing world bears testimony to a similar pattern to that noted in India. In many other developing countries, supermarkets have already become significant players in the retailing of fresh fruits and vegetables (Reardon et al., 2003). In fact, fresh produce sold through supermarkets is already emerging as a more important channel than export in countries in Latin America (Reardon et al., 2003) and in China (Hu et al., 2004). The high standards demanded by the procurement managers of the supermarkets implies that a vast majority of smallholders risk being excluded even in the domestic supply chain, let alone the export market. Barring few exceptions, smallholders are largely excluded from the supermarket-driven agri-food system (Reardon et al., 2009). Exceptions are noted when the procurement manager of the supermarket chain does not have enough large farmers to source from (Reardon et al., 2007; Berdegué et al., 2005), when he finds sourcing from a few larger farmers to be a risky option (Henson and Reardon, 2005) or when smallholders have a comparative advantage over their larger counterparts in crops that demand intensive labour management (Reardon et al., 2009). At times, smallholders successfully participate in the supermarket-driven marketing channel by aggregating themselves as co-operatives (Zuhui et al., 2013, Michelson 2013, Rao and Qaim, 2010). Even within the context of smallholder participation in the supermarket channel, farmers that supply to the supermarket chain are differentiated by their access to irrigation and other non-land assets which indicate their greater ability to meet the exacting standards demanded by the supermarket chain (Michelson, 2013, Hernández et al., 2007, Natawidjaja et al., 2007).

3.5.1 Lessons from Indonesia and China

Even as supermarket has been diffusing very fast over a decade or so in India, it can adopt and adapt models from other countries that have successfully engaged smallholders in supermarket driven supply chain. In this context, lessons learned from Indonesia and China are particularly instructive. Like India, the rural economies of both China and Indonesia are characterized by a predominance of smallholders, many of whom are resource constrained. In China, smallholders with landholding size measuring less than 2 hectares account for 95 per cent of the farmer households. Similarly, Indonesia is home to as many as 17 million small farmers, next only to India and China in Asia (Thapa, 2009). Supermarkets have made early entry into these countries, accounting for a share in total retail which is significantly higher than that in India (Reardon et al., 2003). With the share of supermarkets set to rise in coming decades, India can take lessons from how these two countries, with a significant presence of smallholders in their rural population, deal with the dilemma of incorporating them into the fast-expanding supermarket-driven agri-food system.

In the Chinese horticultural economy, itinerant traders who worked as an intermediary to source fresh produce from smallholders in the traditional marketing system continue to play the same role in the supermarket-driven marketing system (Wang et al., 2009). Case studies of Suago Supermarket, a rural supermarket chain in China, show that these traders, serving as dedicated or semi-dedicated agents of specialized suppliers working with supermarkets, source from the smallholders without compromising on food safety and quality considerations (Huang et al., 2013; Sang, 2013). They source and grade the produce from smallholders at the farm gate, with better quality produce supplied to specialized suppliers and the rest sold at the wholesale market. This model makes good use of the social capital that exists in close-knit village societies in China, as these agents are themselves farmers and source from other farmers living in the same area. There is no formal contract between the specialized suppliers and the agents nor between the agents and the farmers. The proximity with the agent fosters trust and informal relationships with the other farmers, which reduces the transaction costs of sourcing the produce.

Farmer associations or groups have also emerged as an institutional innovation to incorporate smallholders in the supermarket-driven marketing system

(Hu and Gale, 2016; Hu and Dandan, 2013; Qiao and Yu, 2013). These associations are carefully designed to overcome the shortcomings of early co-operative initiatives noted in the literature (Lele, 1981). For example, in Zhejiang province, China, the Farmer Water Melon Co-operative has emerged as an active partner with a number of supermarket chains in the region, thus facilitating smallholder participation in the supermarket-driven marketing system (Zuhui et al., 2013). The success of the co-operatives has been attributed to the preconditions imposed by the management of the co-operatives on new membership, which include ownership of enough capital to buy shares, some ability in organizing production and management, and a minimum of three years of experience in growing melons.

The Chinese government has also played the role of a catalyst in the emergence of farmer associations as an institutional innovation to incorporate small holders in the supermarket-driven supply chain. Apart from providing resources to build collection centres, the government has promoted sourcing through farmer association by giving tax incentives to supermarket chains for such sourcing practices. Of late, the Global Hub Procurement Program that Carrefour has started in China with this program has turned out to be a big success (Hu and Gale, 2016).

In Indonesia, farmer groups are also playing similar roles, as specialized wholesalers to supermarkets are forging partnerships with such collective associations to incorporate smallholders in the supermarket-driven supply chain. Bimandiri, a specialized wholesale company working with Carrefour, serves as a model of how to build capacity among smallholders so that they can meet the standards demanded by supermarkets (Natawidjaja et al., 2007). Bimandiri charges 5 per cent of the total turnover as commission for the services that it gives to the farmer groups, which include introduction of new varieties, provision of inputs through soft loans, quality control, accounting and contract negotiation with buyers. As a specialized wholesaler, it does not take claim of the ownership of the produce that is exchanged between the farmer group and supermarkets, fostering trust and transparency in the relation between different actors in the supply chain.

4 Roadmap for an inclusive and competitive marketing system in India

The agri-food marketing system has undergone significant changes in recent years in response to changes in the food basket of an average Indian, which has moved away from cereals in favour of fruits and vegetables. The available marketing infrastructure has not kept pace with these changes, leading to wastage of fruits and vegetables, which hurts small and marginal farmers more than the others. The government at the centre amended the laws regulating the marketing of fresh fruits and vegetables in early 2000, thereby liberating the regulated sector for private actors. In response to the signals sent by the market, private actors are expected to fill the gap. These changes in the regulatory environment facilitated the entry of new actors, such as supermarkets, which bring both challenges and opportunities. The challenge before India is to promote a marketing system that is both competitive and inclusive. Institutional innovations are required to ensure that smallholders can upgrade their capacity to meet the challenges posed by more demanding actors. Lessons from China and Indonesia show that farmer producer organizations, if carefully designed, can build capacity among smallholders and help them emerge as an attractive option for more demanding buyers such as supermarket procurement managers. In this context, the decision taken by the government to amend the Companies Act, 1956 that gives the rural producers the flexibility to organize themselves as a producer group is a step in the right direction. India can also draw inspiration from the success of its own models, such as Mahagrape (Roy and Thorat, 2008).

Supermarkets are, however, not an unmixed blessing. The evidence from other countries shows that as supermarket share grows, competition among the chains to capture a higher share of market may lead to a situation where the procurement managers of the chains pass on the burden to the suppliers. Delaying payment to farmers, which means that farmer suppliers are subsidizing the supermarket manager through credit at zero interest rate, is one such example. The government should promote good business practices to protect the interests of both farmers and supermarkets by improving contract regulations and enforcement of contracts (Singh, 2010). The government can formulate rules based on lessons learned in other countries, such as Argentina and Malaysia. As a case study from Argentina (Gutman, 2002) shows the government can encourage supermarket chains to develop their own codes of practice to ensure that sourcing fresh produce from smallholders does not turn out to be a 'race to the bottom', where farmers have to face the brunt of a competitive struggle among the supermarket chains. In this context, farmer producer organizations can go a long way in improving the bargaining power of smallholders vis-à-vis supermarkets.

Further, an inclusive agricultural marketing system requires recognition that a well-functioning wholesale market is a key element of a competitive marketing system. The pricing strategy followed by supermarket chain managers shows that procurement managers continue to use prices in the wholesale market as reference prices (Sutradhar, 2015). Moreover, investment in the marketing infrastructure has a public good character; that is, investment in some infrastructure in the wholesale market such as roads leading to the market has benefits that cannot be appropriated by private investors alone because of externality. Despite the amendment in the APMC Act which now allows for private markets, the private sector has not shown enough interest in setting up such markets (Chand, 2012). In this regard, the program taken up by European Bank for Reconstruction and Development (EBRD) to modernize the wholesale market in Hungary is worth emulating (Singh and Singla, 2010). Overall, the policy focus should be to improve the facilities and awareness about grades and standards in the wholesale market so that the demanding actors such as supermarkets and processing companies continue to rely on sourcing from wholesale markets as a dominant strategy. In this context, recent policy decisions taken by the government to create a common national market is a step in the right direction.

Note

1 The rationale behind the procurement prices is that if the produce procured through MSP falls short of required buffer stocks, the government can purchase food grains from the open market through procurement prices, which are higher than MSP. The procurement price, however, does not entail any legal obligation of procurement.

References

Acharya, S. S., 2004. Agricultural Marketing and Rural Credit: Status. *Issues and Reform Agenda*, 17, pp. 372–399.

Alam, G. and Verma, D., 2013. Connecting Small Farmers With Dynamic Markets: A Successful Supply Chain in Uttarakhand, India. In Sharma, V.P., Vorley, B., Huang, J., Suleri, A. Q., Larry, D. and Thomas, R. A. (eds.), *Linking Smallholder Producers to Modern Agri-Food Chains: Case Studies From South Asia, Southeast Asia and China*, Allied Publishers Pvt Ltd, New Delhi, Ch. 4, pp. 76–96.

Balani, S., 2013. *Functioning of the Public Distribution System: An Analytical Report*, PRS Legislative Research, New Delhi, available at www.prsindia.org/administra tor/uploads/general/1388728622~~TPDS%20Thematic%20Note.pdf, accessed 02/04/2017.

Banerjee, A., Mookherjee, D., Munshi, K. and Ray, D., 2001. Inequality, Control Rights, and Rent Seeking: Sugar Cooperatives in Maharashtra. *Journal of Political Economy*, 109(1), pp. 138–190.

Bathla, S., 2016. Organized Fresh Food Retail Chains Versus Traditional Wholesale Markets: Marketing Efficiency and Farmers' Participation. In Rao, N. C., Radhakrishna, R., Mishra, R. K. and Reddy, V. K. (eds.), *Organised Retailing and Agri-Business: Implications of New Supply Chains on the Indian Farm Economy*, Springer, New Delhi, India, Ch. 11, pp. 207–229.

Berdegué, J. A., Balsevich, F., Flores, L. and Reardon, T., 2005. Central American supermarkets' private standards of quality and safety in procurement of fresh fruits and vegetables. *Food Policy*, 30(3), pp. 254–269.

Bhalla, G. S., 2007. *Indian Agriculture Since Independence*, National Book Trust, New Delhi.

Chand, R., 2012. Development Policies and Agricultural Markets. *Economic & Political Weekly*, 47(52), pp. 53–62.

Chandra, P. and Tirupati, D., 2002. *Managing Complex Networks in Emerging Markets: The Story of AMUL*, Indian Institute of Management, Bangalore.

Chandrasekhar, C. P., 2011. The Retail Counter-Revolution. *The Hindu*, available at http://www.thehindu.com/opinion/columns/Chandrasekhar/the-retail-coun terrevolution/article2672067.ece, accessed 31/1/2017.

Dhananjaya, B. N. and Rao, A. U., 2009. Inclusive Value Chains in Fresh Fruit and Vegetables - Case Study 1-Namdhari Fresh Limited. In Malcom, H. (ed.), *Inclusive Value Chains in India*, World Scientific Publishing Co. Pvt Ltd., Ch.3, pp. 31–46.

Fafchamps, M., Hill, R. V. and Minten, B., 2008. Quality Control in Nonstaple Food Markets: Evidence From India. *Agricultural Economics*, 38(3), pp. 251–266.

Gandhi, V. and Namboodiri, N.V., 2002. *Fruit and Vegetable Marketing and Its Efficiency in India: A Study in Wholesale Markets in Ahmedabad Area*, Mimeo, Indian Institute of Management, Ahemdabad, available at www.iimahd.ernet.in/publica tions/data/2004-06-09vpgandhi.pdf, accessed 01/12/2016.

GOI (Government of India), 2001. *Report of the Working Group on Agricultural Marketing Infrastructure*, Ministry of Agriculture, New Delhi.

Gutman, G. E., 2002. Impact of the Rapid Rise of Supermarkets on Dairy Products Systems in Argentina. *Development Policy Review*, 20(4), pp. 409–427.

Harriss-White, B., 1996. *A Political Economy of Agricultural Markets in South India: Masters of the Countryside*, Sage Publications India Pvt Ltd.

Henson, S. and Reardon, T., 2005. Private agri-food standards: Implications for food policy and the agri-food system. *Food policy*, 30(3), pp. 241–253.

Hernández, R., Reardon, T. and Berdegué, J., 2007. Supermarkets, Wholesalers, and Tomato Growers in Guatemala. *Agricultural Economics*, 36(3), pp. 281–290.

The Hindu, 2014. Indian Retail Market to Reach 47 Lakh Crore by 2016/17, available at www.thehindu.com/business/Industry/indian-retail-market-to-reach-47-lakh-crore-by-201617-study/article5677176.ece, accessed 10/10/2016.

Hu, D., Reardon, T., Rozelle, S., Timmer, P. and Wang, H., 2004. The emergence of supermarkets with Chinese characteristics: challenges and opportunities for China's agricultural development. *Development Policy Review*, 22(5), pp. 557–586.

Huang, J., Huang, Z., Niu, X., Zhi, H., Wang, S. and Hu, D., 2013. Market Chain Changes in Small Farm Dominated Economy: A Case Study on Mushroom in China, Linking Smallholder Producers to Modern Agri-Food Chains: Case Studies From South Asia, Southeast Asia and China. In Sharma, V.P., Vorley, B., Huang, J., Suleri, A.Q., Larry, D. and Thomas, R. A. (eds.), *Linking Smallholder Producers to Modern Agri-Food Chains: Case Studies From South Asia, Southeast Asia and China*, Allied Publishers Pvt Ltd, New Delhi, Ch.11, pp. 308–321.

Hu, D. and Dandan, X., 2013. Keys to Inclusion of Small-Scale Producers in Dynamic Markets: Carrefour's Quality Lines in China. In Sharma, V. P., Vorley, B., Huang, J., Suleri, A.Q., Larry, D. and Thomas, R. A. (eds.), *Linking Smallholder Producers to Modern Agri-Food Chains: Case Studies From South Asia, Southeast Asia and China*, Allied Publisher Pvt Ltd, New Delhi, Ch. 10, pp. 275–307.

Hu, D. and Gale, F., 2016. An Innovative Marketing Model for Fresh Produce in China: Farmer-Supermarket Direct-Purchase. In Rao, N. C., Radhakrishna, R., Mishra, R.K. and Reddy, V. K. (eds.), *Organised Retailing and Agri-Business*, Springer, New Delhi, India, pp. 119–138.

Jha, R., Bhanu Murthy, K. V., Nagarajan, H. K. and Seth, A. K., 1997. Market Integration in Indian Agriculture. *Economic Systems*, 21, pp. 217–234.

Kolady, D., Krishnamoorthy, S. and Narayanan, S., 2013. Marketing Cooperative in a New Retail Context: A Study of HOPCOMS. In Sharma, V. P., Vorley, B., Huang, J., Suleri, A. Q., Larry, D. and Thomas, R. A. (eds.), *Linking Smallholder Producers to Modern Agri-Food Chains: Case Studies From South Asia, Southeast Asia and China*, Allied Publishers Pvt Ltd, New Delhi, Ch. 3, pp. 55–75.

Krishnamacharyulu, C. S. G., 2011. *Rural Marketing: Text and Cases, 2/E*, Pearson Education India.

Kumar, P. and Dey, M. M., 2007.Long-Term Changes in Indian Food Basket and Nutrition. *Economic and Political Weekly*, 42(35), pp. 3567–3572.

Lele, U., 1981. Co-Operatives and the Poor: A Comparative Perspective. *World Development*, 9(1), pp. 55–72.

Mangala, K. P. and Chengappa, P. G., 2008. A Novel Agribusiness Model for Backward Linkages With Farmers: A Case of Food Retail Chain. *Agricultural Economics Research Review*, 21(Conference Number), pp. 363–370.

Meenakshi, J. V. and Banerji, A., 2005. The Unsupportable Support Price: An Analysis of Collusion and Government Intervention in Paddy Auction Markets in North India. *Journal of Development Economics*, 76(2), pp. 377–403.

Michelson, H. C., 2013. Small Farmers, NGOs, and a Walmart World: Welfare Effects of Supermarkets Operating in Nicaragua. *American Journal of Agricultural Economics*, 95(3), pp. 628–649.

Ministry of Agriculture, 2013. *Final Report of Committee of State Ministers, In-charge of Agriculture Marketing to Promote Reforms.* A Report prepared by Ministry of Agriculture, Department of Agriculture and Co-operation Government of India.

Minten, B., Reardon, T. and Sutradhar, R., 2010. Food Prices and Modern Retail: The Case of Delhi. *World Development*, 38(12), pp. 1775–1787.

Natawidjaja, R., Reardon, T., Shetty, S., Noor, T. I., Perdana, T., Rasmikayati, E., Bachri, S. and Hernandez, R., 2007. *Horticultural Producers and Supermarket Development in Indonesia.* UNPAD/MSU/World Bank, World Bank Report, Report No 38543.

NCEUS, 2008. *A Special Programme for Marginal and Small Farmers.* A Report prepared by the National Commission for Enterprises in the Unorganized Sector, NCEUS, New Delhi.

Pandey, M., Baker, G. A. and Pandey, D. T., 2013. Supply Chain Re-Engineering in the Fresh Produce Industry: A Case Study of Adani Agrifresh. *International Food and Agribusiness Management Review*, 16(1), pp. 115–136.

Patnaik, G., 2011. *Status of Agricultural Marketing Reforms.* In Workshop Policy Options and Investment Priorities for Accelerating Agricultural Productivity and Development in India, Indira Gandhi Institute of Development Research, Mumbai and Institute for Human Development, New Delhi, pp. 10–11, November.

Pritchard, B., Gracy, C. P. and Godwin, M., 2010. The Impacts of Supermarket Procurement on Farming Communities in India: Evidence From Rural Karnataka. *Development Policy Review*, 28(4), pp. 435–456.

Qiao, H. Z. L. and Yu, S., 2013. Collective Actions of Small Farm Households in Big Markets: Ruoheng Farmer Watermelon Cooperative in China. In Sharma, V. P., Vorley, B., Huang, J., Suleri, A. Q., Larry, D. and Thomas, R. A. (eds.), *Linking Smallholder Producers to Modern Agri-Food Chains: Case Studies From South Asia, Southeast Asia and China*, Allied Publishers Pvt Ltd, New Delhi, Ch.12, pp. 322–345.

Rao, E. J. and Qaim, M., 2010. Supermarkets, Farm Household Income, and Poverty: Insights From Kenya. *World Development*, 39(5), pp. 784–796.

Reardon, T. and Minten, B., 2011. Surprised by Supermarkets: Diffusion of Modern Food Retail in India. *Journal of Agribusiness in Developing and Emerging Economies*, 1(2), pp. 134–161.

Reardon, T. and Timmer, C. P., 2007. Transformation of Markets for Agricultural Output in Developing Countries Since 1950: How Has Thinking Changed? *Handbook of Agricultural Economics*, Elsevier, Vol.3, Ch.55, pp. 2807–2855.

Reardon, T., Timmer, C. P., Barrett, C. B. and Berdegué, J., 2003. The Rise of Supermarkets in Africa, Asia, and Latin America. *American Journal of Agricultural Economics*, 85(5), pp. 1140–1146.

Reardon, T., Barrett, C. B., Berdegué, J. A. and Swinnen, J. F., 2009. Agrifood industry transformation and small farmers in developing countries. *World Development*, 37(11), pp. 1717–1727.

Reardon, T., Timmer, C. P. and Minten, B., 2012. Supermarket Revolution in Asia and Emerging Development Strategies to Include Small Farmers. *Proceedings of the National Academy of Sciences*, 109(31), pp. 12332–12337.

Roy, D. and Thorat, A., 2008. Success in High Value Horticultural Export Markets for the Small Farmers: The Case of Mahagrapes in India. *World Development*, 36(10), pp. 1874–1890.

Sang, N., 2013. Supermarkets Penetrating Chinese Countryside: The Suguo Model and Its Impact on Smallholders and SMEs. In Sharma, V. P., Vorley, B., Huang, J., Suleri, A. Q., Larry, D. and Thomas, R. A. (eds.), *Linking Smallholder Producers to Modern Agri-Food Chains: Case Studies From South Asia, Southeast Asia and China*, Allied Publishers Pvt Ltd, New Delhi, Ch.13, pp. 346–357.

Shah, A., 2011. Retail Chains for Agro/Food products, Inclusive or Elusive. *Economic and Political Weekly*, 46(33), pp. 25–28.

Shilpi, F. and Umali-Deininger, D., 2008. Market Facilities and Agricultural Marketing: Evidence From Tamil Nadu, India. *Agricultural Economics*, 39(3), pp. 281–294.

Singh, S., 2004. Crisis and Diversification in Punjab Agriculture, *Economic and Political Weekly*, 39(52), I, pp. 5583–5589.

Singh, S., 2008. Producer Companies as New Generation Cooperatives. *Economic and Political Weekly*, 43(20), pp. 22–24.

Singh, S., 2009. Inclusive Value Chains in Fresh Fruit and Vegetables- Case Study 4- Spencer's Retail. In Harper, M.(ed.), *Inclusive Value Chains in India*, World Scientific Publishing Co. Pvt Ltd., Ch.3, pp. 81–93.

Singh, S., 2010. Implications of FDI in Food Supermarkets. *Economic and Political Weekly*, 45(34), pp. 17–20.

Singh, S., 2012. New Markets for Smallholders in India: Exclusions, Policy and Mechanisms. *Economic and Political Weekly*, 47(52), pp. 95-105.

Singh, S., 2016. Arthiyas in Punjab's APMC Mandis. *Economic and Political Weekly*, 51(15), pp. 69–70.

Singh, S. and Singla, N., 2010. *Fresh Food Retail Chains in India: Organisation and Impacts*, Centre for Management in Agriculture, Indian Institute of Management (IIM), Ahmedabad *CMA Publication No. 238*, September 24.

Sutradhar, R., 2015. *Organized Retail in Fresh Fruits and Vegetables: An Assessment of Its Impact, With Special Reference to Small Farmers, Based on Field Survey in Rajasthan, India*. Unpublished PhD thesis, Jawaharlal Nehru University, New Delhi.

Thapa, G., 2009. *Smallholder Farming in Transforming Economies of Asia and the Pacific: Challenges and Opportunities*. Discussion on Paper prepared for the Side Event Organized During the Thirty Third Session of IFAD's Governing Council.

Wang, H., Dong, X., Rozelle, S., Huang, J. and Reardon, T., 2009. Producing and Procuring Horticultural Crops With Chinese Characteristics: The Case of Northern China. *World Development*, 37(11), pp. 1791–1801

Williamson, O. E., 1979. Transaction-Cost Economics: The Governance of Contractual Relations. *The Journal of Law and Economics*, 22(2), pp. 233–261.

Williamson, O. E., 1993. The Evolving Science of Organization. *Journal of Institutional and Theoretical Economics (JITE)/Zeitschrift für die gesamte Staatswissenschaft*, 149(1), pp. 36–63.

Zuhui, H., Qiao, L., and Yu, S., 2013. Collective Actions of Small Farm Households in Big Markets: Ruoheng Farmer Watermelon Cooperative in China. In Sharma, V.P., Vorley, B., Huang, J., Suleri, A.Q., Larry, D. and Thomas, R. A. (eds.), *Linking Smallholder Producers to Modern Agri-Food Chains: Case Studies From South Asia, Southeast Asia and China*, Allied Publishers Pvt Ltd, New Delhi, Ch 13, pp. 346–357.

7 Irrigation in India

The post-Green Revolution experience, challenges and strategies

Mrinal Kanti Dutta

1 Introduction

The tremendous growth in agricultural production and productivity in India in the post-Green Revolution period can largely be attributed to the expansion of irrigation infrastructure in the country. Coupled with short duration HYV seeds, fertilizer and pesticides, provisioning of irrigation infrastructure has provided a much-needed boost to Indian agriculture since the later half of 1960s. Irrigation was considered the key instrument in harnessing the huge potential for agricultural productivity in India during the Green Revolution period (Mukherjee, 2016, p. 44). In fact, extension of irrigation facilities has been a central feature of India's agricultural development strategy since independence (Vaidyanathan, 2006, p. 9), and investments in large-scale public irrigation systems were seen as key to increasing agricultural production in the country.

Irrigation-enabled new technology helped farmers to increase production by bringing more area under cultivation and also by increasing yield of crops. Availability of this technology also helped in crop diversification and in the practice of multiple cropping. As per the available data, from about 20,123 thousand hectares in 1966–67, the area sown more than once in the country had gone up to 54,467 thousand hectares in 2012–13, indicating a 2.71 times increase in the area. The corresponding cropping intensity also went up from 114.66 per cent in 1966–67 to 138.92 per cent in 2012–13.

Given the significant role the irrigation sector has played in the overall development of agriculture in India, this chapter is an attempt to assess the development of irrigation in terms of the spread of irrigation over time and across sources. The chapter further discusses certain emerging issues in the sector and future strategies that ought to be taken for the development of the sector. The chapter is comprised of four major sections. The next section reviews the development of irrigation in the post-Green Revolution period in terms of growth in gross irrigated area and quantum of water utilized from various sources. The pattern of investments in the irrigation sector is also examined. Some of the significant emerging issues in irrigation are discussed simultaneously. The third section deals with some key issues concerning future development of the irrigation sector in the country. The necessary data have been collected from various government sources, such as the Directorate of Economics and Statistics, the Ministry of Agriculture and the

Government of India, and from databases, namely, Indiastats.com and Economic Intelligence Service (Centre for Monitoring Indian Economy).

2 Growth of irrigation

The most widely used index of irrigation development is 'area irrigated', which can be divided into net and gross irrigated area (Vaidyanathan, 1999). Figures on net irrigated area give an idea about the area under irrigation during an agricultural year counting the area only once even if two or more crops are irrigated in different seasons in the same land. Gross irrigated area shows the total irrigated area under various crops during the year, counting the area irrigated under more than one crop during the same year as many times as the number of crops grown, crops sown mixed being taken as one crop. Thus, the area irrigated more than once can be obtained by deducting the net irrigated area from the gross irrigated area. There has been tremendous growth in both gross irrigated area and net irrigated area in the country since 1950–51, and particularly since the Green Revolution period. The gross irrigated area almost trebled during 1965–66 to 2012–13, and the net irrigated area increased more than 2.5 times during the same period. When viewed with the land utilization statistics in the country, it is found that in 1950–51, total net irrigated area of the country was 20.8 million hectares, which constituted about 17.56 per cent of the net sown area. The figure shows a moderate increase in the next 15 years, until the Green Revolution was ushered in, in 1966–67. With the introduction of new agricultural technology in 1966–67, the coverage in irrigation experienced rapid growth. While net irrigated area as a percentage of net sown area was 19.34 per cent in 1965–66, the figure stood at 33.61 per cent in 1990–91. In 2012–13, net irrigated area as a percentage of net sown area was 47.24 per cent. During the entire period of 1950–51 to 2012–13, the compound annual growth rates (CAGR) of gross and net irrigated area have been found to be 2.45 per cent and 2.03 per cent, respectively, while the CAGR of gross and net irrigated area since the start of Green Revolution (1966–67 to 2012–13) is found to be 2.27 per cent and 1.93 per cent, respectively.[1] The figures on gross and net irrigated area since 1950–51 are given in Table 7.1.

2.1 Irrigated area by source

Irrigation development in the country, in the initial few decades after independence, was mostly confined to expansion by way of a comprehensive canal network. In the First Five Year Plan (1951–56), a number of multipurpose and major projects were taken up. These include projects such as Bhakra Nangal, Nagarjunasagar, Kosi, Chambal, Hirakud, Kakrapar, Tungabhadra and so on (Government of India, 2011, p. 15). As such, canals contributed the largest share of net irrigated area in the country in the 1950s and 1960s. In 1966–67, canals contributed 42 per cent of the total net irrigated area in the country, followed by wells (including tube wells; 34 per cent), and tanks (16 per cent). However, beset with a number of problems, the relative importance of canal irrigation has come down over time. In 2012–13, the share of canals in the net

Table 7.1 Gross and net irrigated area in India during 1950–51 and 2012–13

Year	Gross irrigated area in million hectares)	Net irrigated area (in million hectares)	Net irrigated area as % of net sown area
1950–51	22.56	20.85	17.56
1955–56	25.64	22.76	17.62
1960–61	27.98	24.66	18.51
1965–66	30.90	26.34	19.34
1970–71	38.20	31.10	22.08
1975–76	43.36	34.59	24.42
1980–81	49.78	38.72	27.6
1985–86	54.28	41.87	29.71
1990–91	63.20	48.02	33.61
1995–96	71.35	53.40	37.56
2000–01	76.19	55.21	39.06
2005–06	84.28	60.84	43.1
2010–11	88.63	63.66	44.97
2011–12	91.53	65.69	46.6
2012–13	92.58	66.10	47.24
CAGR (1966–67 to 2012–13) (in %)	2.27	1.93	

Source: Centre for Monitoring Indian Economy (CMIE), Economic Intelligence Service.

irrigated area of the country was as low as 24 per cent. The problems often associated with surface flow canal irrigation system include problems with command area development, non-completion of proper canal network, conveyance loss, lack of coordination between various agencies involved in delivering water and so on (Chambers, 1988; Saleth, 1996; Dutta, 2011). Explaining the problems of major and medium schemes in general and canal irrigation in particular, Gulati et al. (2005) observed: 'Maintenance is being woefully neglected, leading to poor capacity utilization, rising incidence of water-logging and salinity, and lowering of water use efficiency. On the whole, the growth of irrigated agriculture is threatening to become less sustainable-environmentally as well as financially'. In fact, poor maintenance of the irrigation system and utilization efficiency are caught in a vicious circle. Normally a user fee is collected from the beneficiary farmers of the irrigation project for operation and maintenance of the projects. However, low user charge for irrigation results in under-funding of operation and maintenance, leading to poor system performance, causing farmers' dissatisfaction. The final outcome is even lower payment by farmers for irrigation.

In the 1980s while the growth of canal irrigation slowed down, groundwater development through private investment picked up. Dhawan (1982) pointed out that the high degree of indivisibility in Indian farm conditions was responsible for the non-diffusion of tube well technology during the first half of the 20th century. However, with substantial reduction of tube well indivisibility resulting from easing out of numerous constraints of farm economy, farmers found it convenient to invest in their own tube wells. Compared to the canal-based major and medium irrigation projects, small-scale well irrigation systems (including tube wells) are relatively easy to manage due to their small size and the flexibility of using them as per the requirements of the users. Also, many of these small-scale irrigation systems are owned and operated by farmers themselves. In view of this, the government has also been focusing more on small-scale well-based irrigation systems and has encouraged installation of these systems with government subsidy-driven projects. As a result of this, area irrigated through wells in the country has gone up many times, and in 2012–13, wells contributed as high as 62 per cent of net irrigated area. However, groundwater development in the country is also coupled with numerous issues, such as groundwater over-exploitation at large and in individual states, water quality deterioration (Dhawan, 1995), mounting electricity subsidies and so on. Recent trends show signs of a slowdown in groundwater use, and a renewed interest in surface irrigation is expected (Mukherjee, 2016, p. 44).

The temporal growth of irrigated area by source is presented in Figure 7.1. It is evident from the figure that wells are the most important source of irrigation in the country today. The area under well irrigation today is the maximum, and the growth of area under wells during the Green Revolution period was impressive. At the same time, canals have lost their importance as a source of irrigation and have grown only marginally during the last fifty years. While the area irrigated through tanks has gone down, area irrigated through other sources, has slightly improved.

By contrast, tube wells today constitute the largest proportion of well irrigation in the country. In 2012–13, out of the total area irrigated by wells, as much

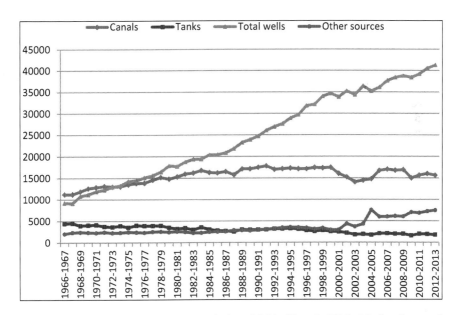

Figure 7.1 Irrigated area by source during 1966–67 and 2012–13 (in thousand hectares)

Source: CMIE, Economic Intelligence Service.

as 73.91 per cent was contributed by tube wells, whereas the share of other wells was only 26.09 per cent. However, at the beginning of the Green Revolution (i.e., in 1966–67), the situation was quite opposite. As much as 81.45 per cent of area under wells was then under other wells. The contribution of tube wells in the area irrigated by wells was much lower (18.55 per cent) (Figure 7.2).

2.2 *Irrigated area across states*

Irrigation development in the country, although having experienced tremendous growth, suffers from the problem of uneven growth. While the northwestern region of the country, the traditional site of the Green Revolution, has experienced relatively high expansion in terms of area irrigated, many other regions have failed to do so. This has resulted in dependence on rainfall for agricultural practices in many states in the country. The eastern region, for instance, has failed to develop irrigation infrastructure although it boasts of huge water reserves (both surface and groundwater). The situation has not changed much in recent years. Taking into account the ratio of gross irrigated area (GIA) to total cropped area (TCA), it is found that there has been some marginal improvement in the ratio for almost all the states in the country during 2001–02 to 2012–13. Table 7.2 provides information on irrigation development across states in India during 2001–02 and 2012–13.

It is clear from Table 7.2 that the ratio of gross irrigated area (GIA) to total cropped area (TCA) for the country as a whole increased from 41.7 per cent in 2001–02 to 47.6 per cent in 2012–13. However, variation has been noticed in the growth of the ratio across states and regions. For example, while this growth has been substantial for some states in eastern, western and central India, such

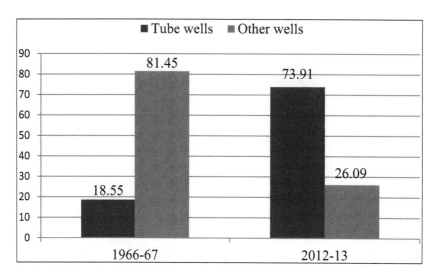

Figure 7.2 Area irrigated by tube wells and other wells in total area irrigated by wells during 1966–67 and 2012–13 (in %)

Source: CMIE, Economic Intelligence Service.

Table 7.2 Irrigated area across states during 2001–02 and 2012–13

States/UTs	2001–02				2012–13			
	Net irrigated area	Gross irrigated area	% of GIA to TCA	Cropping intensity (%)	Net irrigated area	Gross irrigated area	% of GIA to TCA	Cropping intensity (%)
Andhra Pradesh	4,238	5,549	43.5	122.5	4,575	6,268	45.9	122.8
Arunachal Pradesh	42	43	17.4	150.9	57	57	19.9	131.7
Assam	140	174	4.4	143.6	161	160	3.8	149.3
Bihar	3,462	4,539	57.5	139.4	3,053	5,327	68.5	144
Chhattisgarh	1,151	1,227	21.9	116.6	1,449	1,725	30.3	121.8
Goa	23	38	22.9	119.1	36	36	22.4	123.2
Gujarat	2,994	3,572	33.3	111.6	4,233	5,913	46.9	122.3
Haryana	2,938	5,311	84.1	177.2	3,102	5,672	89	181.5
Himachal Pradesh	102	181	18.9	173.9	110	195	20.6	174.2
Jammu & Kashmir	310	449	40.6	147.8	325	487	41.9	156
Jharkhand	141	175	9.5	120.6	210	235	14.2	117.9
Karnataka	2,565	3,089	26.5	116.3	3,421	4,007	34.1	120
Kerala	377	432	14.4	136.6	396	458	17.7	126.5
Madhya Pradesh	4,735	4,899	25.7	128.2	8,550	8,966	38.8	150.7
Maharashtra	3,136	3,727	17.8	121.9	3,244	4,041	18.5	126.1
Manipur	40	40	18.7	100	49	49	15.7	100
Meghalaya	59	76	27.2	120.6	65	125	36.8	119
Mizoram	16	17	19.2	100	14	15	12.6	100
Nagaland	65	80	21.1	113.5	85	92	18.9	128.5
Odisha	1,752	2,546	28.9	150.5	1,248	1,496	29.5	115.6
Punjab	4,056	7,667	96.5	186.7	4,115	7,744	98.4	189.6
Rajasthan	5,420	6,744	32.4	124.1	7,499	9,455	39.5	137
Sikkim	6	12	9.6	157.2	14	19	13.5	185.7
Tamil Nadu	2,801	3,412	54.8	120.4	2,643	2,991	58.2	113.1
Tripura	73	105	37.3	100	60	128	34.9	144.1
Uttarakhand	346	539	44.1	157.3	338	554	49.3	159.2
Uttar Pradesh	12,828	18,220	71.6	151.4	13,929	20,191	78.2	155.9
West Bengal	3,058	5,426	55.5	177.1				
India	56,936	78,371	41.7	133.6	66,103	92,575	47.6	138.9

Note: GIA = Gross Irrigated Area, TCA = Total Cropped Area.

Source: Indiastat.com.

as Bihar, Jharkhand, Chattishgarh, Madhya Pradesh, Gujarat and Rajasthan, the growth is found to be marginal for many other states. The northern state of Haryana also performed creditably during this period. In the case of Punjab, the ratio went up from 96.5 per cent in 2001–02 to 98.4 per cent in 2012–13. Southern states of Karnataka and Kerala also have shown some progress in the ratio of GIA to TCA during this period. Interestingly, however, the performance of northeastern states worsened during this period. As is evident from Table 7.2, gross irrigated area as a percentage of total cropped area in almost all the northeastern states declined during the period from 2001–02 to 2012–13, except for Arunachal Pradesh, Meghalaya and Sikkim.

The regional imbalances in irrigation development in the country are compounded by some paradoxical policy interventions, such as providing free electricity in those areas with limited groundwater potential (for example, the hard rock areas of southern India) and no electricity in the alluvial plains (of eastern India) with rich groundwater potential. Further, the mismatch between the cropping pattern chosen and availability of water resources in the regions should be taken into account when formulating policies for irrigation management in the future (Mukherjee, 2016, p. 46).

2.3 Investment in irrigation

Irrigation works in India are broadly classified into three categories: major, medium and minor irrigation. This classification system evolved during British times and was linked to the quantum of capital resources required for executing irrigation works of varying scale and size. This procedure was followed by Indian planners up to 1978. However, since 1978–79, the criteria used for classification of irrigation works changed from financial to technical norms. The categorization of the schemes is now based on their culturable command areas (CCA) (Swaminathan, 1981).

During the post-Green Revolution period, there has been tremendous growth in public investment in irrigation in the country. There has been a massive increase in plan expenditures on irrigation and flood control over the last 60 years. The bulk of this investment has been on major and medium irrigation projects. As per the data available from the erstwhile Planning Commission, outlays for major and medium irrigation projects increased from Rs. 376 crores in the First Plan to a projected outlay of more than Rs. 165,000 crores in the Eleventh Plan, amounting to a total expenditure of around Rs. 3,51,000 crores over this period. Combined with minor irrigation and command area development, total plan allocation during the First Plan was to the tune of Rs. 442 crores which increased to Rs. 211,700 crores in the Eleventh Plan (Planning Commission, 2013). The relative importance of major and medium irrigation projects in the irrigation scenario in the country has reduced considerably, while the significance of minor irrigation has increased over time. During the First Plan, plan expenditure on major and medium irrigation projects as a share of total expenses on irrigation was 85 per cent, which went down to 78 per cent in the Eleventh Plan. The corresponding share of minor irrigation improved from 15 per cent in the First Plan to 22 per cent in the Eleventh Plan period.

As the data on plan expenditure on irrigation are available only in prices at the time, the comparison across time periods does not carry much meaning. To make the comparison meaningful across different five-year plans, plan expenditure on irrigation has been expressed as a ratio of agricultural GDP of the respective plan periods, as shown in Figure 7.3.

It is clear from Figure 7.3 that irrigation expenditures during the first two plans were rather low, amounting to barely 1.61–1.67 per cent of the agricultural GDP during those two plan periods. However, the increase in the expenditure on irrigation started taking place from the Third Plan and continued thereafter. It reached a high of 4.33 per cent during the Annual Plans of 1978–80. In the recent few plan periods, expenditures on irrigation as a percentage of agricultural GDP have shown a fluctuating trend. For the Eleventh Plan, irrigation expenditure as a percentage of agricultural GDP has been estimated as 3.24 per cent. One of the major problems associated with the major and medium projects in the country is the massive time and cost overruns. As per the Twelfth Plan document, the average cost overrun in major and medium projects has been found to be as high as 1,382 per cent. The Twelfth Plan, therefore, proposed that completion of ongoing projects be given the highest priority and new projects be taken up only when there was a demonstrated need of an outstanding character (Government of India, 2011, p. 147).

Public investment in large irrigation projects has also promoted private investment in tube wells in the command areas of the major and medium schemes. This started happening particularly from the 1970s and continued into the 1980s and 1990s. With the provisioning of subsidies for installation of groundwater structures, the growth of groundwater-based irrigation had been remarkable. In effect, state electricity utilities played a significant role in incentivizing farmers through

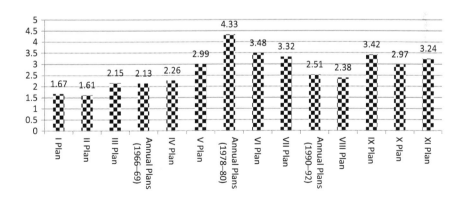

Figure 7.3 Irrigation expenditure as percentage of agricultural GDP during various plans

Source: Plan Document, 12th Five Year Plan, Planning Commission.

subsidized tariffs (or discouraging them through lack of rural electrification, as in eastern India) to tap groundwater. According to Mukherjee (2016), farm power subsidies are estimated at $9 billion annually, up from $6 billion a decade ago. Nevertheless, the pace of investment in groundwater irrigation has slowed down considerably in recent years. The reasons behind this are many. As is evident from available data, the level of the groundwater table has gone down to an extreme low level in many states in the country. A number of Indian states are in a critical groundwater condition, where pumping exceeds the long-term recharge of the aquifers. Groundwater through pumping has become more expensive due to higher tariffs on electricity despite receiving subsidies. The alternative, diesel, has also become costly in recent years with revision of diesel prices every now and then (Mukherjee, 2016, p. 45).

2.4 Irrigation potential created and utilized

Expansion of irrigated area is a poor measure of irrigation development unless it tells about the effectiveness of utilization of irrigation facilities (Vaidyanathan, 1999, p. 64). One of the major issues afflicting major and medium irrigation systems in India is the issue of a large gap between irrigation potential created (IPC) and irrigation potential utilized (IPU).[2] Creating irrigation potential by the major and medium irrigation projects is a costly affair. But in spite of massive public investment in the schemes, utilization of irrigation potential is found to be very low. Interestingly, however, issues relating to utilization of irrigation potential did not receive much attention until the 1980s.

As per the data of the Central Water Commission (CWC), the total irrigation potential of the country is estimated to be 139.86 million hectares (mha) from all sources, namely, major and medium irrigation (MMI), minor irrigation surface (MIS) and minor irrigation groundwater (MIG) (Central Water Commission, 2013). While irrigation potential under major and medium schemes is estimated to be 58.5 mha, the estimated potential under minor irrigation schemes is much higher at 81.4 mha. Groundwater is considered to dominate the total ultimate potential through minor irrigation, contributing about 79 per cent of the total potential.

Table 7.3 shows the change in the potential created and utilized in different plan periods in the country.

It is clear from Table 7.3 that there is a large gap between irrigation potential created and potential utilized, and the gap has worsened over the years. Table 7.3 further indicates that until the end of the Third Plan, IPU closely trailed IPC. Since then, the gap between IPC and IPU has steadily grown from less than 1.5 million hectares during the mid-1960s to over 23 million hectares around 2012, according to Planning Commission figures. The utilization rate (which can be computed as ratio of area utilized to potential created) worked out to be 79.42 per cent in 2012. Interestingly, the gap between irrigation potential created and utilized is found to be much higher in case of major and medium irrigation projects, as compared to the minor schemes. Accordingly, the figures for

Table 7.3 Irrigation potential created and utilized during different plan periods (in million hectares)

Plan		Potential created			Potential utilized		
		Major and Medium	Minor	Total	Major and Medium	Minor	Total
Up to 1951 (Pre-Plan)	Cumulative	9.7	12.9	22.6	9.7	12.9	22.6
I Plan (1951–56)	During	2.5	1.16	3.66	1.28	1.16	2.44
	Cumulative	12.2	14.06	26.26	10.98	14.06	25.04
II Plan (1956–61)	During	2.13	0.69	2.82	2.07	0.69	2.76
	Cumulative	14.33	14.75	29.08	13.05	14.75	27.8
III Plan (1961–66)	During	2.24	2.25	4.49	2.12	2.25	4.37
	Cumulative	16.57	17	33.57	15.17	17	32.17
Annual Plan (1966–69)	During	1.53	2	3.53	1.58	2	3.58
	Cumulative	18.1	19	37.1	16.75	19	35.75
IV Plan (1969–74)	During	2.6	4.5	7.1	1.64	4.5	6.14
	Cumulative	20.7	23.5	44.2	18.39	23.5	41.89
V Plan (1974–78)	During	4.02	3.8	7.82	2.7	3.8	6.5
	Cumulative	24.72	27.3	52.02	21.16	27.3	48.46
Annual Plan (1978–80)	During	1.89	2.7	1.59	1.48	2.7	4.18
	Cumulative	26.61	30	56.61	22.64	30	52.64
VI Plan (1980–85)	During	1.09	7.52	8.61	0.93	5.25	6.18
	Cumulative	27.7	37.52	65.22	23.57	35.25	58.82
VII Plan (1985–90)	During	2.22	9.09	11.31	1.9	7.87	9.77
	Cumulative	29.92	46.52	76.44	25.47	43.12	68.59
Annual Plan (1990–92)	During	0.82	3.74	4.56	0.85	3.42	4.27
	Cumulative	30.74	50.35	81.09	26.31	46.54	72.85
VIII Plan (1992–97)	During	2.21	2.96	5.17	2.13	2.23	4.36
	Cumulative	32.95	53.31	86.26	28.44	48.77	77.21
IX Plan (1997–2002)	During	4.1	3.59	7.69	2.57	1.22	3.79
	Cumulative	37.05	56.9	93.95	31.01	49.99	81
X Plan (2002–2007)	During	4.59	3.52	8.82	2.73	2.82	6.23
	Cumulative	41.64	60.42	102.77	33.74	52.81	87.23
XI Plan* (2007–2012)	During	5.77	4.7	10.47	1.27	1.44	2.71
	Cumulative	47.41	65.12	113.24	35.01	54.25	89.94

*Anticipated
Source: Planning Commission, 2013.

utilization rates are relatively lower for the major and medium irrigation projects vis-à-vis the minor irrigation schemes. As evident from Table 7.3, the utilization rate for major and medium irrigation projects was anticipated to be 73.85 per cent in 2012, compared to 83.31 per cent for the minor schemes.

The factors contributing to the large gap between potential created and utilized are both technical and institutional. While irrigation development through canals requires extensive expansion of canal networks, including construction of the main canal, subsidiaries and water courses, and so on, the process often gets stuck due to a host of technical, socio-economic and institutional reasons. While in many cases, problems crop up due to the slow pace of the command area development programme and the paucity of non-plan funds for maintenance of irrigation systems (Government of India, 2015), some institutional issues, such as not involving stakeholders in managing the irrigation systems, also contribute towards under-utilization of irrigation potential created. Some other reasons may be implementation issues, such as faulty project designs, poor lining and de-silting, shoddy maintenance of distribution channels, lack of coordination between concerned department officials (resulting in delays in implementation and implementation without proper technical assessment), inadequate technical and managerial capacity of irrigation department staff and so on (Dutta, 2011)

The problem is relatively less acute in the case of minor irrigation schemes, in general, and privately owned and operated minor irrigation schemes in particular. A study carried out in certain districts in Assam has shown that private shallow tube wells have much better utilization efficiency compared to government-owned and operated major and medium irrigation projects (Dutta, 2011), though there is still scope to improve the utilization rate of the installed capacity of tube well-based irrigation projects. In certain circumstances, the emergence of groundwater markets has helped overcome the problem of a low utilization rate of the privately owned shallow tube well-based irrigation in the state (Dutta, 2011).

3 Some other issues in irrigation development

While India has experienced tremendous growth of irrigation infrastructure during the post-Green Revolution period, a number of issues have also emerged in the process which India needs to look into while managing its water resources and irrigation infrastructure. The current challenge in the irrigation development in the country is no longer about creating large infrastructure for irrigation; rather it is the better management of irrigation systems so as to improve effectiveness of the created infrastructure, among others. Obviously, institutional issues for making better use of the existing potential should be given preference. As Mukherjee (2016, p. 46) has pointed out 'The current challenges in the irrigation sector . . . are . . . about improving water use efficiency, providing last mile connectivity, offering better service to farmers by treating them as clients instead of beneficiaries, finding creative ways of solving water disputes, and ensuring that groundwater and surface water resources are neither overexploited, nor polluted'. Some of the issues which merit discussion in irrigation development in India are discussed below.

3.1 Large irrigation projects vs. small irrigation schemes

Traditionally, large dam projects have been the mainstay of the irrigation effort in the country. However, it is now increasingly recognized that there are definite limits to the role they can play in providing economically viable additional large water storage. Compared to the minor irrigation schemes, the area covered by major and medium schemes could be much higher, facilitating irrigation to more farmers. However, the quantum of capital expenditure involved in major and medium irrigation projects is also much higher, whereas the utilization efficiency is much lower than for small projects. Besides, lack of coordination among different agencies involved in delivering water to the field complicates the management and utilization of such projects. Small surface works are relatively cheaper, take less time to complete and are more conducive to management by user communities. Groundwater irrigation, by its very nature and because it is in the hands of individual farmers, is deemed to be more efficient (Vaidyanathan, 1999). The flexibility of operating small-scale irrigation projects such as shallow tube wells makes it a good option in so far as utilization is concerned. However, there is a need to look into various geological and technical issues before developing the small-scale (usually groundwater-based) irrigation projects. Those regions/ states which have already witnessed severe fall in the groundwater table due to excessive reliance on groundwater may not be conducive for further exploitation of groundwater resources. In those regions, there may be no alternative to development of surface irrigation systems, although associated efficiency may not be great. On the other hand, in those regions where groundwater reserves are relatively better and are not properly utilized, there is a scope for utilization of the resource keeping in view better utilization efficiency. Groundwater-based tube well irrigation systems can be a good alternative for irrigation development in those regions. However, from the point of view of greater water use efficiency and effectiveness of irrigation, there are now calls for development of micro irrigation systems, such as sprinkler and drip irrigation, as substitutes for the conventional irrigation systems. In drip irrigation, water is applied at a low rate directly into the plant's root zone through a low-pressure delivery system. Although mostly suitable for horticultural crops, drip irrigation is also used for such as crops as pulses, oil seeds, cotton and sugarcane. The greatest advantage of drip irrigation technology is the conservation of the scarce resource of water while enhancing yield. Because of lesser rainfall and lesser abundance of water in many states in India, drip irrigation technology is gaining popularity. In 2014–15, 3.38 million hectares of land in India were under drip irrigation systems (Narayanamoorthy, 2017). Although the fixed cost of generating irrigation through these systems is said to be high, the idea may be encouraged as the process involves huge positive externalities in terms of lesser amount of water required per crop. This positive externality may outweigh the cost in the long run.

3.2 *Participation in irrigation management*

The relatively below-par performance of many major and medium irrigation projects is found to be structural. The investments in these systems are carried out by the government, and the systems are also operated by government agencies. The structural rigidities in the system do not allow involvement of stakeholding farmers in the operation and management of the systems. Studies have shown that in the case of large irrigation systems, if stakeholders are made part of the operation and management of the system, performance of the system in terms of utilization rate and effectiveness increases considerably (Dutta, 2011). In recent years, however, there has been an attempt to make 'participation' an important ingredient in the overall irrigation management in the country. The concept of participatory irrigation management (PIM) has gained importance in view of the failure of government mechanisms in the management of irrigation. These reforms are directed at improving the performance of irrigation by involving farmers, who have the greatest stake in irrigation, in the management of irrigation systems (Gulati et al., 2005, p. 171). PIM refers to the participation of irrigation users, the farmers, in the management of the irrigation system not merely at the tertiary level of management but spanning the entire system. Participation, here, is not construed as mere consultation with farmers. The concept of PIM refers to management by irrigation users at all levels of the system and in all aspects of management. The involvement of farmers in the management of an irrigation system can be ensured by forming water users associations (WUA).[3] Existence of a WUA enables the stakeholding farmers to play an active role in management and distribution of water within a system. It also helps farmers to collectively resolve common water and agricultural problems. Members of WUAs benefit from increased crop yields through more efficient water use.

4 Conclusion

Considering the fact that irrigation has contributed tremendously towards production and productivity of agriculture in India, irrigation is and will remain central to India's agricultural policy. However, being a state subject, the sector has received varied attention in various states, and accordingly, development of irrigation varies across states.

In spite of the substantial amount of public investment that has gone into the sector, effective use of irrigation water remains as an issue. The increased gap between potential created and utilized, especially in the case of large irrigation projects, does not augur well for the overall effectiveness of irrigation. Since large irrigation systems are beset with a number of technical and institutional issues, there are initiatives to promote small and micro irrigation, such as drip or sprinkler irrigation.

In view of the problems the irrigation sector is currently experiencing, there may be a need for technical as well as institutional reforms in the sector. However, issues in the irrigation sector should be looked into with the issues of water governance at large. Questioning the present practice of water governance in the country, some recent studies have advocated for bringing an ecosystem perspective to our water management and governance. The perspective considers water in its natural state as essentially in the common pool, to be shared equitably by all (Vijayshankar, 2016, p. 19).

In so far as future development of irrigation in the country is concerned, a uniform strategy may not work. The policy for irrigation development should be based on the resource endowment, cropping pattern and soil conditions of the different regions. In view of the already deteriorating groundwater levels in some states of north, west and south India, there will perhaps be no alternative to canal-based major and medium irrigation schemes in these states. In the states of eastern India, which until now have a relatively better groundwater reserve, irrigation development through investment in well irrigation, particularly in tube well irrigation, may reap better returns in terms of utilization, effectiveness and efficiency. Further, development of micro irrigation schemes such as drip irrigation should also be given importance. Given that installation of infrastructure for drip irrigation is expensive, it may be promoted by giving subsidies, which can be justified on account of the positive externality generated by this type of irrigation.

Notes

1 Compound annual growth rate in the irrigated area is estimated using the following semi:log linear trend equation:

$$ln Y_t = \beta_0 + \beta_1 T + \mu_t \tag{1}$$

where, $ln Y_t$ is the logarithmic value of irrigated area, β_0 and β_1 are the constant and coefficients terms to be estimated and μ_t is the random error term. T is the trend variable in the model. Ordinary Least Square estimation technique was used to determine the value of the respective coefficients. Using coefficient β_1, compound annual growth rate (CAGR) can be estimated as follows:

$$CAGR = \left(e^{\beta_1} - 1\right) \times 100 \tag{2}$$

2 Although there are variations in the definition of the concept of irrigation potential, the commonly accepted definition is as follows: "Irrigation potential is the gross area that can be irrigated from a project in a design year (1st July to 30th June of the succeeding year) for the projected cropping pattern and assumed water allowance on its full development. The gross irrigated area will be the aggregate of the areas irrigated in different cropping seasons, the areas under two seasonal and perennial crops being counted only once in a year" (Dutta, 2011). It may, however, be mentioned that full utilization of irrigation potential, especially under major canal systems, although desirable, is of merely notional importance due to a number of factors. Proper development of the command area and proper construction of the main canals, subsidiaries and the water courses are some important prerequisites for achieving full potential under a canal irrigation system. Conveyance loss due to incomplete and improper construction of subsidiaries and water courses is very common in canal irrigation systems. Taking these various aspects into account, Wade (1978) suggested that

about 90 per cent utilization can be considered good enough. According to Satpathy (1984), at the commencement of water supply from a project, partial under utilization may be tolerated as a transitional problem.

3 A water users association (WUA) is a voluntary, non-governmental, non-profit entity established and managed by a group of farmers located along one or several water course canals. Water users consist of farmers, peasants and other owners who combine their financial, material and technical resources to improve the productivity of irrigated farming through equitable distribution of water and efficient use of irrigation and drainage systems. A WUA has a leader and it handles disputes internally, collects fees from the members and manages the system.

References

Central Water Commission, 2013. *Water and Related Statistics.* Water Resources and Information Directorate, New Delhi, available at http://www.cwc.nic.in/main/downloads/Water%20and%20Related%20Statistics-2013.pdf, accessed 27/12/2016

Chambers, R., 1988. *Managing Canal Irrigation.* Oxford University Press and IBH Publishing Company, New Delhi.

Dhawan, B. D., 1982. *Development of Tube well Irrigation in India,* Agricole Publishing Academy, New Delhi.

Dhawan, B. D., 1995. *Groundwater Depletion, Land Degradation and Irrigated Agriculture in India,* Commonwealth Publishers, New Delhi.

Dutta, M. K., 2011. *Irrigation Potential in Agriculture of Assam,* Concept Publishing Company (P) Ltd., New Delhi.

Government of India, 2011. *Report of the Working Group on Major & Medium Irrigation and Command Area Development for the XII Five Year Plan (2012–2017),* Ministry of Water Resources Development, New Delhi.

Government of India, 2015. *Raising Agricultural Productivity and Making Farming Remunerative for Farmers.* An Occasional Paper, NITI Aayog, available at http://niti.gov.in/writereaddata/files/Raising%20Agricultural%20Productivity%20and%20Making%20Farming%20Remunerative%20for%20Farmers_0.pdf, accessed 17/05/2017.

Gulati, A., Meinzen-Dick, R. and Raju, K. V., 2005. *Institutional Reform in Indian Irrigation,* Sage, New Delhi.

Mukherjee, A., 2016. Evolution of Irrigation Sector. *Economic and Political Weekly,* 51(52), pp. 44–47.

Narayanamoorthy, A., 2017. Farm Income in India: Myths and Realities. *Indian Journal of Agricultural Economics,* 72(1), pp. 49–75.

Planning Commission, 2013. *Twelfth Five Year Plan (2012–2017) Faster, More Inclusive and Sustainable Growth,* Vol. 1, Sage Publications, New Delhi.

Saleth, R. M., 1996. *Water Institutions in India: Economics, Law and Policy,* Commonwealth Publishers, New Delhi.

Satpathy, T., 1984. *Irrigation and Economic Development,* Asish Publishing House, New Delhi.

Swaminathan, M. S., 1981. *Irrigation and Our Agricultural Future.* First Ajudhia Nath Khosla Lecture, delivered at the University of Roorkee, Reproduced by Centre for Monitoring Indian Economy, Mumbai.

Vaidyanathan, A., 1999. *Water Resource Management Institutions and Irrigation Development in India,* Oxford University Press, New Delhi.

Vaidyanathan, A., 2006. *India's Water Resources Contemporary Issues on Irrigation*, Oxford University Press, New Delhi.

Vijayshankar, P. S., 2016. All Is Not Lost, But Water Sector Reforms Must Go Ahead. *Economic and Political Weekly*, 51(52), pp. 19–20.

Wade, R., 1978. Water Supply as an Instrument of Agricultural Policy – A Case Study. *Economic and Political Weekly*, 13(12), pp. A9–A13.

8 Technology adoption in Indian agriculture and its determinants

An inter-state analysis

Bibhunandini Das and Amarendra Das

1 Introduction

As discussed in chapter 1, adoption of the Green Revolution technology in the mid-1960s made India self-sufficient in food grain production by the mid-1970s. In fact, India now has a huge buffer stock of food grains. Though the availability of food grains is not a problem now, there can hardly be any scope for complacency. In order to feed the burgeoning population, production has to be sustained, and farmers need to adopt productivity-boosting and ecologically sustainable agricultural technologies for that purpose. Policy makers have been giving importance to developing new agricultural technology and using those technologies to boost agricultural productivity. Against this backdrop, this chapter has the following objectives:

1. To examine the extent of technology adoption by farmers in India
2. To understand the factors that determine the use of modern technology by farmers

The rest of the chapter is organized into five sections. Section 2 is a discussion on the literature related to the objectives of the study. Section 3 elaborates on the data and methodology used in the analysis. Section 4 discusses the results of the data analysis. Section 5 concludes.

2 Insights from literature: theoretical perspectives and empirical evidence

In order to understand the diffusion of modern agricultural technology among the farmers, it is pertinent to understand the general principles or process of diffusion of general technology. Technology adoption/diffusion[1] comes at the third stage of technological change. Schumpeter (1951) in his theory of linear progression states that during the first invention stage, new ideas are generated. In the second stage, inventions go through an innovation process for transforming the new idea into marketable products and processes. During the third stage comes diffusion or adoption of new technology. During the last stage, new products and processes spread across the potential market (Mansfield, 1968). Theoretical literature on technology diffusion emerged in the 1950s with the epidemic approach. This approach compares the adoption of new technology to infectious diseases. In the initial stage, there will be a certain number of users of new technology. Over the years, with the interaction of users, non-users become users. This interaction is basically transfer of information from the user to the non-user (Stoneman, 2002). In a similar line, Brown (1981) discussed the differential rate of adoption and the underlying generative process through different processes of technology diffusion. He argues that adoption occurs mostly due to three factors: individual characteristics (adoption perspective), diffusion agencies (market and infrastructure perspective), and continuity of innovation (economic history perspective).

The adoption perspective basically emphasizes the demand aspects that determine diffusion. This perspective stresses the learning, communication and interaction among the potential adopters that lead to diffusion of innovation. In the market and infrastructure perspective, the accent is on the way innovations are made available to potential adopters. It focuses upon the role of diffusion agencies and how they can increase the adoption of innovation among potential adopters. The adoption and market and infrastructure perspectives assume innovation to be the same throughout the diffusion process. The economic history perspective focuses on continuity of innovation. Economic historians developed the dynamic approach and believe that hardly any innovation during its life cycle remains static because it evolves in tune with the changing environment in which it is being used. They said that the continuity of innovation affects the temporal as well as spatial diffusion in both the supply and demand side.

From the above discussion it appears that innovation and diffusion are complex processes. The diffusion process hinges upon the nature of innovation, adopters' characteristics and institutional factors. It varies over time and space. All three perspectives – adoption, market and infrastructure, and economic history – remain incomplete if analyzed independently, since all the perspectives have their limitations. Integration of these three may give a clearer picture.

2.1 Empirical literature

Various studies have focused on adoption of agricultural technology in order to improve the productivity (Vaidyanathan, 2010; Abdullah and Samah, 2013; Shaffril et al., 2009; Samah et al., 2009; Adrian et al., 2005; Ghosh and Ganguly, 2008). In Asian countries, the adoption of improved agricultural technologies was considered as a major factor in the success of the Green Revolution (Chen and Ravallion, 2004).

In India's case, notwithstanding the substantial increase in food grain production following the Green Revolution, a high prevalence of poverty and inequality calls for augmenting agricultural produce in a sustained manner (Kannan and Sundaram, 2011). Under these circumstances, importance has been given to improving productivity growth in the agricultural sector by introducing modern technology, like high-yielding varieties of seeds, fertilizer application, biotechnological innovation and so on, as well as institutional policies in the sector.

Mani and Santhakumar (2011) have emphasized the role of an articulated regulatory policy mechanism for the diffusion of agricultural technology in India. Using a sectoral system of innovation (SSI) framework, the authors have argued that due to the presence of an articulated regulatory policy mechanism for natural rubber, new technologies that were generated by the research arm could be adopted by the farmers. Contrary to this, due to a lack of cohesiveness with a multiplicity of actors operating at sub-optimal scales in the coconuts sector, the diffusion of new technologies has been low. This has resulted in the highest level productivity in natural rubber and relatively low productivity in coconuts.

A study by Kasirye (2013) on the determinants of use of two improved agricultural technologies – improved seeds and fertilizer – found that farmers in Uganda with low education and land holdings are less likely to adopt improved seeds or fertilizer. A study in Malayasia found that farmers' perceptions, levels of education, extension workers' knowledge, management of the extension programme and the physical conditions of the area are the factors that affect technology adoption among farmers (Abdullah and Samah, 2013). By focusing on Malaysian agriculture, Shaffril et al. (2009) and Samah et al. (2009) in their studies concluded that education, negative perceptions, lack of capital, small land areas and ineffective infrastructure facilities are some of the major factors that affect technology adoption. Analyzing row crop farmers in the southeastern United States, Adrian et al. (2005) found that attitude of confidence, perceptions of net benefit, farm size and farmers' educational levels positively influence the intention to adopt precision agriculture technologies.

Other than adoption of improved seeds and fertilizer and pesticides applications in agriculture, countries are now also moving towards biotechnological innovations in the form of 'gene technology' in agriculture for some perceived advantage either to the producer or consumer of these foods. In spite of having several challenges in approving genetically modified (GM) crops, there are socio-economic considerations over the adoption of GM crops on different grounds among the developing countries. Socio-economic assessments are important as non-GM crops, particularly cereals, are an important source of export revenue for many developing countries (Chaturvedi et al., 2012). For instance, in India, the controversy over Bt brinjal gives ideas about the concerns and anxiety over the use of these biotechnological innovations. Analyzing the controversy over the usefulness of transgenic crops, Herring and Rao (2012) studied Bt cotton cultivation in India by looking at the differences between Bt farms and non-Bt farms and the experience of farmers before growing Bt and after switching to Bt. The study found that the insect-resistance trait from the Bt transgene generally resulted in better yields of harvested cotton with less spraying of toxins, which improved farmer incomes across size of holding and social categories. The study also concluded that farmer behaviour mostly hinders the failure of Bt cotton in India.

In India, adapting to the evolving dietary patterns which favour greater protein consumption, agriculture requires a new paradigm with the following component:

increasing productivity by getting 'more from less' (GoI, 2016).[2] Addressing India's multiple challenges in agriculture will require significant upgrading of the country's national agriculture research and extension systems. India's National Agricultural Research System (NARS) (comprising the Indian Council of Agricultural Research [ICAR], other central research institutes, and national research centres set up by ICAR), together with agriculture research universities, played a key role in the Green Revolution. In more recent years, however, agriculture research has been plagued by severe under investment and neglect (Government of India, 2016). Along with poor agricultural research, diffusion of modern technologies among farmers remains a major challenge due to poor extension services and the inability of farmers to access information on modern technologies using information communication technologies (ICTs) such as television, radio, internet, mobile phone, newspaper and so on. As a result, the productivity of Indian agriculture remains far below the world average and major advanced countries. Table 8.1 provides the yield of three major crops in some major countries of the world. India's yield of paddy per hectare is only 82 per cent of the world average and less than half of that of the United States. Similarly, the yield of maize per hectare in India is far below the world average and that of the United States. However, the yield in wheat in India is higher than the world average and that of the United States, but it is much less than the yield of France (7,599 quintals) and Germany (7,328 quintals).

In order to ensure food and nutritional security, India needs to augment the yield not only in food and cereal crops but also in other cash crops such as pulses, fruits and vegetables etc.

The discussion on the relevant theoretical and empirical literature suggests that the adopters' characteristics (in our study, farmers' characteristics) and institutional and technological factors affect the adoption of any technology. Against this backdrop, our study seeks to answer the following research questions: Who uses technology in agriculture? What are the associates of technology use in agriculture? How do farmers obtain information on modern technology? Is technology use limited to specific crops?

Table 8.1 Comparison of yields of major crops (yield in kg/hectare in 2012)

Country	Paddy	Wheat	Maize
World	4,548	3,090	4,888
India	3,721	3,177	2,556
USA	8,349	3,115	7,744
China	6,775	4,987	5,870
Brazil	4,786		5,006
Russian Federation	5,490	1,773	4,239

Source: Government of India, *Agricultural Statistics at a Glance 2014*

3 Data sources and methodology

In order to answer the above research questions, the present study used the secondary data provided by the National Sample Survey Office (NSSO) in its 70th round. The Situation Assessment Survey of Agricultural Households was conducted in the NSS 70th round (January–December 2013) to collect information on various aspects of farming, such as farming practices and preferences, availability of resources, awareness of technological developments and access to modern technology in the field of agriculture, level of living standard measured in terms of consumption expenditures, and income and indebtedness of agricultural households[3] in rural India. The survey covers 35,200 households in 4,529 sample villages.

3.1 Methodology

The key objective of this paper is to examine the technology adoption of farmers across Indian states. Different researchers use different indicators for this purpose, such as use of high-yield variety seeds, fertilizers, pesticide, modern equipment etc. We have taken use of machinery by the farmers for this purpose. In order to identify the farm households using modern technology, we looked at the farm households that reported expenditure on machinery with the assumption that technology is embodied in the machinery. Expenditures on machinery include the rental and purchase price of machinery, diesel, and electricity. These expenditures may be incurred in the use of tractors, pump sets for irrigation, machinery for tilling land and harvesting crops and so on. Therefore, households reporting expenditure in these categories are considered to have used modern technology. To understand the extent of machinery use, the paper starts with a descriptive analysis. Further to analyze the factors that determine the extent of machinery use in cultivation, the study uses logistic regression. We have used an estimated binary logit model to identify the specific attributes of households which influence the decision as to whether to adopt technology or not.

$$
\begin{aligned}
Y_i = {} & \beta_1 + \beta_2 Sources + \beta_3 Crop + \beta_4 Education + \beta_5 Age + \beta_6 lnMPCE \\
& + \beta_7 MSP_{Share} + \beta_8 HHS_{Size} + \beta_9 Crop_{Ins} + \beta_{10} Training + \beta_{11} OBC \\
& + \beta_{12} SC \,\&\, ST + \beta_{13} Irrigation + \beta_{14} leased + \beta_{15} Land\ Size + \beta_{16} Sale \\
& + \beta_{17} PSI + U_i
\end{aligned}
$$

Where,

Y_i represents the outcome dummy variable, which has two outcomes: s (i) the household uses machinery and (ii) it does not use machinery. From the NSS data, this variable has been constructed as follows: a household gets the value 1 if it reports use of machinery and 0 otherwise. The notations, descriptions and expected signs of the explanatory variables used in the regression model are presented in Table 8.2.

Table 8.2 Hypothesis and variable construction

Variables	Notation	Description	Expected sign
Source	Sources	The variable is entered as 1 if farmers are accessing any one sources for technical knowledge and 0 otherwise.	+
Crop	Crop	Crops with more use of machinery (1) and crops with less use of machinery (0)	+
Education	Education	The variable is entered as 1 if household head is literate and 0 otherwise.	+
Age	Age	Age of the household head	–
Monthly per capita consumption expenditure	lnMPCE	Natural logarithm of Monthly per capita consumption expenditure as proxy for income	+
Minimum support price	MSP_{Share}	Awareness of minimum support price	+
Household size	HHS_{Size}	Total member of the household	–
Crop insurance	$Crop_{Ins}$	Dummy variable with households having crop insurance (1) and not having crop insurance (0)	+
Training	Training	Dummy variable with formally trained (1) and untrained farmers (0)	+
Social group	OBC SC & ST	The variable has entered the model as dummy, and two dummies have been considered – SC/ST and OBC. Others are reference category.	–
Irrigation	Irrigation	Irrigated land (1) and unirrigated land (0)	+
Leased-in area	Leased	Leased-in land (1) and others (0)	–
Land holding	Land Size	Total land of the household	+
Sale	Sale	Farmers with marketable surplus (1) and 0 otherwise	+
Primary source of income	PSI	Dummy variable: farmers for whom agriculture is the main source of income (1) and 0 otherwise	+

4 Analysis

4.1 Agricultural households receiving formal training

Traditionally the skills required for farming have been transferred through family instruction. Although the indigenous knowledge on farming has helped in understanding local climate variations and crop-specific requirements, such as timing of crop plantation and harvest, lack of exposure to modern technologies keeps agricultural productivity low. In that context, we are presenting the percentage of households with formal training received (see Table 8.3). At the all-India level, a very low percentage (4.41 per cent) of farm households received formal training on agriculture. Tamil Nadu has the highest share of farm households with formal training (12.48 per cent), followed by Tripura (10.23 per cent), Karnataka (10.16 per cent) and Meghalaya (10.15 per cent). Sikkim has

Table 8.3 State-wise percentage of farm households receiving formal training

States	Received formal training	Did not receive formal training
Andhra Pradesh	2.58	97.42
Arunachal Pradesh	3.5	96.5
Assam	3.39	96.61
Bihar	4.51	95.49
Chhattisgarh	6.33	93.67
Goa	4.4	95.6
Gujarat	2.13	97.87
Haryana	5.25	94.75
Himachal Pradesh	2.88	97.12
Jammu & Kashmir	1.69	98.31
Jharkhand	3.76	96.24
Karnataka	10.16	89.84
Kerala	6.55	93.45
Madhya Pradesh	2.99	97.01
Maharashtra	3.97	96.03
Manipur	2.54	97.46
Meghalaya	10.15	89.85
Mizoram	0.58	99.42
Nagaland	2.56	97.44
Odisha	2.61	97.39
Punjab	4.54	95.46
Rajasthan	1.55	98.45
Sikkim	0.64	99.36
Tamil Nadu	12.48	87.52
Telengana	2.62	97.38
Tripura	10.23	89.77
Uttar Pradesh	1.89	98.11
Uttaranchal	3.68	96.32
West Bengal	5.35	94.65
All India	**4.41**	**95.59**

Source: NSSO Unit level Data, 2013.

the lowest proportion of farm households that received formal training on agriculture. Eighteen out of 29 states have a low proportion of farm households with any formal training.

With the vast majority of the agricultural households not receiving any formal training, there is a serious negative implication for farm productivity. Farmers would not have the capability to adapt modern technology and diversify agriculture.

4.2 Subsistence or commercial farming

We can divide the farmers into two groups: those who do subsistence farming to get the basic minimum food and those who farm for profit. We presume that the second type of farmers would go for better adoption of modern technology and the former would not go for the same. Therefore, before we proceed to other analysis, in this section we see what proportion of farmers have a marketable surplus.

Table 8.4 provides an overview of the percentage of households growing different crops. At the all-India level, about 50 per cent of agricultural households grow cereals and pulses. Backward states like Odisha, Bihar, Chhattisgarh and Jharkhand show heavy dependence on cereals and pulses. Kerala has the lowest percentage of agricultural households growing cereals and pulses (less than 1 per cent), and Chhattisgarh has the highest percentage (87.68 per cent).

At the all-India level, about 21 per cent of agricultural households grow fruits and vegetables. Sikkim has the highest and Goa has the lowest percentage of farm households that grow fruits and vegetables. Many northeastern states have a higher percentage of farm households that grow fruits and vegetables. In aggregate, only 7 per cent of farm households in the country grow plantation crops. Kerala has the highest percentage (70 per cent) of farm households that grow plantation crops. There are a large number of states (Bihar, Chhattisgarh, Gujarat, Haryana, Himachal Pradesh, Jammu and Kashmir, Jharkhand, Manipur, Punjab, Rajasthan, Sikkim, Telangana and Uttaranchal) that have almost no households that grow plantation crops. Only 5 per cent farm households at the all-India level grow spices. A relatively higher percentage of farm households in the northeastern states grow spices. At the all-India level, around 17 per cent of farm households grow non-food crops. Punjab has the highest percentage of farm households growing non-food crops, followed by Haryana, Gujarat and Maharashtra. Thus, it is clear that the economically advanced states have a higher percentage of farm households that go beyond the traditional cereals and pulses and grow commercial crops.

What proportion of farm households get marketable surplus, and where do they sell their surplus? The sale point for farmers would be a source of differential return received by the farmers. These questions have been answered in Tables 8.5 and 8.6, which provide a summary of the agricultural households reporting sale of selected crops during kharif (July–December 2012) and rabi (January–June 2013) seasons.

Table 8.4 Percentage of farm households growing different crops

States	Cereals and pulses	Fruits and vegetables	Plantation	Spices	Non-food crops
Andhra Pradesh	45.89	30.63	4.23	2.23	17.02
Arunachal Pradesh	52.92	28.18	1.37	16.49	1.03
Assam	44.43	22.41	19.75	5.70	7.71
Bihar	80.90	11.23	0.00	1.51	6.37
Chhattisgarh	87.68	8.00	0.00	4.32	0.00
Goa	44.29	0.00	55.71	0.00	0.00
Gujarat	42.39	12.82	0.00	0.86	43.92
Haryana	33.84	11.57	0.00	3.06	51.53
Himachal Pradesh	33.50	35.81	0.00	15.51	15.18
Jammu & Kashmir	50.59	25.88	0.00	11.62	11.91
Jharkhand	78.82	19.61	0.00	1.45	0.13
Karnataka	44.49	20.22	20.05	1.99	13.26
Kerala	0.92	4.17	69.78	24.04	1.09
Madhya Pradesh	39.21	50.18	0.12	0.65	9.85
Maharashtra	35.43	28.26	0.79	0.87	34.65
Manipur	52.62	32.39	0.00	14.57	0.42
Meghalaya	13.77	31.54	19.76	26.95	7.98
Mizoram	18.37	48.19	3.01	28.01	2.41
Nagaland	60.68	29.34	0.28	9.12	0.57
Odisha	85.56	8.68	1.94	1.88	1.94
Punjab	15.73	0.72	0.00	0.00	83.54
Rajasthan	42.40	26.16	0.00	0.34	31.10
Sikkim	2.97	52.81	0.00	39.27	4.95
Tamil Nadu	32.18	22.81	22.72	4.60	17.68
Telengana	34.64	8.38	0.00	0.70	56.28
Tripura	68.53	23.26	6.72	1.37	0.12
Uttar Pradesh	58.96	21.05	0.02	0.84	19.13
Uttaranchal	53.31	29.04	0.00	9.19	8.46
West Bengal	65.03	10.22	2.43	3.11	19.21
All India	**49.68**	**21.27**	**7.05**	**4.82**	**17.17**

Source: Same as for Table 8.3

Overall we observe that more farm households reported sale of crops during rabi season. Along with that, we also observe that a larger proportion of households that grow commercial crops like sugarcane, soya bean, cotton, jute and groundnut reported sales, compared to the households that grow cereal crops like paddy, jowar, bajra, maize, ragi and so on.

4.3 Use of modern technology by agricultural households

Farm productivity largely depends upon the use of modern technology. In order to identify the farm households using modern technology, we looked at the farm households who reported expenditure on machinery with the assumption that technology is embodied in the machinery. Expenditures on machinery include

Table 8.5 Number per 1000 of agricultural households reporting sale of selected crops during khariff season (July–December 2012)

Crop	No. per 1000 households reporting sale by agency							
	Local private trader	Mandi	Input dealer	Cooperative or government agency	Processors	Others	All	Estimated no. of households reporting sale of crops
Paddy	234	80	37	39	7	28	411	186,734
Jowar	200	70	7	3	0	21	298	15,092
Bajra	117	114	9	1	0	7	243	17,487
Maize	222	105	23	2	1	8	354	34,563
Ragi	148	26	4	0	0	16	190	3,549
Arhar(tur)	190	215	38	1	0	6	449	15,507
Urad	343	128	29	4	0	12	503	18,783
Moong	209	191	16	2	0	10	427	8,227
Sugarcane	192	59	14	376	209	45	880	36,000
Potato	346	122	60	4	1	22	510	8,625
Groundnut	371	182	59	25	0	28	654	15,509
Coconut	379	50	6	14	0	37	457	9,571
Soya bean	416	413	45	12	1	5	884	45,017
Cotton	482	222	120	54	18	11	885	57,158
Jute	684	198	46	0	10	1	919	9,038

Source: NSSO Report 2013.

rental and purchase price of machinery, diesel, and electricity. These expenditures may be incurred in the use of tractors, pump sets for irrigation, machinery for tilling land and harvesting crops and so on. Therefore, households reporting expenditure in these categories are considered to have used modern technology. Table 8.7 presents the percentage of households across states that reported expenditure on diesel, electricity and machinery for farming. At the all-India level, around 17 per cent of the farm households reported expenditure on diesel. The proportion varies widely across states. The Green Revolution belt (Punjab, Haryana and Uttar Pradesh) shows a higher proportion of farm households spending on diesel. Northeastern states, where fewer households grow traditional cereals and pulses, reported a lower proportion of households spending on diesel. This could be due to the reason that most of the northeastern states are hilly terrain and use of machinery is not conducive in hilly regions. Use of electricity by farmers not only depends upon the use of modern technology but also is largely influenced by states' policies in this regard. From time to time, state governments have announced schemes like free power for agricultural purposes. In such cases more farmers are likely to use electricity for farming purposes. At the all-India level, only 8.51 per cent of farm households reported spending on electricity. This also varies widely across states. Haryana reported having the largest proportion of households spending on electricity, followed by Maharashtra

Table 8.6 Number per 1000 of agricultural households reporting sale for selected crops during rabi season (January–June 2013)

Crop	No. per 1000 households reporting sale by agency							Estimated no. of households reporting sale of crops
	Local private trader	Mandi	Input dealer	Cooperative or government agency	Processors	Others	All	
Paddy	460	95	47	28	6	12	638	54,578
Jowar	155	105	12	0	1	7	278	4,565
Maize	514	136	61	19	0	5	719	19,581
Wheat	181	128	34	25	1	4	368	129,991
Barley	78	50	12	0	0	0	140	1,432
Gram	223	249	58	2	0	3	532	33,190
arhar(tur)	156	122	36	0	0	2	317	3,517
Moong	391	38	4	6	0	3	442	6,893
Masur	219	84	91	0	0	0	393	7,352
sugarcane	215	49	10	417	255	7	943	20,558
Potato	383	126	32	1	1	2	534	24,679
Onion	362	142	33	7	0	5	543	5,955
groundnut	457	166	37	13	1	20	689	6,770
rapeseed/mustard	211	209	38	2	1	1	456	36,155
coconut	412	51	4	15	0	18	491	11,084
Cotton	415	229	234	11	35	1	923	10,753

Source: Same as for Table 8.5

Table 8.7 Percentage of households reporting expenditures on diesel, electricity for farm use, and agricultural machinery

States	Diesel	Electricity	Machinery
Andhra Pradesh	17.61	12.03	44.07
Arunachal Pradesh	0.64	0.64	5.41
Assam	11.41	0.36	29.49
Bihar	33.21	0.91	51.15
Chhattisgarh	7.91	5.54	53.01
Goa	2.20	2.20	12.09
Gujarat	17.54	16.70	50.04
Haryana	32.49	46.53	49.07
Himachal Pradesh	11.98	10.38	29.23
Jammu & Kashmir	4.49	2.25	27.67
Jharkhand	13.47	0.91	28.37
Karnataka	7.37	7.37	47.18
Kerala	2.27	9.79	10.11
Madhya Pradesh	12.31	13.70	46.93
Maharashtra	11.22	19.51	51.23
Manipur	0.53	0.27	42.59
Meghalaya	4.21	0.19	9.39
Mizoram	0.29	0.00	0.00
Nagaland	0.28	0.57	24.43
Odisha	5.88	2.08	50.06
Punjab	56.67	1.51	58.46
Rajasthan	10.39	11.35	67.92
Sikkim	0.00	0.00	0.32
Tamil Nadu	9.04	0.15	30.82
Telengana	5.10	42.80	80.76
Tripura	4.93	2.65	39.59
Uttar Pradesh	39.46	8.84	48.44
Uttaranchal	12.71	3.34	14.05
West Bengal	23.61	4.80	64.96
All India	17.04	8.51	44.26

Source: NSSO Unit level Data 2013.

and Gujarat. Compared to diesel and electricity, a relatively higher proportion of farmers reported expenditure on renting or using machinery for farming purpose. At the all-India level, 44.26 per cent of farm households reported expenditure on machinery. Farmers from Telangana reported the highest proportion of households spending for machinery for farming purpose, followed by Rajasthan and West Bengal. Northeastern states reported a lower proportion of farm households spending on machinery for farm purposes.

4.4 Sources of technical advice

For increasing farm productivity, it is important to transfer new technologies developed by agricultural research institutes and universities to farmers. There are several mediums through which this knowledge can be transferred to the farmers, including extension agents (EA), Krishi Vigyan Kendra (KVK), agricultural universities or colleges (AU), private commercial agents (PCA), progressive farmers (PF), radio/tv/newspaper/internet (ICTs), veterinary departments (VD), nongovernmental organizations (NGOs) and so on. Table 8.8 presents the percentage of farm households accessing technical advice from different sources. At the all-India level, only 38 per cent of farm households use at least one of the eight sources. Among these eight sources, a relatively higher percentage of farmers (around 24 per cent) use ICT sources (radio, TV, newspaper or internet), followed by progressive farmers, extension agents, PCA, KVK and NGOs. The percentage of farm households using any one of the eight sources varies widely across states. Kerala has the highest percentage of farmer households (70.47 per cent) using any of the eight sources, followed by Jammu and Kashmir and Karnataka. Sikkim reports the lowest proportion of farm households using any one of the eight sources.

4.5 Determinants of technology adoption by farm households

What determines the adoption of technology by farm households? In order to answer this question, a logistic regression model has been estimated in this section. We have used STATA 13 version to compute the logistic regression model. In our regression model, only the variable formal training comes out statistically insignificant. All other variables are statistically significant and have shown results in the expected direction, except education. Though education is significant, the coefficient is negative.

In Table 8.9 we have presented the coefficients, odds ratio and marginal effect statistics along with the p value to show the level of significance. In order to test the fitness of the model, we have also reported the receiver operating characteristics (ROC) in the table. STATA 13 automatically drops the variable in case of multi-collinearity. Therefore, our model does not have any problem of multi-collinearity. Among all the variables we have included in the model, crop category has the highest marginal effect. The probability of using machinery increases by 44 per cent for households that grow cereal and pulses, fruits and vegetable, and non-food crops, compared to the agricultural households that grow plantation crops and spices. Farmers using at least some information source, such as ICT, extension workers etc. for obtaining agricultural information have a 9 per cent higher chance of using machinery in agriculture compared to those who do not use any sources. Agricultural households with illiterate heads have a 2 per cent less chance of using machinery, compared to households with literate households. This could be because use of machinery does not depend on education per se, but rather requires specific skills. These skills can be acquired from other farmers in the locality or through learning by doing. The marginal effects of age of the household head and size of the household are almost zero. From the summary statistics, we observed that very few households have received formal training in agriculture. This is probably the reason for the insignificant result of formal training on expenditure incurred on machinery. Awareness of farmers about the minimum

Table 8.8 Percentage of agricultural households accessing technical advice from different sources

States	EA	KVK	AU	PCA	PF	ICTs	VD	NGO	Any one
Andhra Pradesh	24.77	2.58	1.06	30.05	35.80	31.22	16.67	0.12	49.14
Arunachal Pradesh	6.56	3.47	0.00	0.00	2.32	0.39	1.16	0.77	9.87
Assam	9.39	0.52	1.55	2.98	17.42	36.20	11.10	1.88	45.78
Bihar	6.91	3.18	0.32	2.48	22.18	19.00	4.37	0.43	34.55
Chhattisgarh	23.40	5.77	1.76	6.25	43.43	15.22	8.97	2.88	56.33
Goa	1.43	1.43	0.00	0.00	0.00	0.00	0.00	0.00	2.20
Gujarat	9.09	6.51	2.20	7.56	44.50	24.78	11.20	1.82	44.04
Haryana	8.52	7.86	7.64	9.17	16.59	33.84	23.14	1.10	41.96
Himachal Pradesh	3.47	4.46	2.64	0.17	5.45	31.02	22.28	0.17	43.13
Jammu & Kashmir	0.44	13.24	12.79	1.76	14.56	54.56	32.11	4.42	63.06
Jharkhand	0.26	2.51	0.26	0.66	8.18	13.32	1.32	3.43	24.48
Karnataka	12.27	7.55	3.07	10.95	31.18	45.69	33.25	1.16	60.80
Kerala	13.14	26.04	2.66	1.91	17.30	60.23	18.80	1.83	70.47
Madhya Pradesh	5.28	2.25	0.30	3.14	22.78	17.62	4.33	0.95	36.01
Maharashtra	8.88	5.51	1.79	7.48	19.82	23.37	7.75	0.31	37.39
Manipur	1.15	3.45	0.00	0.29	9.91	19.83	6.32	1.01	27.77
Meghalaya	15.46	0.00	0.00	0.60	1.41	5.62	7.83	6.85	26.25
Mizoram	26.20	0.00	0.30	0.30	9.94	37.05	16.87	3.33	43.77
Nagaland	1.47	4.11	2.35	0.00	4.99	12.32	2.93	0.00	20.17
Odisha	11.40	3.52	0.33	5.08	24.23	17.39	8.40	1.31	38.24
Punjab	5.79	5.98	12.14	10.87	18.66	25.72	28.68	1.09	39.75
Rajasthan	4.32	2.12	0.21	1.99	15.00	9.45	3.22	0.27	24.13
Sikkim	0.66	0.33	0.00	0.00	0.66	0.00	0.00	0.33	1.92
Tamil Nadu	13.70	2.74	7.87	7.87	17.42	35.01	21.84	1.50	31.43
Telengana	4.19	1.54	0.28	3.36	33.43	14.27	4.90	0.42	40.05
Tripura	21.02	0.87	0.00	1.24	9.33	6.97	15.05	0.87	35.98
Uttar Pradesh	1.91	1.91	0.89	8.03	14.49	18.62	4.65	0.67	28.71
Uttaranchal	0.37	4.78	1.47	0.74	5.51	18.38	9.19	0.74	25.75
West Bengal	4.71	1.93	0.56	14.46	24.32	21.22	7.28	0.51	41.87
All India	**7.91**	**4.29**	**1.85**	**6.12**	**19.52**	**23.74**	**10.57**	**1.16**	**37.88**

Note: EA = Extension Agent; KVK= Krishi Vigyan Kendra; AU = Agricultural University or College; PCA = Private Commercial Agents; PF = Progressive Farmers; ICTs = Radio/TV/Newspaper/Internet; VT = Veterinary Department.

Source: Same as for Table 8.7

Table 8.9 Factors influencing the use of machinery by farmers

Independent variable		Dependent variable: use of machinery (Yes = 1, No = 0)			
		Coefficient	Odd ratio	Marginal effect (dy/dx)	P value
Constant		−4.11			0.000
Source		0.372	1.45	0.09	0.000
Crop		2.351	10.50	0.44	0.000
Education		−.073	0.928	−0.02	0.005
Age		.001	1.00	0.00	0.098
HHS Size		−.010	0.989	−0.002	0.027
Training		−.044	0.956	−0.01	0.455
MSP		0.016	1.01	0.003	0.000
Crop insurance		0.771	2.16	0.19	0.000
Caste	OBC	0.162	1.17	0.04	0.000
	SC & ST	−0.328	0.720	−0.07	0.000
LnMPCE		0.141	1.15	0.03	0.000
Irrigation		0.246	1.28	0.06	0.004
Leased-in		0.301	1.35	0.08	0.000
Sale		0.261	1.29	0.06	0.000
Income source		0.114	1.12	0.03	0.000
Land size		0.028	1.02	0.01	0.000
Log likelihood				−20229.244	
LR x$^2_{(16)}$				7839.74	
Pseudo R^2				0.162	
Total observation				35170	
ROC				0.74	

support price also has little impact on the adoption of machinery in agriculture. Caste still plays some role in the adoption of machinery in agriculture. SC and ST farm households have a 7 per cent less chance of using machinery in agriculture compared to the other category farm households. However, OBC farm households have a 4 per cent higher probability of using machinery in agriculture compared to the other farm households. Farm households having crop insurance have a 19 per cent higher chance of deploying machinery in agriculture compared to those who do not have agricultural insurance. With a 1 per cent increase in the monthly per capita consumption expenditure, the probability of using machinery in agriculture increases by 3 per cent. Irrigated lands have a 6 per cent higher chance of use of machinery. Farmers who have a marketable surplus have a 6 per cent higher chance of using machinery compared to those who do not have a marketable surplus. Farmers who have leased-in land have an 8 per cent higher probability of using machinery compared to those who did not lease in land. With a 1 per cent increase in land size, the probability of adopting machinery in agriculture increases by 1 per cent. Agricultural households for whom agriculture is the main source of income have a 3 per cent higher chance of using machinery compared to those for whom agriculture is not the main source of income.

5 Conclusion

In this chapter, we sought to comprehend the technological capability of farmers in India by assessing the percentage of agricultural households across states who received formal agricultural training and to understand the use of modern agricultural technology and the sources used by farmers for obtaining valuable information on modern agricultural practices. We also attempted to understand the factors influencing the use of modern technology by the farmers. In order to answer these questions, we used the NSS 70th round data.

We found that a very small proportion (4.41 per cent) of agricultural households in India received formal training in agriculture. This proportion varied across states, and the numbers are far from satisfactory. Tamil Nadu has the highest share of farm households (12.48 per cent) with formal training, followed by Tripura (10.23 per cent), Karnataka (10.16 per cent) and Meghalaya (10.15 per cent). Sikkim has the lowest proportion of farm households that have received formal training on agriculture.

At the all-India level, only 38 per cent of farm households use at least one of the eight sources for obtaining information on modern agricultural practices. Among these eight sources, a relatively higher percentage (around 24 per cent) of farmers use ICT sources, such as radio, TV, newspaper and internet, followed by progressive farmers, extension agents, PCA, KVK and NGOs.

In order to increase farm productivity, use of modern technology is a prerequisite. For measuring the technology use by farmers we looked at the machinery use by farmers, assuming that technology is embodied in the machinery/physical capital. Further, an econometric analysis was carried out in order to identify the factors that influence technology use by the farmers. We found that crop category has the greatest influence on the decision to use machinery in agriculture. The other variables that influence the use of machinery in agriculture are crop insurance, use of any source for obtaining modern agricultural information, irrigation, marketable surplus and leased-in area. We also found that SC and ST households are in a disadvantaged position as far as the use of machinery in agriculture is concerned, relative to the general category households. However, a greater proportion of OBC farm households use agricultural machinery as compared to the general households.

Thus we conclude that a vast majority of farmers in India have low technological capability. In order to increase their technological capability, farmers should be encouraged to use various sources to obtain information on the latest technologies developed by the agriculture universities and research institutes. The government extension service network can play an important role in this context.

Notes

1 In this paper we have used adoption and diffusion interchangeably. However, there is a difference between adoption and diffusion. Metcalfe (1988) in his paper differentiated between adoption and diffusion. For him, adoption analysis considers the decision taken by the agents to incorporate a new technology into their activities. It is concerned more with the process of decision making and less with propositions

linking the nature and timing of adoption decisions to specified characteristics of adopters, such as the size of firms or their socio-metric position within a communication network. By contrast, diffusion analysis is concerned with how economic significance of a new technology changes over time.

2 Economic Survey of India, 2015–16, chapter on agriculture.
3 Agricultural households were defined as households receiving some value of produce more than Rs. 3,000 from agricultural activities and having one member self-employed in agriculture either in the principal status or in subsidiary status during last 365 days.

References

Abdullah, F. A. and Samah, B. A., 2013. Factors Impinging Farmers' Use of Agriculture Technology. *Asian Social Science*, 9(3), p. 120.

Adrian, A. M., Norwood, S. H. and Mask, P. L., 2005. Producers' Perceptions and Attitudes Toward Precision Agriculture Technologies. *Computers and Electronics in Agriculture*, 48(3), pp. 256–271.

Brown, L. A., 1981. *Innovation Diffusion; a New Perspective*, Methuen Publications, London.

Chaturvedi, S., Srinivas, K. R., Joseph, R. K. and Singh, P., 2012. Approval of GM Crops: Socio-Economic Considerations in Developing Countries. *Economic & Political Weekly*, XLVII(23), pp. 53–61.

Chen, S. and Ravallion, M., 2004. How Have the World's Poorest Fared Since the Early 1980s? *The World Bank Research Observer*, 19(2), pp. 141–169.

Ghosh, G. N. and Ganguly, R., 2008. *Development Challenges of Indian Agriculture*. Background Technical Papers, The National Medium Term Priority Framework, Government of India and FAO.

Government of India, 2015. *Agricultural Statistics at a Glance 2014*, New Delhi, Oxford University Press.

Government of India, 2016. *Economic Survey of India 2015–16*, Ministry of Finance, Department of Economic Affairs.

Herring, R. J. and Rao, N. C., 2012. On the Failure of Bt Cotton: Analysing a Decade of Experience. *Economic and Political Weekly*, XLVII(18), pp. 45–53.

Kasirye, I., 2013. *Constraints to Agricultural Technology Adoption in Uganda: Evidence From the 2005/06–2009/10 Uganda National Panel Survey*, Economic Policy Research Centre, Uganda.

Kannan, E. and Sundaram, S., 2011. *Analysis of Trends in India's Agricultural Growth*. The Institute for Social and Economic Change, Bangalore Working Paper, No. 276.

Mani, S. and Santhakumar, V., 2011. Diffusion of New Technologies and Productivity Growth in Agriculture: Natural Rubber vs Coconuts. *Economic and Political Weekly*, XLVI(6), pp. 58–64.

Mansfield, E., 1968. *Industrial Research and Technological Innovation; an Econometric Analysis*, W. W. Norton, New York.

Metcalfe, J. S., 1988. The Diffusion of Innovation: An Interpretative Survey. In Dosi, G., Freeman, C., Nelson, R., Silverberg, G. and Soete, L. (eds.), *Technical Change and Economic Theory*, Printer Publishers Ltd., London.

NSSO, 2013a. Key *Indicators of Situation of Agricultural Households in India*, Government of India, New Delhi, India.

NSSO, 2013b. *Situation Assessment Survey of Agricultural Households, 70th Round, CD-ROM*, Government of India, New Delhi, India.

Samah, B. A., Shaffril, H. A. M., Hassan, M. S., Hassan, M. A. and Ismail, N., 2009. Contribution of Information and Communication Technology in Increasing Agro-Based Entrepreneurs Productivity in Malaysia. *Journal of Agriculture and Social Sciences*, 5(3), pp. 93–98.

Schumpeter, J. A., 1951. *Essays: On Entrepreneurs, Innovations, Business Cycles, and the Evolution of Capitalism*, Transaction Publishers, New Brunswick, NJ.

Shaffril, H. A. M., Hassan, M. S. H. J. and Samah, B. A., 2009. Level of Agro-Based Website Surfing Among Malaysian Agricultural Entrepreneurs: A Case of Malaysia. *Journal of Agriculture & Social Sciences*, 5, pp. 55–60.

Stoneman, P., 2002. *The Economics of Technological Diffusion*, Blackwell Publishing, Oxford.

Vaidyanathan, A., 2010. *Agricultural Growth in India: The Role of Technology, Incentives, and Institutions*, Oxford University Press, Oxford.

9 Trade liberalization and Indian agriculture[1]

Smitha Francis, Anirban Dasgupta and Murali Kallummal

1 Introduction

It is well known that the Indian economy has undergone major changes in the quarter century since liberalization was adopted as an active policy goal in 1991. Agriculture, which contributed nearly 30 per cent to national output and more than 60 per cent to overall employment in 1991, expectedly has also been impacted by these changes. This paper presents an overview of the structural changes in the agricultural sector that are directly linked to the opening up of the Indian economy post-1991, specifically focusing on the composition of trade and price movements in primary commodities.

Before delving into empirical details, it is instructive to conceptualize the various channels through which liberalization is expected to impact agriculture in an economy like India (Francis and Kallummal, 2009). First and the most obvious is the trade-induced channel. Most countries, both developed and developing, have historically had strong barriers to trade in agricultural commodities. These restrictions in the form of tariffs and non-tariff measures have been enacted primarily in the interest of domestic consumers by ensuring them access to wage goods at affordable and relatively stable prices (Nayyar and Sen, 1994). Additionally, in India's closed domestic markets, governments also protected the interest of agricultural producers by intervening through mandated minimum support prices for major crops. The framework under the World Trade Organization (WTO) was designed to reduce and eventually eliminate the protectionist measures adopted by national governments and pave the path for a notionally optimal global free-trade regime in agricultural commodities. In a simple (and possibly simplistic) understanding of allocative efficiency, such opening up of the agricultural sector is expected to have an impact on the production mix, which is in line with the country's comparative advantage. The reality, of course, is more complicated. The majority of Indian farmers are not positioned to compete effectively in open agricultural markets, particularly given the high levels of per capita subsidies enjoyed by agricultural producers in developed countries. The lack of market access for developing country agricultural exports in developed country markets due to the latter's use of specific duties and peak tariffs on products of interest to them as well as increasing use of sanitary and phytosanitary (SPS) measures has exacerbated the situation (Kallummal, 2015). Thus it remains an empirical task to ascertain how greater integration with global markets has transformed India's agricultural trade performance.

The second route through which the opening up of the economy impacts agriculture is the liberalization of capital flows that has taken place in phases since the early 1990s. This includes the significant flow of foreign direct investment (FDI) into different upstream and downstream activities related to agri-product value chains, including in wholesale and retail trade in food products (Francis and Kallummal, 2009). A third channel unfolds through the working of international finance capital, which has been increasingly involved in developing instruments of financial speculation in primary commodities (Ghosh, 2010).

It is evident that all the above three channels of liberalization causing deeper external integration of the domestic agricultural sector will have significant effects on prices and therefore on the production dynamics of the agricultural sector. This chapter will limit itself to an investigation of trade-induced changes, leaving the other two causal links for future research. It should be kept in mind that these effects of external liberalization are in addition to the profound effect of the drastic reduction in public expenditure and formal credit on the agricultural sector. Clearly, it is difficult to delineate the impacts of domestic and external liberalization policies. But the attempt here is to understand the linkage between trade liberalization and agricultural production through the mediating impacts of trade composition changes and price movements.

The second section will summarize the major changes that have taken place in Indian agricultural trade policy in the post-liberalization period. Section 3 will present an overview of Indian agriculture, including its contribution to national output, the crop-mix and extent of international trade. Section 4 will investigate the compositional changes in India's agricultural exports and imports and also analyze the movements of international and domestic prices of top exports in the quarter century since 1991. Section 5 will conclude and indicate areas of future research.

2 Evolution of India's agricultural trade policies

India's pre-reform agricultural policies were centred around self-sufficiency and price stability – ensuring food security for a rapidly growing population through a twin-track approach: keeping food prices low for consumers and incentivizing agricultural production through guaranteed remunerative prices to farmers and domestic support measures. Apart from subsidized credit, the latter took the form of input subsidies for fertilizers, electricity, irrigation water and seeds across crops, and minimum support prices (MSP) for selected crops. These objectives also guided agricultural trade policies, which protected the sector through import tariffs and non-tariff barriers such as trade bans or quantitative restrictions, canalization through state trading corporations, import and export licensing, and trade price controls. These regulations were maneuvered depending on the domestic supply and demand scenario to contain large fluctuations in domestic prices – allowing exports when domestic production was in surplus and increasing imports when there was domestic shortage. Occasionally, the need for raw materials at reasonable prices for industries like food processing, textiles and clothing, etc. also influenced agricultural trade policy decisions.

However, from around the mid- to late 1980s onwards, it was argued that the overvalued exchange rates and excessive protection to industry that had been in place for promoting domestic industrialization had worsened the terms of trade for agriculture and introduced an inbuilt bias against agricultural production and exports. Consequently, since the early 1990s, currency devaluation and agricultural trade liberalization have been carried out in India (along with some liberalization of domestic agricultural markets and prices), with the purported aim of improving the profitability of investments in agriculture by providing the correct price signals. The underlying theme of the new policy package in India thus included a move towards freer export and import of agricultural commodities so that the level and structure of product prices can be brought in line with international prices, thereby facilitating specialized production on the basis of comparative advantage (Singh, 1995). The rupee devaluation of mid-1991 was followed by the removal of export subsidies on agricultural commodities such as tea and coffee, which were India's traditional agricultural exports. Apart from the removal of the export restriction on rice and minimum export price requirements on a number of crops including durum wheat and rice in 1994, the devaluation and the reduced protection provided to the manufacturing sector were also supposed to improve the terms of trade and export prospects for agriculture.

The process of progressive reduction or removal of agricultural trade restrictions of various types accelerated from the mid-1990s in tune with WTO agreements and involved liberalization of remaining export controls, liberalization of quantitative controls on imports and some decontrol of domestic trade. Despite concerns that the WTO's Agreement on Agriculture will not provide a level playing field to developing countries like India in the world markets because of the huge subsidization of developed country agricultural production, it was argued by official and other liberal circles that it will enlarge the access of Indian exports in the world market (Gulati and Sharma, 1994) and thereby bring in greater efficiency in resource use in the agricultural sector (Singh, 1995). While several export restrictions continued, such as those on groundnut oil, sugar, agricultural seeds, wheat and wheat products, butter, rice, pulses and cotton, all these were removed in April 2000 (WTO, 2011). Almost all agricultural products are now allowed to be freely exported. Major exceptions are pulses and oil seeds, which have seen a huge increase in domestic consumption demand, while exports of onions and niger seeds continue to be canalized through state trading corporations.

On the import side, trade liberalization has been associated with the reduction of tariffs as well as the removal of quota control. Under the WTO commitments, all import restrictions that did not take the form of tariffs had to be converted to tariffs – a process known as tariffication. During the Uruguay Round in 1995, such non-tariff restrictions had to be replaced by tariffs representing the same level of protection, and subsequently, average tariffs had to be reduced by 36 per cent within 2000 for developed countries and by 24 per cent within 2005 for developing countries.

India completed the implementation of its Uruguay Round tariff commitments in 2005, and all agricultural tariff lines have been bound since then (WTO, 2015a).[2] While the range of bound rates (10 per cent–300 per cent) is considerably high when compared to the non-agricultural sector, India's average applied tariff on agricultural products has dropped continuously, as tariffs have been substantially reduced over the years autonomously. As seen in Figure 9.1, the average most favoured nation (MFN) applied tariff rate for agricultural products, which was about 83 per cent in 1988, dropped sharply in the first half of the 1990s and stood at 30 per cent in 1997. However, due to increased tariffs mainly on grains, oil seeds, live animals and fats (WTO, 2002) during a phase of relatively low global prices, applied tariffs increased between 1997–98 and 2001–02. The average applied rate dropped again from 2007 onwards owing to the drop in import duties on edible oils during the hike in global prices, before increasing slightly after 2010. The increase in the applied tariff from 31 per cent in 2010–11 to about 36 per cent in 2014–15 was mainly due to an increase in tariffs for oil seeds and cereals in the late 2000s.

In principle, the gaps between India's higher WTO-bound tariff levels compared to the applied rates for many agricultural products allow the government to raise applied tariff rates within these bindings in response to domestic and international market conditions. However, apart from the occasional adjustment in the tariffs on some agricultural commodities in the face of high volatility in international food prices (as seen above), in most cases tariffs have been reduced

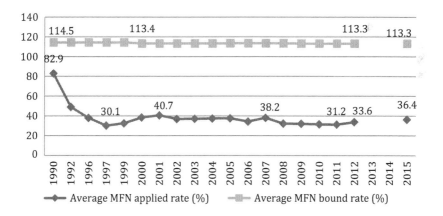

Figure 9.1 Trends in agricultural tariffs, MFN bound and applied rates

Source: Authors' calculation based on UN Comtrade data from WITS and Trade Policy Report, WTO.

rather than raised and have generally been continued at the lower levels (WTO, 2015b, p. 14). In fact, tariff rates have been relatively stable despite tremendous volatility in world trade prices (WTO, 2015b). This may be because the government used non-tariff measures to a larger extent than tariffs.

As Sathe and Deshpande (2006, p. 5338) stated, even in a more liberalized environment, India has basically followed the policy of allowing imports when domestic production has fallen short of demand. Thus, even though some quantitative restrictions on imports were removed in 1991, the import of nearly all agricultural products was subject to other non-tariff measures like import licensing or control by state trading corporations. For instance, until 2011, natural rubber (along with raw silk) was permitted to be imported only against a license. Similarly, cashew kernel and areca nuts imports are restricted (i.e., subject to a licence) when their import price (cost inclusive of insurance and freight, or the c.i.f. price) is lower than the stipulated minimum import price.

Canalization has also continued for a number of agricultural products even after the removal of most remaining quantitative restrictions on imports in 2000–2001. Apart from allowing imports only when there is a domestic shortage, the canalization policy has been followed to obtain better terms of trade through bulk transactions. Imports have also been subject to non-tariff barriers, such as packaging, quality and sanitary requirements, apart from restrictions imposed on grounds of health, safety, moral and security reasons, and for self-sufficiency and balance of payments concerns.

India also continues to maintain tariff rate quotas (TRQs) on imports of several commodities. For instance, during the period 2012–14, in the skimmed milk powder and whole milk powder product group, while imports of up to 10,000 tonnes may come in annually at an in-quota tariff rate of 15 per cent, 60 per cent tariffs were imposed on imports above this quota level. The rates are the same for imports of maize, for which the current tariff quota released on 30 May 2001 is 400,000 tonnes (WTO, 2002, 2015a).

India continues to use trade policy as a means to regulate domestic supply, inflation and fluctuations in commodity prices (WTO, 2015a, p. 26). Export taxes, minimum export price and import duties are adjusted depending on the situation. For instance, the government had imposed export bans on non-basmati rice and wheat during 1996–2000 and 2007–2011 to insulate domestic prices from international price fluctuations. Similarly, export prohibitions have been in place on edible oils since March 2008, with some exceptions introduced on 8 June 2013. Export restrictions and minimum export prices are also used periodically for other agricultural exports, including onions, potatoes, sugar and pulses (WTO, 2002, 2015a). Import policy has also been adjusted based on domestic supply considerations. In the case of sugar, for instance, import duties were lifted temporarily in 2012 to allow an increase in imports in face of excess domestic demand, but it was reintroduced at 10 per cent in July 2012 (WTO, 2015a, p. 27).

Against this backdrop of significant trade policy changes, we will now examine the overall changes in the agricultural sector in terms of its contribution to GDP, crop composition and aggregate trade patterns.

3 Overview of agricultural production and trade

In the two and a half decades since the advent of economic liberalization, Indian agriculture has evolved significantly. While more than 60 per cent of workforce was employed in the sector in 1994, producing 28.4 per cent of GDP, in 2013 approximately 48 per cent of employment based in the sector was producing about 18 per cent of GDP. The absolute value added in agriculture in constant prices (2010 USD) nearly doubled from $168 billion in 1992 to $325 billion in 2015. Even the value added per agricultural worker increased substantially from $771 in 1992 to $1,147 in 2015 (both measured in 2010 USD). The average growth rate of agricultural production also accelerated from 2.5 per cent in the decade 1994–95 to 2004–05 to 4 per cent in the subsequent period from 2005–06 to 2013–14. Since then the growth rate has fallen again due to severe drought and other adverse weather events in 2014–15.

In addition to the aggregate movements mentioned above, there have also been important structural changes within the agricultural sector in terms of cropping pattern as well as output.

Although the proportion of gross cropped area devoted to main cereals like rice and wheat has remained stable (for rice)[3] or increased (as in the case of wheat), that for coarse cereals has declined rapidly. Area under pulses has remained almost constant despite the huge demand for them being met by large quantities of imports (Table 9.1). Among commercial crops, cotton and coffee gained significantly, followed by less pronounced increases for oil seeds, sugarcane, and tea (Table 9.2).

Among other crops not covered in Tables 9.1 and 9.2, the most significant increase in cropped area has been for horticultural crops, for which the percentage of area (as a share of gross cropped area) increased from 6.9 per cent in 1991–92 to about 12 per cent in 2014–15 (Government of India, 2016). The largest

Table 9.1 Percentage of gross cropped area under different crops

Year (TE)	Rice	Wheat	Coarse cereals	Pulses	Food grains	Non-food grains
1990–91	22.7	12.9	20.2	12.8	68.6	31.4
2000–01	24.2	14.5	16.0	11.7	66.4	33.6
2015–16	22.5	15.8	12.6	12.6	63.6	36.4

Source: *Agricultural Statistics at a Glance 2015*, and RBI Database on the Indian Economy

Table 9.2 Percentage of gross cropped area under selected commercial crops

Year (TE)	Oil seeds	Sugarcane	Tea	Coffee	Cotton
1990–91	12.36	1.88	0.22	0.12	3.98
2000–01	12.18	2.27	0.32	0.17	4.78
2015–16	13.79	2.59	0.29	0.22	6.28

Source: Same as for Table 9.1

growth within this group has been for flowers, for which area covered increased nearly eight times and production increased more than six times in the same period. Substantial growth was also observed for fruits and vegetables. Another key development is the significant growth in meat production from 1.9 million tonnes in 1998–99 to 5.9 million tonnes in 2012–13 (Government of India, 2014), a three-fold growth in one and a half decades. Within this group, the biggest increase has been in the category of buffalo meat in recent years.

When it comes to agricultural trade, it is seen that after some decline in the early 1990s, India's agricultural imports have grown steadily since 2001 (with the exception of 2004–06) and even more strongly and steadily since 2008. But given that non-agricultural imports registered higher growth, the relative share of agricultural imports as a share of India's total imports showed a decline in the post-2000 phase. As a result, imports of agricultural products, which stood at nearly 10 per cent of total merchandize imports in 1988–90 on the eve of the economic reforms, was only 4 per cent of total imports during 2012–14 (Table 9.3). This increased to about 6 per cent in 2015, as agricultural import growth was positive in 2014 and 2015 after rebounding from the negative growth rate in 2013, while there was a heavy drop in non-agricultural imports in these three years.

The fact that India's agricultural import dependence has been rising steadily is reflected in the rise in the agricultural imports–agricultural GDP ratio, which increased from 2.6 per cent in 1988 to more than 4 per cent in the late 1990s and stood at 7.5 per cent in 2012. There was a significant spurt in the ratio from 2007 onwards.

Table 9.3 Sectoral shares in merchandize trade

	Percentage share in total merchandize exports				
	1988–90	*1996–98*	*2004–06*	*2012–14*	*2015*
Agricultural exports	15.9	16.7	9.3	12.7	11.3
Non-agricultural exports	84.1	83.3	90.7	87.3	88.7
Total merchandize exports	100.0	100.0	100.0	100.0	100.0

	Percentage share in total merchandize imports				
	1988–90	*1996–98*	*2004–06*	*2012–14*	*2015*
Agricultural imports	6.2	6.9	9.3	4.3	5.9
Non-agricultural imports	93.8	93.1	90.7	95.7	94.1
Total merchandize imports	100.0	100.0	100.0	100.0	100.0

Source: Authors' calculation based on UN Comtrade data from WITS

The share of agricultural exports in total merchandize exports, which stood at an average 16 per cent on the eve of reforms (1988–90) and showed a marginal decline in the early 1990s, grew strongly during 1994–96 (Table 9.3). Although there was a decline in the late 1990s, agricultural exports registered strong growth performance again from 2000 onwards. However, their relative share in total merchandize exports declined to a low of about 9 per cent during 2004–06 because of the boom in manufactured exports. Subsequently, with manufactured exports showing lower growth rates from 2010, the share of agricultural exports in total merchandize exports increased again to about 13 per cent during 2012–14. The rise in global food prices from 2007 until 2011 was also a factor in stimulating export growth (See Figure 9.2). But agricultural exports registered negative growth and slumped in 2014 and 2015 (as in 2009).

Importantly, as a percentage of agricultural GDP, agricultural exports increased from 3 per cent in 1988 to 15 per cent in 2012. With exports contributing nearly double the share of imports to agricultural GDP, India's agricultural trade has been in surplus throughout the study period, peaking in 2013. However, agricultural exports declined sharply after 2013, while agricultural imports grew further in 2014 and 2015 (Figure 9.2). Apart from a narrowing trade surplus, the phase-wise trend growth rates (exponential) in agricultural exports and imports during 1988–2006 and 2007–15 also clearly point towards the increasing importance of imports in India's agricultural trade. At 11 per cent and 15 per cent during 1988–2006 and 2007–15, import growth rates were greater than export growth rates at 7 and 13 per cent, respectively.

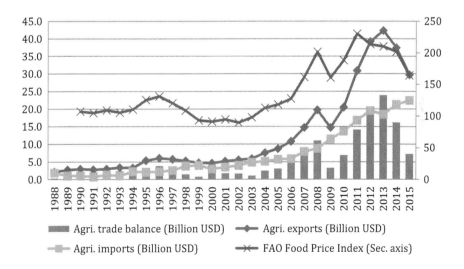

Figure 9.2 Values of agricultural exports, imports and trade balance

Source: Authors' calculation based on UNCOMTRADE trade data from WITS for 1988–96, DGCIS trade data for 1996–2004, and GDP data from RBI Statistics

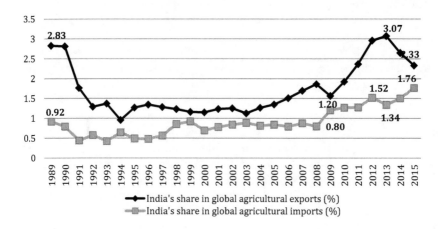

Figure 9.3 India's share in global agricultural trade, 1989–2015

Source: Authors' calculation based on UN Comtrade data from WITS.

These trends are mirrored in India's share in global agricultural trade. India's share in global agricultural exports was higher than her share in global agricultural imports throughout the study period (Figure 9.3). The largest increase in export share took place with a lag during the period of the global food price crisis of 2007–2012. However, after peaking at 3.1 per cent in 2013, there was a distinct drop in India's share in global agricultural exports in 2014 and 2015, even as India's share in agricultural imports increased further despite a drop in 2013 (Figure 9.3).

In fact, even as agriculture's share in total global imports has shown a decline from 10 per cent in 1989 to 8.3 per cent in 2015, India's share in global agricultural imports increased from 0.9 per cent to 1.8 per cent between 1989 and 2015. The fastest growth in India's agricultural imports happened after 2008, wherein in just seven years India's share in global agricultural imports more than doubled.

Given these trends in India's agricultural trade, we now examine the changes in commodity composition that contributed to these shifts and to what extent increase in India's agricultural exports and imports has been driven by increase in quantity as opposed to a price effect.

4 Changes in agricultural trade composition and price movements

During 1988–90, India's three most important agricultural import categories were animal or vegetable fats and oils, edible vegetables and tubers, and cereals.

The import share of the top-most category, vegetable and animal oils and fats, has increased steadily. Within this category, while refined palm oil was the most dominant import in the 1990s, crude palm oil became the most important import from 2000 onwards. Crude palm oil alone constituted more than one-fourth of total agricultural imports during 2012–14 (Table 9.4). The import share of other vegetables oils like crude soya bean oil has also risen after 2000, while that of crude sunflower oil has risen from 2008 onwards. By contrast, the import share of cereals, composed primarily of other wheat and meslin followed by rice, decreased in a dramatic fashion from 1990.

Edible vegetables as well as edible fruits and nuts have been the second and third largest agricultural import sectors since the 1990s. Edible vegetables were

Table 9.4 Composition of India's agricultural imports at the product category level (HS 6-digit), 1988–2015 (period average percentage share in total agricultural imports)

S. No.	Product category	1988–90	1996–98	2004–06	2012–14	2015
1	Crude palm oil	4.6	0.6	15.9	27.7	23.8
2	Palm oil (excl. crude) and liquid	8.4	27.1	9.3	8.5	7.5
3	Crude soya bean oil	2.1	0.0	12.6	7.7	9.5
4	Crude sunflower seed and safflower	0.8	0.8	0.8	6.9	6.6
5	Cashew nuts, fresh or dried	4.3	7.4	7.6	4.7	5.1
6	Dried peas, shelled	6.4	2.4	3.8	3.5	3.5
7	Dried beans, shelled	0.5	0.2	1.4	2.4	2.8
8	Almonds in shell, fresh or dried	1.5	2.0	2.2	2.4	2.8
9	Cotton, not carded or combed	1.9	1.4	3.2	2.3	2.1
10	Raw cane sugar, in solid form	0.0	2.2	2.2	2.2	2.2
11	Dried lentils, shelled	2.1	0.5	0.3	2.0	3.0
12	Dried leguminous vegetables, shelled	3.5	3.0	2.6	1.8	2.0
13	Dried chickpeas, shelled	4.0	2.3	1.5	1.5	1.5
14	Greasy wool (excl. shorn), not card	6.0	2.8	1.7	1.2	1.1
15	Other preparations of a kind used in	0.1	0.6	0.7	1.1	1.1
16	Crude palm kernel or babassu oil	0.1	0.0	1.1	1.1	1.1
17	Apples, fresh	0.0	0.0	0.3	1.1	1.1
	Cumulative share of the above	46.3	53.1	67.3	**78.1**	76.7

Note: # The table contains only those products which have at least a 1 per cent and above average share in total agricultural imports during 2012–14.

Source: Authors' calculation based on UN Comtrade data from WITS.

dominated by dried peas, beans, lentils and other shelled leguminous vegetables (Table 9.4). India is the world's largest producer and importer of pulses. It must be noted that while an import duty of 5 per cent was initially levied on pulses in June 2001, which was increased to 10 per cent in March 2003, the duty was reduced to 0 per cent from June 2006 (Vishandass and Lukka, 2013, p. 26). While the edible fruits and nuts category has been dominated by cashew nuts, almonds have steadily increased their share (Table 9.4). Imports of apples have also gone up significantly since 2007.

Meanwhile, the shares of wool, cereal preparations, dairy produce, raw hide and skin, silk, and vegetable saps and extracts, which were among the largest imports during 1988–90, have all declined over the years.

The import share of coffee, tea and spices, however, show an increasing trend, dominated by coffee. Similarly, the import share of beverages and spirits, dominated by whiskies, undehydrated ethyl alcohol and sweetened waters, has increased. Despite a decline in its average share, cotton has been among the major imports. The other rising import category was sugar and sugar confectionary. The import share of raw cane sugar started rising from 1997 onwards, and the share of various kinds of sugar confectionary have also become important in recent years. Three other sectors that have become more important among imports are oil seeds, residues and waste from food industries and animal fodder, as well as cocoa and cocoa preparations. These were in fact among the fastest growing imports in terms of trend growth rates during 2007–15.

Some of these import trends could also be related to the accelerated agricultural tariff liberalization through the preferential route under India's free trade agreements (FTAs) with Sri Lanka, ASEAN, South Korea, Japan, etc. For instance, under the India-ASEAN FTA, crude palm oil, refined palm oil, coffee, black tea and pepper saw major tariff reductions from 2014 (Francis, 2011, p. 49).[4] However, a detailed analysis of different FTAs involving agricultural trade liberalization is beyond the scope of this paper.

On the other side, when we analyze agricultural exports (Table 9.5), it is seen that coffee, tea, mate and spices (dominated by black tea, followed by pepper), the single most important export category during 1988–90, declined in share steadily. The second largest agricultural export category until about 2010, residues and waste from food industries and animal fodder, has also declined in share since then. While they remain among the top ten agricultural exports from India, these two sectors are becoming important in India's imports, as we saw above. Similar is the case of edible fruits and vegetables, dominated by cashew nuts, whose high export shares have declined dramatically, while they continue to be important imports. Thus it is observed that some product categories whose export shares have declined significantly have begun showing rising import shares. This would imply that at least some of our traditional primary exports have faced severe competitive pressure from imports and have lost out, with possible adverse implications for the regions that have been primarily growing these crops.

At the same time, the categories which have shown declining import dependence coincide with the ones that show export dynamism. Thus cereals have

Table 9.5 Composition of India's agricultural exports at the product category level (HS 6-digit), 1988–2015 (percentage share in total agricultural exports during each phase) #

S. No.	HS code	Product category	1988–90	1996–98	2004–06	2012–14	2015
1	100630	Semi-milled or wholly milled rice	9.6	19.3	15.4	17.7	19.4
2	20230	Frozen boneless bovine meat	1.3	2.0	5.6	10.2	12.0
3	520100	Cotton, not carded or combed	6.5	3.8	5.5	9.2	8.4
4	130232	Mucilages and thickeners of locust beans/guar seeds	1.5	2.5	2.2	9.0	4.8
5	230400	Oil-cake and other solid residues from soya bean	8.3	11.3	9.2	5.1	4.1
6	100590	Maize (excl. seed)	0.0	0.0	1.0	2.7	2.0
7	100190	Spelt, common wheat and meslin	0.2	0.9	2.0	2.3	1.9
8	80130	Cashew nuts, fresh or dried	8.4	6.6	6.1	2.2	2.4
9	170199	Cane or beet sugar, in solid form	0.1	1.0	1.4	2.0	2.2
10	151530	Castor oil and its fractions	0.8	2.6	2.3	1.8	1.9
11	120220	Shelled groundnuts, not roasted or otherwise cooked	0.8	1.6	1.1	1.7	1.6
12	240120	Tobacco, partly or wholly stemmed	2.6	0.6	1.8	1.7	1.8
13	120740	Sesamum seeds	1.7	1.2	1.9	1.7	1.8
14	90240	Black tea (fermented and partly fermented)	14.5	4.2	3.2	1.6	1.7
15	170111	Raw cane sugar, in solid form	0.3	0.6	0.6	1.4	0.8
16	90111	Coffee, not roasted or decaffeinated	6.7	5.8	2.6	1.4	1.5
17	90420	Fruits of genus Capsicum or Pimenta	0.6	0.8	1.2	1.2	1.4
18	70310	Onions and shallots, fresh or chilled	1.8	1.0	2.0	1.0	1.2
		Cumulative share of the above	65.7	65.8	65.1	**73.8**	71.0

Note: # The table contains only those products which have at least a 1 per cent and above average share in total agricultural imports during 2012–14.

Source: Authors' calculation based on UN Comtrade data from WITS.

become the most important agricultural exports from India despite the fact that the government has imposed export bans on non-basmati rice and wheat, as seen earlier. The export share of cereals has increased continuously in the post-1991 period. Rice alone came to account for one-fifth of total agricultural exports in 2015. India had emerged as the world's largest exporter of rice in 2011, replacing Thailand. Exports of corn also began increasing in the 2000s and were followed by wheat (Table 9.5).

The second, third and fourth most important export categories by the end of 2000s were cotton, mucilages and thickeners from gaur seeds (known as guargum meal), and frozen boneless meat of bovine animals. Significantly, all of these categories are dominated by their raw material and semi-processed forms (Table 9.5). Guargum meal is a raw material for the food processing industry. Apart from maize and wheat, mentioned above, another agricultural product that has seen increased shares in exports is cane sugar, while soya bean oil cake, cashew nuts and castor oil have remained among the top 10 agricultural exports despite the decline in their shares.

An analysis of the quantities of the top 10 agricultural exports (Figures 9.4 to 9.7) clearly reveals that exports of rice and bovine meat experienced significant increases in their volumes following the global price rise in the late 2000s.

While export quantities of soya bean oil-cake, maize and cotton, followed by guargum meal, also witnessed increases, these were subject to annual fluctuations. Similar was the case with cane sugar and wheat, in whose case the fluctuations can be directly related to the changes in export policies during this phase. While castor oil export quantities also increased, the growth was from a very low base.

It is also observed that the drop in India's agricultural exports after 2013 was contributed to by declines in the quantity exported of all these major products, dominated by soya bean oil-cake, wheat, maize and cotton, except cane sugar.

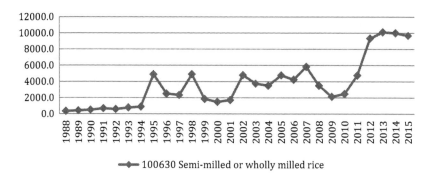

Figure 9.4 Quantity trends in rice exports, 1988–2015 (metric tonne)

Source: All quantities are in US$/kg and are authors' calculations based on UN Comtrade data from WITS.

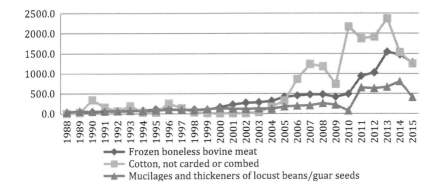

Figure 9.5 Quantity trends in bovine meat, cotton and guargum meal exports, 1988–2015 (metric tonne)

Source: All quantities are in US$/kg and are authors' calculations based on UN Comtrade data from WITS.

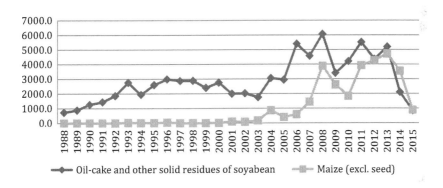

Figure 9.6 Quantity trends in soya bean oil-cake and maize exports, 1988–2015 (metric tonne)

Source: All quantities are in US$/kg and are authors' calculations based on UN Comtrade data from WITS.

The quantity of rice exports declined only slightly when compared to the other major exports. On the other side, cashew nut exports appear to be relatively stable at a low base.

We now consider the price movements of the major exports in order to understand how India's export prices have fared in comparison with their trend in export growth (Table 9.6). When the unit prices of the top 20 major exports with increasing shares in India's agricultural exports were analyzed for the time

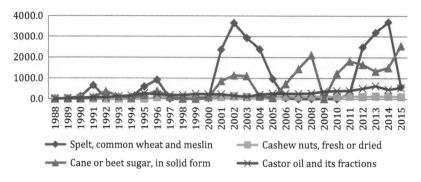

Figure 9.7 Quantity trends in wheat, cane sugar, castor oil and cashew nut exports, 1988–2015 (metric tonne)

Source: All quantities are in USD/kg and are authors' calculations based on UN Comtrade data from WITS.

period 1992–2012, it was found that only 3 products out of these 20 major exports – guargum meal, frozen bovine meat, and maize – were found to exhibit a significant positive correlation between their shares in agricultural exports and unit export prices. Four other products showed weak positive correlation. In the case of products which showed a negative correlation (as their unit export prices declined), we infer that farm prices would not have experienced any increase.

Ironically, in the case of rice, India's most important agricultural export during 2010–12, unit export prices showed a negative correlation with the export share of rice in this period. That is, even though India was exporting large volumes of rice during a period of global price rise, the unit export prices received by India were not increasing. This would indicate that farmers in the regions dependent on rice production not have benefitted from the increased exports.

This gets confirmed when we compare the international and domestic price movements as well as India's unit export prices and producer prices for the major exports. The divergence between domestic and export prices is clear from Figures 9.8 to 9.12, which plot the international and Indian unit export prices for some major export products, along with India's domestic wholesale prices and minimum support price (MSP).

It is evident that Indian domestic market prices for rice were significantly lower than export prices and experienced any major increase only during the initial phase of the global food price rise of 2007–11. However, the MSP was even lower than the domestic wholesale prices, let alone the export prices obtained by Indian exporters, even during 2007–11 and 2013–15 when India's unit export prices were higher than international prices.[5]

Table 9.6 Correlation between export shares and unit export prices of India's major agricultural exports

S.No.	HS code	Product category	Correlation between export shares and unit export prices (21 years; 1992–2012)	Average share during 2010–12 (%)
1	100630	Semi/wholly milled rice w/n polished/glazed	−0.39	12.9
2	520100	Cotton, not carded or combed	0.48	11.6
3	130232	Guargum meal	0.84	8.2
4	20230	Boneless meat of bovine animals, frozen	0.83	8.0
5	230400	Oil-cake and other solid residue w/n grnd/in pellets form obtained from soya bean oil extraction	−0.20	6.9
6	170199	Refined sugar not containing flavouring/colouring matter	−0.01	3.2
7	100590	Other maize (corn)	0.61	2.9
8	80130	Cashew nuts fresh/dried w/n shelled/peeled	0.48	2.5
9	151530	Castor oil and its fractions	−0.06	2.5
10	120220	Shelled groundnuts w/n broken	0.54	2.4
11	90240	Other black tea/other partly fermented tea	−0.41	2.3
12	240120	Tobacco partly or wholly stemmed/stripped	0.50	2.0
13	170111	Raw cane sugar not containing flavouring/colouring matter	0.19	1.9
14	90111	Coffee neither roasted nor decaffeinated	0.09	1.9
15	120740	Seasamum seeds w/n broken	0.28	1.8
16	90420	Fruits of gens capsicum/pmnta, dried/crushed/grnd	0.56	1.6
17	70310	Onions and shallots, fresh or chilled	0.29	1.4
18	330190	Essential oils, terpenic by-products etc., nes.	0.19	0.9
19	100190	Other wheat and meslin	−0.31	0.7
20	100110	Durum wheat	0.07	0.6

Source: Authors' calculation based on UN Comtrade data.

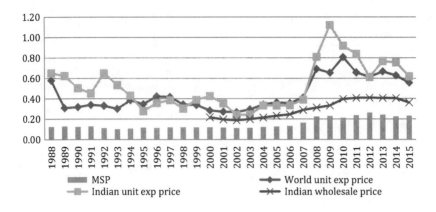

Figure 9.8 Trends in export unit prices, domestic prices and producer prices of rice, 1988–2015 (USD/per kg)

Source: Authors' calculations. Global and Indian unit export prices were derived based on export value and quantity figures from UN Comtrade data. Indian wholesale prices were obtained from the FAO GIEWS. MSP series was taken from the Reserve Bank of India Database on the Indian Economy.

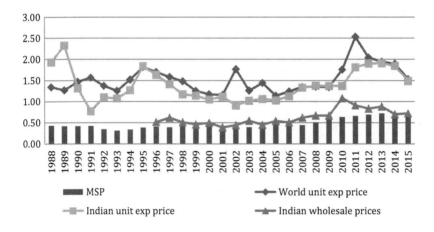

Figure 9.9 Trends in export unit prices, domestic prices and producer prices of cotton, 1988–2015 (USD/per kg)

Source: Authors' calculations. Global and Indian unit export prices were derived based on export value and quantity figures from UN Comtrade data. Indian wholesale prices for cotton were the national averages derived from data available from the Cotton Corporation of India Ltd. MSP series was taken from the Reserve Bank of India Database on the Indian Economy.

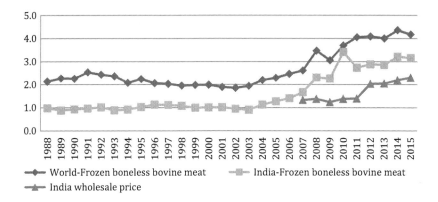

Figure 9.10 Trends in export unit prices and domestic prices of frozen bovine meat, 1988–2015 (USD/per kg)

Source: Authors' calculations. Global and Indian unit export prices were derived based on export value and quantity figures from UN Comtrade data. Indian wholesale prices were obtained from various volumes of Agricultural Price Statistics, Government of India.

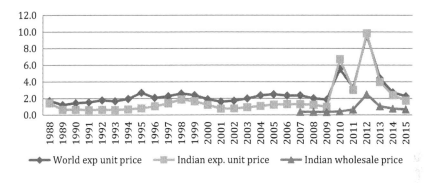

Figure 9.11 Trends in export unit prices and domestic prices of guargum meal, 1988–2015 (USD/per kg)

Source: Authors' calculations. Global and Indian unit export prices were derived based on export value and quantity figures from UN Comtrade data. Indian wholesale prices were obtained from various volumes of Agricultural Price Statistics, Government of India.

A comparison of international and domestic prices for the next three major export crops also shows that domestic wholesale prices for cotton, bovine meat and guargum meal were below India's export prices for these commodities. This lack of congruence between domestic and international prices, particularly in the immediate period around the global food crisis in 2007–8, is borne out by other studies (Acharya et al., 2012).

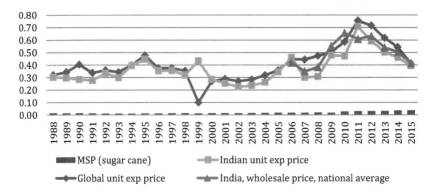

Figure 9.12 Trends in export unit prices, domestic prices and producer prices of sugar, 1988–2015 (USD/per kg)

Source: Authors' calculations. Global and Indian unit export prices were derived based on export value and quantity figures from UN Comtrade data. Indian wholesale prices were obtained from the FAO GIEWS. MSP series was taken from the Reserve Bank of India Database on the Indian Economy.

Significantly, in the case of cane sugar, another major export product,[6] despite the fact that domestic wholesale prices were better aligned with export prices compared to the above crops (and higher than export prices in some years), the MSP was again much lower than wholesale prices.

Even though producer price data was not available, it is possible to infer that farm gate prices would have been lower than domestic wholesale prices in the case of all these products. This indicates that farmers may not have been the major gainers from the post-liberalization export growth.

5 Concluding remarks and areas of further research

Indian agriculture has been faced with significant multilateral tariff liberalization since the 1995 Uruguay Round multilateral negotiations. However, trade in some important agricultural products continues to be regulated through non-tariff measures, mainly in the form of export/import restrictions and minimum trade prices to take care of domestic price situations. These relate in particular to pulses, oil seeds and vegetable oils on the import side, and rice, wheat, sugar, cotton, onions, etc. on the export side. Despite the non-tariff regulation that remains in support of domestic agricultural producers and consumers, import growth has been clearly higher than export growth. As a result, there has been a narrowing of India's agricultural trade surplus after 2013. Some of this could be related to the accelerated agricultural tariff liberalization through the preferential route under India's FTAs. An analysis of FTAs is therefore critically important in this context but is beyond the scope of this paper.

On the basis of the preliminary analysis presented in this chapter, it is possible to link trade liberalization with the change in domestic output levels for crops which in their raw or processed forms have emerged as important in India's trade basket in recent decades. While a detailed analysis is beyond the scope of this paper, the production figures of relevant crops give some indication about the impact of the emerging trade patterns. Rice, cotton and guargum meal (derived from guar seeds) are among the top agricultural exports for India in recent years, apart from bovine meat. For all four crops/products, production was seen to have increased substantially in the post-liberalization period, albeit at different rates. This is in line with the expectation that reduction of trade barriers will incentivize at least partial specialization in some commodities with a consequent increase in output.

Another observation on production is related to oil seeds – an aggregate of nine different varieties including direct raw materials for sunflower and soya bean oil, which are prominent in India's agricultural import basket. Palm oil, by far the top import item, is also a popular and cheap edible oil and a substitute of sunflower and soya bean oil. There has been a significant increase in the volume of oil seeds output in the last two and half decades consequent to the rapid increase in edible oil demand. This implies that imports have increased not at the cost of domestic production but in conjunction with it in the case of these crops. The same can be said of another major import commodity, cashew nuts, for which domestic production has increased significantly. However, there are other crops, such as coconut, rubber, etc., where increased imports of substitutes (palm oil and synthetic rubber) have impacted the livelihood of domestic farmers adversely (Kallummal, Ratna and Sharma, 2016). The nature of the exact impact of import growth on farmers of various crops needs further investigation.

Even in cases where there is evidence of increased production consequent upon trade liberalization, it is important to ascertain the conditions under which this has happened and the returns that it generates for farmers. A comparison of international and domestic prices for India's top export crops shows that their domestic wholesale prices remained far below India's export prices. It is reasonable to infer that the gap between export prices and that received by farmers is even larger. The long chain of intermediaries between the farmer and the market (domestic as well as export) and the inadequate marketing infrastructure (Mahendra Dev, 2012) has been a major factor that erodes the prices obtained by farmers. However, another reason is the adjustment in MSPs (along with export and import quantities) with the policy objective to maintain stability in domestic prices. When we consider the gradual withdrawal of the state from the agrarian sector both in terms of public investment and subsidies in conjunction with the divergence between domestic and international prices seen above, there emerges a worrying picture for the Indian farmer. The worsening of returns to agriculture that has been well documented across regions and crops can be explained to some extent by the low price for output received by farmers even for export crops with thriving international demand. Further, whether increased international competition though freer trade has led to a tendency of differentiation along farm size, capital use or any other relevant criteria will be important to examine in future research.

What is clear from this study is that the promise of a remunerative agriculture through relative equalization of domestic and international prices following trade liberalization has remained largely unfulfilled. This may be partly attributed to the continued regulation of agricultural trade due to the need to balance various domestic policy objectives given that the vast majority of Indian farmers are small and marginal, and therefore net buyers of food. Given that this will continue to be of critical importance, it is more than evident that the current imperfect institutional arrangements in the Indian agricultural marketing system that prevent farmers from obtaining remunerative prices need the long overdue restructuring. An important part of this effort would be to increase farmers' bargaining strength and marketing capabilities through government support for the creation of farmers' cooperatives.

Notes

1 The authors are grateful to Binoy Goswami and an anonymous referee for their comments, which helped improve the paper substantially. The usual disclaimer applies.
2 India had initially bound several tariff lines at very low levels given that tariff rates for many agricultural commodities were low or zero in the early 1990s (which in turn was largely because quantitative restrictions on imports were far more important policy instruments than tariffs). These bound tariffs were subsequently re-negotiated.
3 Rice output increased in the tune of 40 per cent between early 1990s and mid-2010s.
4 Kallummal, Ratna and Sharma (2016) has shown that ASEAN countries became the dominant import suppliers for these products by 2016.
5 India is currently the single largest rice exporter with a global export share of 32–33 per cent.
6 Based on Table 9.5, however, the selection of export crops for price analysis was conditioned by the availability of price data for at least some years.

References

Acharya, S. S., Chand, R., Birthal, P. S. and Negi, D. S., 2012. *Market Integration and Price Transmission in India: A Case of Rice and Wheat With Special Reference to the World Food Crisis of 2007/08*, Food and Agriculture Organization, Rome.
Francis, S., 2011. The ASEAN-India Free Trade Agreement: A Sectoral Impact Analysis of Increased Trade Integration in Goods. *Economic & Political Weekly*, 46(2), pp. 46–55.
Francis, S. and Kallummal, M., 2009. *Financial Liberalisation and the Agriculture: An Overview of the Challenges before Developing Countries*. Paper presented at the International Seminar on Financial Structures and Economic Development: Financing Theories and the New Standards, UNAM, Mexico.

Ghosh, J., 2010. The Unnatural Coupling: Food and Global Finance. *Journal of Agrarian Change*, 10(1), pp. 72–86.

Government of India, 2014. *Basic Animal Husbandry and Fisheries Statistics*, Ministry of Agriculture, New Delhi.

Government of India, 2016. *Horticultural Statistics at a Glance*, Ministry of Agriculture and Farmers Welfare and Oxford University Press, New Delhi.

Gulati, A. and Sharma, A., 1994. Agriculture Under GATT: What It Holds for India. *Economic and Political Weekly*, 29(29), pp. 1857–1863.

Kallummal, M., 2015. North-South Imbalances in the Doha Round: The Use of Specific Duties as a Trade Policy Instrument. *Agrarian South: Journal of Political Economy*, 4(1), pp. 85–124.

Kallummal, M., Ratna, R. S. and Sharma, S. K., 2016. *India's Agricultural Imports: Under the Shadow of Free Trade Agreements*. Paper presented at the 5th International Conference on WTO, Trade and Agriculture: Issues and Challenges for Developing and Least Developed Countries, Centre for WTO Studies, New Delhi, October 20–21.

Mahendra Dev, S., 2012. *Small Farmers in India: Challenges and Opportunities*. IGIDR Working Paper No. 2012–14.

Nayyar, D. and Sen, A., 1994. International Trade and the Agricultural Sector in India. *Economic and Political Weekly*, 29(20), pp. 1187–1203.

Sathe, D. and Deshpande, R. S., 2006. Sustaining Agricultural Trade: Policy and Impact. *Economic and Political Weekly*, 41(52), pp. 5337–5344.

Singh, S., 1995. Structural Adjustment Programme and Indian Agriculture: Towards an Assessment of Implications. *Economic and Political Weekly*, 30(510), pp. 3311–3314.

Vishandass, A. and Lukka, B., 2013. *Pricing, Costs, Returns & Productivity in Indian Crop Sector During 2000s*, Commission for Agricultural Costs and Prices (CACP), Ministry of Agriculture, New Delhi.

WTO, 2002. *Trade Policy Review: India*. Report by the WTO Secretariat, Geneva.

WTO, 2011. *Trade Policy Review: India*. Report by the WTO Secretariat, Geneva.

WTO, 2015a. *Trade Policy Review: India*. Report by the WTO Secretariat, Geneva.

WTO, 2015b. *Trade Policy Review: India*. Report by Government of India, Geneva.

10 Indian agriculture through the turn of the century

Gathering stress and farmers' distress

M. P. Bezbaruah and Mofidul Hassan

1 Introduction

The spurt in India's food grain production in the late 1960s sprouted from successful deployment of HYV seeds-fertilizers technology in the wheat belt of Punjab, Haryana and western Uttar Pradesh. In the subsequent period, the harvests from this technological breakthrough expanded in a sustained way as the technology package was adapted for other crops and other parts of the country, and even smaller farmers gradually joined in the process of adopting the new cultivation practices (Bezbaruah, 1994, pp. 15–27). Consolidation of the gains of the Green Revolution during the 1970s and 1980s transformed India from a country of chronic food shortages to one of food self-sufficiency with even a buffer stock to see itself through the occasional bad years that pop up in agricultural cycles.

In 1991 India embarked upon a market-oriented structural reform of its economic regime, as a result of which state control over economic activities was softened, a more open orientation towards international trade and inflow of foreign capital was adopted, and some measure of fiscal discipline was sought to be enforced in both central and provincial governments. Following the onset of this reform process, the Indian economy shifted to a higher growth trajectory (Panagariya, 2008, pp. 4–11). But in contrast to the step-up in the growth rate of the economy as a whole, the part of gross domestic product (GDP) originating in agriculture started decelerating after the mid-1990s (Bezbaruah, 2014). The result has been a steady decline in agriculture's share in the GDP, which came down to below 15 per cent by 2013–14. Such a trend, of course, is a common feature in the process of transition of an economy from a relatively less developed state to an advanced one. However in the case of India, the decline in the share of agriculture in GDP was not accompanied by a concomitant shift in occupational distribution of the workforce away from agriculture, leaving the agriculture sector to accommodate about a half of country's work force even today. Consequently, labour productivity in agriculture now stands at only around one-fourth of the average labour productivity for the entire economy. Meanwhile, signs of degradation of the soil, water and ecological resource base from relentless pursuit of Green Revolution-induced cultivation practices became discernible. Consequent escalation of the cost of cultivation and declines in the rates of returns from cultivation of major crops meant that Indian agriculture had finally slipped into a phase of fatigue after the prolonged run of the HYV seed and fertilizer technology. That the malady afflicting the agriculture sector of the country was heading towards a crisis is borne out by the fact that the rate of suicide among farmers in many parts of the country shot up around the mid-1990s and remained high for several years thereafter. In the present chapter we recount the factors that had gone into brewing this crisis (section 2) and have a closer examination of data for a better understanding of the magnitude of the phenomenon of farmers' suicide (section 3). We conclude with a discussion of the policy options for strengthening farmers' natural resilience for better coping with the uncertainties they typically encounter.

2 Build-up of the stress

Since the slow-down of agricultural growth and the upsurge of farmers' suicide rate coincided with the period when the effects of India's market-oriented structural adjustment programme also started manifesting, some scholars attribute the agricultural crisis to the reform process itself (Reddy and Misra, 2009). However a little deeper digging for the genesis of the crisis has led us to locate the seed of the crisis in the very policy measures that were instrumental in making the Green Revolution a resounding success. Struck by two successive monsoon failures and deprived of the easy imports of food grains under PL 480[1] from the United States, India was pushed into a corner by a severe food crisis in the mid-1960s. The high-yielding varieties (HYV) of wheat and rice developed respectively in Mexico and the Philippines then came as a ray of hope for the country. To induce farmers to extract the potentials of the new varieties, the government came out with a policy package to comprehensively support the farmers who would adopt the new technology. HYV seeds, the complementary inputs of fertilizers and other agro-chemicals like pesticides, and irrigation water were made available at subsidized rates. Electricity was extended free to farmers in several states so that water could be drawn to fields with the minimum of costs. So that farmers responding to such incentives by producing larger output were also assured of remunerative prices, the government came out with the policy of announcing minimum support prices (MSP) well in advance of harvesting season and public procurement of grains in the post-harvest period (Balasubramanyam, 1984, p. 85). In the context of the difficult food situation of that time and the overarching national compulsion of increasing domestic production of food grains, the support measures to farmers were fully justified. However, from the point of view of efficient and sustainable use of agricultural resource base, the policy measures had adverse implications.

Agro-chemicals have well-known negative externalities. Excessive and prolonged use of fertilizers can damage soil health. Indiscriminate use of pesticides is not only a threat to local ecology but to human and animal health. Any standard textbook of microeconomics would suggest that to mitigate such negative externalities these inputs should be taxed rather than subsidized. Groundwater is an open-access resource for all who can dig a well and pump the water up. Efficient and sustainable use of this natural resource requires appropriate regulation of extraction. Such regulations have been either non-existent or ineffective in most states. On top of that, subsidization of the cost of extraction through free supply of electricity to farms accentuated over-exploitation of groundwater reserves. The result is manifestation of a typical 'tragedy of commons' phenomenon, especially in areas where rates of recharge of the aquifers are low due to insufficient precipitations. The adverse environmental consequences of not phasing out of subsidies had manifested, especially in Green Revolution areas, in the 1980s (Bidwai, 1988). Continued and often excessive price support to cereals, especially rice, also created a bias towards these crops in the cropping pattern, accentuating degradation of soil and water recourses in parts of the country.

Once the Green Revolution had materialized and the HYV technology started getting diffused, measures such as fertilizer subsidies and free power supply should have been phased out, and the procurement policy and price support mechanisms should have been rationalized. But by late 1970s, the big farmers of the Green Revolution belt had acquired not only substantial economic prosperity but also considerable political clout, and the privilege given to them in the form of input subsidies and price support for bringing about the Green Revolution could not be taken away (Misra and Chand, 1995). Some of the support measures actually got expanded as the years rolled by. It was only when India was forced to adopt wide-ranging economic and fiscal reforms in 1991 that the agricultural subsidies could be brought under the ambit of the reform process.

Fiscal consolidation constituted a part of the structural adjustment program of India launched in 1991.Since subsidy reforms constituted a component of the broader fiscal reforms, subsidies to agriculture naturally became a subject of attention and action. Proposals for reducing fertilizer subsidies, however, met with resistance and hence could be implemented only partially. In particular, lowering of subsidy on nitrogenous fertilizer was strongly opposed and the resultant slower reduction of subsidy on this type nutrient caused an imbalance in application of N, P and K among some farmers. Indeed fertilizer subsidies have been known to be beset with inefficiencies and ill-targeted, but suitable reforms in this area are yet to be effectively implemented. Electricity charges and other user charges have since been in effect in most states of India. Notwithstanding the imperfections and inadequacies in the reforms of farm input subsidies, the direction of these reforms has been towards correction of inefficiencies of resource use. In this sense, the reforms should indeed be welcomed. However, these reforms also meant that the social cost in the form of negative externalities arising from input subsidization process were now being internalized and shifted to the farmers' accounts. This adversely impacted the financial performance of those farmers who were prime beneficiaries of the old subsidy regime. The decline in financial performance of these farms in turn adversely affected the balance sheets of banks that had lent to the farmers. On their part, banks started being wary of lending to these clients as, post-reforms, financial institutions were expected to adhere to more stringent prudential norms and show better financial performance of their own business.

Another factor which is believed to have contributed to the crisis was the slow-down of public investment in agriculture. Chand (2009) shows that from 1974 to 1980, real fixed capital formation in Indian agriculture grew rapidly at an annual compound rate of 8.9 per cent, with both public and private investment rising in tandem, and public investment taking the lead. But in the following decade, public sector investment declined steadily, and private sector invest-ment also decelerated somewhat, leaving agriculture as a whole with a marginally negative growth rate of real fixed capital formation. In the post-reform decade (1991–2001), the decline of public investment was arrested, and there was some increase in the growth rate of private sector investment, resulting in some revival in the growth of real gross fixed capital formation in agriculture. But the high rate of the 1970s, which presumably contributed immensely in the success of the Green Revolution, has not been revived. It is worth noting that the slowdown of public sector investment had been underway a decade before the market-oriented reforms were even launched. In the post-reform period, the decline was actually arrested, though not reversed in any significant manner.

A brief reference to the discourse on the nature of relation between public and private investment in Indian agriculture may be in order here before get-ting back to the causes and consequences of the decline in public investment in agriculture, particularly in the crucial component of major and medium irrigation projects. The rise in public and private investment in agriculture in the period leading up to 1980 induced many scholars to conclude that private investment in Indian agriculture enjoys significant complementarities with public investment in the sector, implying thereby that public investment actually 'crowds in' rather than 'crowds out' private investment (Shetty, 1990; Rao, 1994). It is not hard to understand that public investment in agricultural and rural infrastructure can induce complementary private investment. For instance, development of major and medium irrigation, which in the Indian context could take place through public investment, obviously induces private investment by farmers for develop-ing feeder channels and levelling of the land. But sustained growth of private investments in the subsequent period, despite the decline and stagnancy of pub-lic investment, indicates that private investment in more contemporary Indian agriculture is influenced by other independent factors, such as the movement of terms of trade (Gulati and Bathla, 2001). Moreover, to the extent that private investment in minor irrigation during this period had to be stepped up for aug-menting irrigation in the face of stagnancy, or even decline, of supply from state-owned major and medium irrigation systems, private investment at least in part took place in lieu of public investment.

Two important factors causing the stagnancy or even decline in public sector real investment discussed in the literature are not strictly economic in nature. Gulati and Narayanan (2003) point out that burgeoning subsidies in the post-Green Revolution period competed with scarce resources in the government budget. Given the political inexpediency of capping the subsidies and also con-taining the procurement prices, budget constraints of the government implied that capital expenditure had to be eased out. As stated in the Approach Paper to the Tenth Five Year Plan, 'subsidies have "crowded out" public agricultural investments in roads and irrigation and expenditure on technological upgrading' (Government of India, 2001, p. 26).

The other factor which discouraged and restricted public investment, especially in major and medium irrigation projects, is the forceful rise of environmentalist movements, domestic as well as foreign, against these systems during the 1980s. As Misra and Chand (1995, p. A-75) state, 'By obstructing the construction of these systems the domestic environmentalists incredibly added and continue to add to their gestation lags and thereby to the costs. Foreign environmentalists succeeded in stopping bilateral and multilateral aid or making its release conditional, including desired change in the design of the system. . . . Finally, incredible as it might seem, the federal character of the Indian state itself became a severe constraint on public capital formation in irrigation systems. The endemic problem of inter-state disputes about water sharing became more severe as political parties came increasingly to rule the states which were different from the party ruling at the centre'.

Notwithstanding the apprehension of environmentalists regarding major and medium irrigation projects, it is worth noting that the absence of capacity expansion in the major and medium irrigation sectors actually resulted in some serious environmental and economic costs. As farmers were required to depend on extraction of groundwater, the water tables started to go down rapidly, particularly in low recharge areas. This necessitated deepening of the borewells, frequently involving additional capital expenditure. Moreover, the cost of lifting the water from deeper levels also added to the operational costs. In short, the farmers got trapped in a mutually reinforcing downward spiral of lowering the groundwater tables and deepening the borewells. The need for repeated investment in deepening wells and more powerful water-lifting equipment just to extract the same or even lesser volume of water has been identified as a contributing factor to lowering of returns from cultivation and worsening of finances for farm households, accentuating the crisis in Indian agriculture (Reddy and Misra, 2009).

The other development which contributed to the agricultural crisis by increasing exposure of farmers to price uncertainties in the post-reform period is not directly related to India's domestic reforms but to implementation of international trade agreements involving India that came into force in the mid-1990s. Conclusion of the Uruguay Round of multilateral trade negotiation in 1994 and subsequent formation of the World Trade Organization (WTO), which would oversee implementation of the Uruguay Round agreements and other standing multilateral agreements under GATT, was initially received with considerable apprehension and public debate in India. The Agreements on Agriculture (AoA) for the first time brought international trade in agricultural products for negotiation under the GATT multilateral framework. In principle, AoA aimed to eliminate distortions[2] in agricultural trade by reducing subsidies on export and production and import barriers. In practice, this goal was to be achieved through tariffication (i.e., conversion of all non-tariff barriers to equivalent tariffs), tariff reduction, limitations on domestic support and phasing out of export subsidies.

Initially there was considerable apprehension in India about these agreements. It was feared that the requirement to limit domestic support to farmers would result in abandoning public procurement of food grains and the public distribution system. But it turned out that the prevailing domestic support to farmers in India was well within the permissible limits of aggregate measures of support.[3] The apprehensions then gave way to optimism regarding prospects of enhanced export of agricultural products, of which India had considerable stockpiles at that time (Gulati et al., 1999). But as India liberalized trade in agricultural goods, the country had to wake up to a rude shock when cheaper imported wheat and rice appeared in Indian markets. The government of India quickly moved to restrict the free import of food grains by requiring that import of such food grains would have to be canalized through the Food Corporation of India, the public sector agency dealing with procurement, storage and distribution of food grains across the nation. Though the farmers of the country producing food grains were thus protected from international competition, the incident exposed their lack of competitiveness, not just with the highly state-supported farmers of Europe and North America, but even with those from their fellow developing countries of Thailand and Vietnam.

While farmers growing food grains were shielded from external competition, not all crops could be protected from such exposure to freer international trade. The spice farmers of Kerala, for instance, were exposed to stiff international competition following India opening up trade in agricultural products under WTO obligation (Jeromi, 2007).

3 Farmers' suicides: the casualties and the causalities

A crisis had been brewing in Indian agriculture, putting its farmers under increasing stress. The gravity of the situation received due attention from the public and policy makers only when reports of farmers resorting to suicide started pouring in with alarming frequency from different parts of the country in the mid-1990s. The magnitude and pattern of this tragic phenomenon has since been extensively studied. Here we attempt to summarize the findings of some of these studies and add our own findings from updated data.

Most studies attempting to fathom the magnitude of the tragedy fall back on the same data source, namely, *Accidental Deaths & Suicides in India*(ADSI), an annual publication of the National Crime Records Bureau (NCRB) of the Ministry of Home Affairs, Government of India (http://ncrb.nic.in/accdeaths.htm). The reports present data on suicide mortality in fair amount of detail, with state-wise, gender-wise and occupation-wise classification since 1995. A general pattern revealed by the dataset is that suicide rates are generally higher among males than females across most categories, including farmers. The category 'farmers' comprises both cultivators and agricultural labourers. Data for the cultivators and the agricultural labourers are shown separately only from 2014.

Despite using the same set of data, researchers have come out with different estimates of suicide mortality rates (SMR) among farmers. Reddy and Misra (2009),

Nagraj (2008) and Mishra (2014), for instance, estimate SMR among farmers in India – male farmers in particular – to be much higher in all or most of the years since 1995. In contrast, more recent studies by Banarjee (2016) and Basu et al. (2016) find the SMR among farmers to be significantly lower than among the non-farmer population. These latter estimates are consistent with the findings drawn from a detailed countrywide sample survey by Patel et al. (2012). Our scrutiny of the results tends to suggest that Reddy and Misra (2009), Nagraj (2008) and Mishra (2014) overestimate the SMR of farmers by taking an inappropriately smaller denominator than the latter group.[4] Our estimates based on the same data source corroborate with those of Banarjee (2016) and Basu et al. (2016).

Contrary to popular impression and as shown in Figure 10.1, the SMR among male farmers has generally been significantly lower than that among their non-farming counterparts. It is arguable, therefore, that being used to coping with weather-related and other uncertainties, farmers are indeed more resilient than others and not prone to giving up easily. But the fact remains that despite their resilience, farmers in larger numbers and greater proportions took to taking their own lives during the decade from 1995 to 2004. Obviously the stress on India's agriculture sector and the resulting farmers' distress assumed a crisis proportion during that decade. Thereafter, even as the SMR among non-farmers continued to increase, the rate started declining for farmers, almost reaching the level of 1995 by 2013. Two factors seem to have contributed to this mitigating effect on the farmers' SMR after 2005. First, there was some recovery in the farmers' income growth (Chand, 2017, p. 4). Second, this period of decline of SMR corresponds to the years of implementation and expansion of the MGNREGA[5] programme meant to extend relief and work to rural households. Relief extended under the programme seems to have had some mitigating effect on the distress in agricultural households. Since 2014 the rate has increased a little again. In both the years of 2014 and 2015, farming and farmers were affected by adverse weather conditions. In particular, the rabi crop harvest was severely hit in 2015 by unseasonal rains and hailstorms in the pre-harvesting period in central and northern India (Bera, 2016).

For the two years of 2014 and 2015, the data on incidence of suicide are available separately for cultivators and agricultural labourers. We looked at the numbers to see if any further insights could be gathered about the phenomenon. Figure 10.2 reveals that the suicide rate is higher among cultivators than among agricultural labourers. This is understandable as the cultivators have to bear the whole uncertainty of their agricultural operations, from sowing to reaping and disposing of the produce. An agricultural labourer may also be adversely affected due to reduced availability of work during a downswing of agricultural operations. But their exposure to risk should be limited as receipts for their work delivered are assured by pre-decided contracts. Accordingly, a cultivator is more vulnerable to the vagaries of uncertainties inherent in agriculture than the agricultural labour. The point is further supported by the fact that SMR among cultivators shot up in 2015, a year in which harvests of rabi crops, including wheat, were badly affected by unexpected and severe weather conditions.

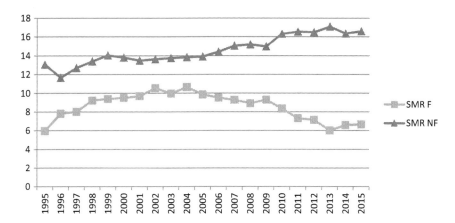

Figure 10.1 Estimated suicide mortality rates (suicide death per 100,000 of respective population) among male farmer and male non-farmer populations of India

Note: Data on number of suicides taken from *Accidental Deaths & Suicides in India*(ADSI), published annually by the National Crime Records Bureau (NCRB) of the Ministry of Home Affairs, Government of India. Basic population data are taken from Census of India reports. Population for inter-census years have been interpolated using the calculated annual compound growth rate during successive censuses. Populations for 2012 to 2015 are adjusted projected population figures after equalization of 2011 actual census and projected population figures of Census of India.

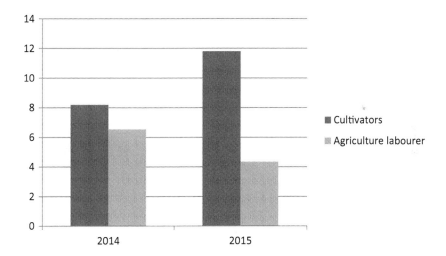

Figure 10.2 Suicide mortality rate among cultivators and agricultural labourers

Note: Data on number of suicides taken from *Accidental Deaths & Suicides in India*(ADSI), published annually by the National Crime Records Bureau (NCRB) of the Ministry of Home Affairs, Government of India. Basic population data are taken from Census of India reports. Population for inter-census years have been interpolated using the calculated annual compound growth rate during successive censuses. Populations for 2012 to 2015 are adjusted projected population figures after equalization of 2011 actual census and projected population figures of Census of India.

Going beyond the above-narrated countrywide trend and pattern of suicides among farmers, it is worthwhile to note that the intensity of the phenomenon and the underlying causal factors have been varied across different parts of the country. Incidences of farmers' suicides have been reported in larger numbers and relatively higher proportions from the states of Maharashtra, Andhra Pradesh, Karnataka, Kerala and Punjab. But the tragedy has by no means been confined to these states only. Farmers committing suicide have been found to be predominantly young males in the age group of 25 to 50 years. But they did not disproportionately belong to disadvantaged caste groups, nor were they disproportionately small and marginal farmers everywhere. While a multiplicity of factors seems to have conspired to compel farmers to take such an extreme course, one common factor associated with all such cases is high indebtedness, not necessarily to moneylenders, but also to other informal sources like friends and relatives and even to institutional sources like banks. Thus despondency due to high debt burden and a hopelessness regarding the prospect of repaying seem to be the common proximate cause of farmers' suicide. While the suicides almost invariably seem to be triggered by indebtedness, the underlying causes are found to be varied across regions and even from case to case within a region. But these factors can be traced to stresses that farmers in India are having to go through in the post-Green Revolution period.

In Green Revolution states like Punjab, the falling rate of returns from food grain production due to the rise in cost of cultivation, in which degradation of the natural resource base had a hand, has been reported as the prime cause of the crisis (Sidhu, 2002). The Approach Paper to the Tenth Five Year Plan elaborates, 'The intensity of private capital is increasing at a faster rate for Green Revolution areas and for large farmers. The weight of fertilizers, pesticides and diesel that accounted for mere 14.9 per cent of total inputs in 1970–71 in the country increased to 55.1 per cent in 1994–95. For a large farmer in commercialized region it could be as high as 70 per cent. . . . Whereas the need for resources to purchase these inputs has been increasing, the marketable surplus has been increasing at a slower rate to absorb this. It is not surprising that repayment of loans is such a problem in Indian agriculture and has even led to suicides in some cases' (Government of India, 2001, p. 28). This explanation corroborates with those found by scholars studying the phenomenon in Punjab (Gill and Singh, 2006).

Among cash crop growers of Maharashtra, Andhra Pradesh, Karnataka and Kerala, market and technology-related factors also have been at work. Many cotton growers in Vidarbha (Maharashtra) took to cultivation of high-cost Bt cotton even under unfavourable conditions, reportedly succumbing to the lure of aggressive marketing by Bt cotton seed companies. Government extension services, which should have educated farmers about the risks involved in using these varieties under their farming conditions and guided them through the process of adopting the new technology, were found to be absent. Farmers adopting such risky ventures had no support to fall back upon when their enterprises encountered problems. The plight of cotton growers was further compounded by a fall in the price of their produce due to a glut in the international market induced allegedly by manipulation by the United States (Meeta and Rajivlochan, 2006; Mishra, 2006). The spice farmers of Kerala also faced distress due to sudden exposure to international competition following India opening up trade in agricultural products under WTO obligation (Jeromi, 2007).

These stresses often reduce a farmer's threshold in coping with external shocks, and the prospect of poor rainfall or floods can be enough to push a vulnerable farmer over the edge (as was seen in the unseasonal heavy rains in the wheat harvesting season of 2015). Social factors such as worries about family obligations as well as loss of self-esteem and prestige in the society for defaulting on loans, especially those from friends and relatives (Dandekar and Bhattacharya, 2017), have also been found to push farmers to this extreme step in some cases.

It is often said that in this post-IT, post-globalization era, Indian society – especially its youth, has become highly inspirational. If so, the young Indian farmer cannot be expected to be an exception. But with the aspiration of moving up, many young farmers stepped into the pitfall of taking up highly risky ventures. Repeated failures in such ventures have pushed many to indebtedness to multiple lending sources, leaving no escape route out of the trap (Rao, 2009).

4 Conclusion: mitigating farmers' vulnerability

The high rate of farmers' suicides in the decade of 1995–2004 had the effect of drawing serious attention from researchers and policy makers to the long-brewing crisis in Indian agriculture. Though the suicide rates started receding in subsequent years, the resurgence of Indian agriculture is yet far from complete. Given the complexity of the tangle, policy measures required to put India's agriculture sector back on a resurgent track will have to be comprehensive. The National Commission on Farmers (NCF), constituted in November 2004 under the chairmanship of eminent agricultural scientist Professor M. S. Swaminathan, was mandated to go into the entire gamut of issues related to this crisis. The commission's recommendations, penned in its five reports submitted over the two years of 2005–06, form an extensive and comprehensive list of measures, starting from completing the long-pending land reform measures to enhancing social security arrangements for farmers (National Commission on Farmers, 2006). Comprehensive as the suggestions are, a strategic vision for getting farmers and farming in India back on track and ready to face emerging challenges of the 21st century was somewhat lost in the reports. Indeed some of the suggestions, such as benchmarking minimum support prices at 50 per cent above cost of cultivation and including agricultural laborers in the category of farmers, have been criticized for not being founded on adequate rationales (Chand, 2017, pp. 3–4). But a significant impact of these reports has been moving the focus of Indian agricultural policy from 'increasing production' to 'increasing farmers' welfare and income'. This shift of focus has since caught the imagination of policy makers and researchers, so much so that Prime Minister Narendra Modi in a public speech in 2015 announced a target of doubling the income of farmers by 2022, the year in which India will complete 75 years of independence from colonial rule.

The goal of increasing farmers' income and welfare, however, is not necessarily in conflict with the traditional goal of increasing agricultural production, especially of food grains, which was imperative in view of the chronic food shortages until the mid-1960s. But in the single-minded obsession with production growth, such concerns as longer-run sustainability of the natural resource base of agriculture and the need to raise the income of the farm households, perhaps did not receive the attention they deserved. To ensure that a sustained increase in the volume of farm production also gets translated to a sustained increase in farm income, several other conditions will have to be met. Some of these are (a) better resource use efficiency to keep the rise in cost of cultivation in check;(b) market outlets for farm produce to secure a remunerative price by farmers;(c) diversification of income sources in farm households through shifts in production composition towards potentially more rewarding activities, such as horticulture and livestock product and even to non-farm activities;(d) shift of population from farming to non-farm occupations, which in itself can increase the income of the farmers on a per capita basis; and (e) a mechanism to stabilize farm income and conserve farmers' credit worthiness through the cycles of good and bad years that agricultural production is typically subjected to. Several of these issues have been discussed in detail in different chapters of this volume. Consolidation of such discussion will be attempted in the concluding chapter. Here we confine our discussion to the limited point of stabilization of farm income through the weather-, nature- and/or market-generated ups and downs in agricultural production and prices.

One of the ways to protect farmers' income in the event of natural calamity or weather-related loss of production is to cover them under a programme of crop insurance. The possibility is worth some discussion as the Government of India brought out the much-publicized Pradhan Mantri Fasal Bima Yojana (PMFBY, or Prime Minister's Program/Scheme for Insuring Harvest) in January 2016. Just as individuals and organizations may seek to protect themselves from damage due to an unfavourable turn of events, such as fire, accident, sickness, etc., by buying insurance coverage in the market, it may seem feasible to protect farmers from the loss due to crop damage from unfavourable weather conditions, natural calamities or pest attacks by providing crop insurance. However, as these risks are usually covariate and not independent, that is, when one farmer in a particular area is affected other farmers are also likely to be affected, commercial insurers are likely to treat such risks as uninsurable. Thus state support is essential for such insurance to be available. Evaluation studies of crop insurance schemes in different countries have shown that such schemes have been financially burdensome and often unsustainable in both developing and developed countries (Skees et al., 1999). Moreover such government-supported schemes have also been prone to moral hazards with risky farmers and regions benefiting more at the expense of the government (Mcleman and Smit, 2006). Indian experience in this regard has not been spectacular either.

When a crop insurance scheme was introduced by the government of India in 1985, it was more an insurance for crop loans for banks rather than for farmers' income from crop failure. Whenever a crop loan was advanced, the bank would deduct the insurance premium from the principal. Thus, in the event the farmer was unable to repay the loan, the bank's investment was protected. For the farmer, this insurance only served the limited purpose of preserving his/her credit worthiness for the next round of crop loans. Subsequently, several schemes were introduced which were compulsory for a loanee farmer but open to non-loanee farmers too. In reality, participation by non-loanee farmers remained negligible. Even those who participated were mostly the large and medium farmers; the small and marginal farmers had virtually opted out of the program (Swain, 2013). The PMFBY of 2016 is cast more or less in the same mould, with the promise of nationwide coverage and procedural reforms for speedier settlement of claims. Government subsidies may be needed not only for keeping premiums within reach of the farmers but also to payout compensation in the event of an adverse state of nature. The professionalism and expertise of the financial institutions are to be brought in by getting banks and insurance companies to implement the scheme. Whether the new scheme will serve the purpose of protecting farmers from nature-induced crop failure better is to be seen only in the future. Given the experience of such schemes around the globe, it is difficult to be overly optimistic. Yet the scheme can be one of the components of a strategy for reducing farmers' exposure to production risk, along with measures that encourage farmers to diversify their income sources to include less risky activities, avail themselves more of irrigation to reduce dependence on rainfall, and adopt crops and varieties that are less prone to pest attacks and diseases.

For ensuring farmers remunerative prices for their produce, the National Commission for Farmers (2006) has recommended expanding the system of announcing minimum support prices for crops. When India introduced minimum support prices, backed up by the policy of public procurement of food grains in the mid-1960s, the policy served several useful purposes. It ensured a minimum price for wheat and rice growers, which encouraged them to go all out in adopting HYV seeds and make the Green Revolution a resounding success. It helped the government to build up a buffer stock for smoothing food grain supply in the country across the good and bad agricultural years. But the policy has been criticized for several undesirable consequences. While the government currently announces MSP for 23 crops, the minimum prices are guaranteed only for a few crops, like wheat, rice and cotton, which are procured by public agencies. Moreover, guaranteed minimum prices for rice and wheat have created a bias in favour of these two cereals at the expense of other important crops, such as pulses and oilseed. This induced bias in production pattern, especially towards water-intensive rice, has contributed to depletion of water resources, soil degradation and deterioration in water quality in some states like Punjab, which is traditionally not a rice-growing state (Government of India, 2001, p. 26; Singh and Kalra, 2002). Additionally, the price support mechanism has also discriminated against eastern states where procurement at the MSP is minimal or non-existent. Thus, in its present form, expansion of the price support system is neither desirable nor, as stated in a NITI Ayog document, feasible: 'It is neither possible nor desirable for the government to buy each commodity in each market in all regions. Financial cost of such a policy would place fiscal consolidation at risk and administrative burden would put challenge to the capacity of the bureaucracy' (NITI Ayog, 2015, p. 29). With suitable reforms the practice may be retained for some major crops and extended to cover pulses and oilseeds.

For other farm outputs, such as livestock and horticultural products, which are becoming increasingly important in view of recent patterns of diversification within the Indian farm sector and also the shift of consumer preference across all income strata, procurement-backed MSP may not be an effective way of mitigating price risk. Here, linking farmers to an organized post-harvest value chain can play an important role. The chain involves several links, from aggregation, storage and processing to retailing. Farmers may be inducted to a value chain through any or many of the alternative routes, such as a producer cooperative, a producer company, a contract farming agreement or simply direct retailing. Policy interventions are required for putting enabling infrastructure – such as connectivity and cold storage – and institutions in place. Lastly, anachronistic restrictions on movements of farm products leading to regional fragmentation of markets need to be replaced by policy measures for creation of common national agricultural markets.

Notes

1 Under Public Law 480, the United States used to provide food aid to countries, including India. Under the arrangement, popularized as "Food for Peace" under President John F. Kennedy, India received food supply from the United States until the mid-1960s, for which payments could be made in Indian rupees. During the tenure of President Lyndon B. Johnson, who succeeded Kennedy, supply from the source to India became virtually unavailable as a fall out of Cold War politics.
2 Distortions increase domestic production, reduce domestic consumption, increase exportable surpluses and depress global price. The result is inefficiency and income loss.
3 The issue resurfaced around the time of the Ninth Ministerial Conference of the WTO in Bali, Indonesia, in December 2013. The contention was about the way of calculating the aggregate measure of support. A decision on the issue was postponed. For further details on the subject, see Basnett (2013). According to Narayanan (2014), it may not be necessary for India to negotiate for special provision under the WTO to enable the National Food Security Act.
4 While the numerator is the number of suicides by male farmers, which includes both cultivators and agricultural laborers, the denominator seems to include only the male cultivator population in these estimations.
5 The Mahatma Gandhi National Rural Employment Guarantee Act (MGNREGA) of 2005 was initiated as a way of fulfilling the 'Right to Work' inducted earlier as a statute-guaranteed right in the Indian legal system. In effect, at least 100 days of wage employment in a financial year are guaranteed under the programme to every household whose adult members volunteer to do unskilled manual work. A secondary but significant aim of MGNREGA is to create durable public assets, such as village roads, by engaging the labour employed under it. Starting from 200 districts on 2 February 2006, the programme covered all the districts of India from 1 April 2008. Details can be accessed from http://nrega.nic.in. Despite reports

of some imperfections and leakages in implementation, the programme has been retained and expanded even after the change of government in New Delhi in 2014. Some of the loopholes have also been plugged by taking recourse to information technology for benefit transfer. The World Development Report 2014 hailed the programme as an interesting case of improving 'outreach to poor people living in rural areas through the introduction of government-to-person payments using a bank account' (World Bank, 2013, p. 30).

References

Balasubramanyam, V. N., 1984. *The Economy of India*, Weidenfeld and Nicolson, London.

Banarjee, D., 2016. *Inequality and Farmers' Suicides in India*. NIAS Working Paper: WP5-2016 National Institute of Advanced Studies, Indian Institute of Science Campus, Bengaluru.

Basnett, Y., 2013. *WTO Bali Declaration: What Does It Mean?* Available at www.odi. org.uk/opinion/8056-wto-bali-declaration-least-development-countries-trade-facilitation-agriculture-doha-round, accessed 06/12/2016.

Basu, D., Das, D. and Misra, K., 2016. *Farmer Suicides in India: Levels and Trends Across Major States, 1995–2011*. Working Paper 2016–01, University of Massachusetts – Amherst, available at http://scholarworks.umass.edu/econ_workingpaper, accessed 26/02/2017.

Bera, S., 2016. Crops Damaged in 6 States Due to Unseasonal Rains. *Live Mint*, available at www.livemint.com/Politics/nlfDP24oSqWripI1hwl6XI/Unseasonal rainsdamagecropsinsixstates.html, accessed 15/03/2016.

Bezbaruah, M. P., 1994. *Technological Transformation of Agriculture*, Mittal Publications, New Delhi.

Bezbaruah, M. P., 2014. Agricultural Development in India: Post-reform Experience. *Arthabeekshan*, 22(4), pp. 159–172.

Bidwai, P., 1988. India's Agriculture in Crisis: Wages of Ecological Devastation. *The Times of India*, February 20, New Delhi.

Chand, R., 2009. Capital Formation in Indian Agriculture: National and State Level Analysis. In Reddy, D. N. and Misra, S.(eds.), *Agrarian Crisis in India*, Oxford University Press, New Delhi, Ch.2.

Chand, R., 2017. Doubling Farmers' Income: Strategy and Prospect. *Indian Journal of Agricultural Economics*, 72(1), January–March, pp. 1–23.

Dandekar, A. and Bhattacharya, S., 2017. Lives in Debt: Narratives of Agrarian Distress and Farmer Suicides. *Economic and Political Weekly*, LII(21), May 27, pp. 77–84.

Gill, A. and Singh, L., 2006. Farmers' Suicides and Response of Public Policy: Evidence, Diagnosis and Alternatives From Punjab. *Economic and Political Weekly*, XLI(26), June 30, pp. 2762–2768.

Government of India, 2001. *Approach Paper to the Tenth Five Year Plan (2002–2007)*, Planning Commission, New Delhi.

Gulati, A. and Bathla, S., 2001. Capital Formation in Indian Agriculture: Re-Visiting the Debate. *Economic and Political Weekly*, 36(20), pp. 1697–1708.

Gulati, A., Mehta, R. and Narayanan, S., 1999. From Marrakesh to Seattle: Indian Agriculture in a Globalising World. *Economic and Political Weekly*. 34(41). pp. 2931–2942.

Gulati, A. and Narayanan, S., 2003. *The Subsidy Syndrome in Indian Agriculture*, Oxford University Press, New Delhi.

Jeromi, P. D., 2007. Farmers' Indebtedness and Suicides: Impact of Agricultural Trade Liberalization in Kerala. *Economic and Political Weekly*, 42(31), August 4, pp. 3241–3247.

Mcleman, R. and Smit, B., 2006. Vulnerability to Climate Change Hazards and Risks: Crops and Flood Insurance. *Canadian Geographer*, 50(2), pp. 217–226.

Mishra, S., 2006. *Suicide of Farmers in Maharashtra*, Indira Gandhi Institute of Development Research, Mumbai.

Mishra, S., 2014. *Farmers' Suicides in India, 1995–2012: Measurement and Interpretation*. Asia Research, Center Working Paper 62, London School of Economics.

Misra, S. N. and Chand, R., 1995. Private and Public Capital Formation in Indian Agriculture Comments on Complementarities Hypothesis and Others. *Economic and Political Weekly*, 30(24), pp. A-64–A-79.

Nagraj, K., 2008. *Farmers' Suicides in India: Magnitudes, Trends and Spatial Patterns*, available at www.macroscan.org/anl/mar08/pdf/farmers_suicides.pdf, accessed 09/04/2017.

Narayanan, S., 2014. The National Food Security Act vis-à-vis the WTO Agreement on Agriculture. *Economic & Political Weekly*, XLIX(5), February 1, pp. 40–46.

National Commission on Farmers, 2006. *Serving Farmers and Saving Farming: Towards Faster and More Inclusive Growth of Farmers' Welfare*, Ministry of Agriculture, Government of India, New Delhi.

NITI Aayog, 2015. *Raising Agricultural Productivity and Making Farming Remunerative for Farmers*. An Occasional Paper, Government of India, available at niti.gov.in/writereaddata/files/document_publication/RAP3.pdf, accessed 05/02/2017.

Panagariya, A., 2008. *India, the Emerging Giant*, Oxford University Press, Oxford.

Patel, V., Ramasundarahettige, C., Vijaykumar, L., Thakur, J. S., Gajalakshmi, V., Gururaj, G., Suraweera, W. and Jha, P., 2012. Suicide Mortality in India: A Nationally Representative Survey. *Lancet*, 379, pp. 2343–2351.

Rajivlochan, M., 2006. Farmers' Suicide: Facts and Possible Policy Interventions. *YASHADA*, available at www.yashada.org, accessed 25/04/2017.

Rao, C. H. H., 1994. *Agricultural Growth, Rural Poverty and Environmental Degradation in India*, Oxford University Press, New Delhi.

Rao, V. M., 2009. Farmers' Distress in a Modernizing Agriculture – The Tragedy of the Upwardly Mobile: An Overview. In Reddy, D. N. and Misra, S.(eds.), *Agrarian Crisis in India*, Oxford University Press, New Delhi, Ch.5.

Reddy, D. N. and Misra, S., 2009. Agriculture in the Reforms Regime. In Reddy, D. N. and Misra, S.(eds.), *Agrarian Crisis in India*, Oxford University Press, New Delhi, Ch.1.

Shetty, S. L., 1990. Investment in Agriculture, Brief Review of Recent Trends. *Economic and Political Weekly*, XXV(7–8), February 17–24, pp. 389–398.

Sidhu, D. S., 2002. Crisis in Agrarian Economy in Punjab: Some Urgent Steps. *Economic and Political Weekly*, 37(30), 27 July, pp. 3132–3138.

Singh, K. and Kalra, S., 2002. Rice Production in Punjab: Systems, Varietal Diversity, Growth and Sustainability. *Economic and Political Weekly*, 37(30), July 27, pp. 3139–3148.

Skees, J., Hazell, P. and Miranda, M., 1999. *New Approaches to Crop Yield Insurance in Developing Countries*. Environment and Production Technology Division

Discussion Paper No. 50, International Food Policy Research Institute, Washington, DC.

Swain, M., 2013. Agricultural Risk and Efficacy of Crop Insurance Schemes in Odisha. In Chandra, S. S., Babu, S. S. and Nath, P. K. (eds.), *Agrarian Crisis in India: The Way Out*, Academic Foundation, New Delhi, Ch.17.

World Bank, 2013. *World Development Report 2014: Risk and Opportunity – Managing Risk for Development*, World Bank, Washington, DC.

11 Shift of rural work force from farm to non-farm employment

Some determinants

Upasak Das and Udayan Rathore

1 Introduction

The stress that surfaced in Indian agriculture in the aftermath of the Green Revolution continued to increase in the post-reform period. This has been discussed in fair detail in the previous chapter. As the resulting farmers' distress assumed a crisis proportion by the mid-1990s, the growth of the rural non-farm sector emerged as an additional and alternative source of rural livelihood in the rural economy. The expansion of this sector opened up opportunities for gainful employment, especially for the young and the educated (Binswanger-Mkhize, 2012, p. 2). For example, there has been a substantial rise in non-agricultural sector employment due to a massive expansion in the construction sector, both in rural and urban areas (Chowdhury, 2011, p. 25). We postulate that since liberalization, these changes may have resulted in a movement of the work force away from agriculture to non-agricultural activities in the rural sector of the economy. In fact, census figures also suggest so. Between 2001 and 2011, the number of total workers engaged in agricultural activities declined by 3.2 percentage points. In this context, we use nationally representative individual-level data for 1993–94 and 2011–12 to identify the factors that influence the probability of a person remaining engaged in the agriculture sector in these two periods. Since policies need time to take root, it is highly unlikely that market conditions would have changed massively as compared to the pre-reform period in 1993–94. Thus, these data are expected to conform to the agrarian employment scenario before the reform process. The latter round was conducted in 2011–12 and is expected to capture the current scenario.

More specifically, we look at the age profile of the working individuals and examine whether they are likely to be engaged in agriculture and allied areas now (2011–12) as compared to the earlier years (1993–94). The underlying reasons for such preference deserve attention. In this chapter, we argue that one reason for movement out of agriculture and allied activities is possible preference for avoidance of the increased risk associated with agriculture, which has been magnified, especially after the introduction of hybrid seeds and fertilizers. Using a limited dependent variable regression model, we find that youths are more likely to be drawn towards working in the non-agricultural sector now as compared to earlier years.

The rest of the chapter proceeds as follows. Section 2 provides a detailed description about the data. Section 3 describes the variables used in the regression model. Section 4 presents the findings from descriptive statistics, graphical analysis and regression. Section 5 ends with a discussion of the findings and then concludes.

2 Data

We used publicly available data from the employment and unemployment schedule of the 50th and 68th rounds of the National Sample Survey (NSS), conducted by the Government of India for the years 1993–94 and 2011–12, respectively. The NSS survey is an individual-level nationally representative survey. The 68th round survey covered the whole of the Indian Union *except* (i) interior villages of Nagaland situated beyond five kilometres off the bus route and (ii) villages in Andaman and Nicobar Islands which remained inaccessible throughout the year. The number of households surveyed was 101,724, and the number of individuals surveyed was 456,999, including rural and urban sectors. From the rural areas, information for 59,700 households comprising a total of 280,763 individuals was gathered. The 50th round survey covers the whole of India except certain parts of the states of Nagaland, Andaman Nicobar Islands and Jammu and Kashmir. The survey covered 115,409 households consisting of 564,740 individuals from the two sectors. Information for 356,351 individuals from 69,230 households was collected from rural parts of the country. Both of the surveys are unique in the sense that they are designed to gauge the employment-unemployment scenario of the country with data on demographic characteristics, employment details and household consumption. The details of the 1993–94 and 2011–12 surveys are available in the respective survey reports (Government of India, 1997, 2013).

3 Variables

3.1 Outcome variable

The outcome variable of interest in this analysis is the likelihood of an individual residing in a rural area, in the age group 14 years to 60 years, of being predominantly engaged in the agricultural sector. We identify this by using the Usual Principal Status (USP) of each individual in the specified age group as collected by the survey. The USP informs about the activity status on which the individual spent his/her major time during the 365 days preceding the date of the survey. According to the schedules of the 50th and 68th round surveys, the broad activity statuses have been further sub-divided into several detailed activity categories. These are stated as follows:

(i) Working or being engaged in economic activity (engaged in labour):

(a) worked in household enterprise (self-employed) as an own-account worker
(b) worked in household enterprise (self-employed) as an employer
(c) worked in household enterprise (self-employed) as 'helper'

  (d) worked as regular wage/salaried employee
  (e) worked as casual wage labour in public works
  (f) worked as casual wage labour in other types of works

(ii) Not working

  (a) Did not get work but was available for working
  (b) attended educational institution
  (c) attended to domestic duties only
  (d) attended to domestic duties and was also engaged in free collection of goods,
  (e) tailoring, weaving, etc., for household use
  (f) recipient of rent, pension, remittance, etc.
  (g) not able to work due to disability
  (h) others

Out of all the working individuals (i.e., those engaged in economic activity), those engaged in agriculture and allied activities have been segregated according to the National Classification of Occupation (NCO). The 50th round of the NSS records the 1968 NCO codes, whereas the 68th round uses the 2004 NCO codes. These have been harmonized.

Individuals recorded as cultivators, farmers, agricultural labourers, plantation labourers and related workers, other farm workers, forestry workers, hunters and related workers, and fishermen and related workers are taken as those engaged in agriculture and allied activities and are coded as 1 (as described in the NSS data). Those working individuals not falling into these NCO codes are coded as 0. Given this categorization, we estimate the probability of a rural working individual in the age group of 14–60 years of being mainly employed in the agriculture sector. Besides this, we take all the working individuals in the age group 14–60 years who are self-employed and estimate the probability of them being engaged in agriculture. An individual is allocated a code of 1 if he/she is self-employed in agriculture and a code of 0 if he/she is self-employed in a non-agricultural sector. Similarly, we separate all the individuals in the specified age group who are working as casual wage labourers and estimate the probability of them being an agricultural labourer. An individual is allocated a code of 0 if he/she is working as a casual labourer in a non-agriculture sector and a code of 1 if he/she is in the agricultural sector.

3.2 *Variables of interest and other controls*

The probability of a rural working person being engaged in agriculture or his/her movement away from agriculture to a non-agriculture sector could be conditional upon several factors. We hypothesize that in the post-liberalization era, since the non-farm sector has offered more diversified opportunities, which are generally less risky than agricultural sector, the younger generations are more driven towards the non-farm sector. Hence one of our primary variables of interest is age. To gauge the heterogeneous association of movement away from agriculture with different age groups, we created age bands as follows:

(i)   14 to 20 years
(ii) 21 to 30 years
(iii) 31 to 40 years
(iv) 41 to 50 years
(v)   51 to 60 years (taken as the reference group in the regression model).

These age bands are introduced in the regression as dummies. We start from 14 years of age since in India a labourer is not considered as a child labourer if he/she is 14 years or above. Sixty years was chosen as the upper limit because it is the retirement age in many of the formal sectors in India.

We add other possible factors which may affect the likelihood of moving away from agriculture. Since the focus of our study is rural areas, it can be broadly considered that the status quo occupation of an individual could be to be engaged in some activities associated with agriculture. We argue that if the conditions or the factors are conducive to the individual, he/she would prefer to leave working in agriculture and allied work and move into the non-agricultural sector. Accordingly, we incorporate independent controls which might affect this movement from agriculture to the non-agriculture sector, making use of published literature on the determinants of individual labour participation taking the Indian context into consideration (Ferber, 1982; Powers, 2003; Faridi et al., 2009). The group of independent variables can be divided into two types: variables pertaining to individual characteristics and those pertaining to the household. The former include gender dummy, marital status dummy and educational dummies (illiterate [taken as reference], below primary, primary and middle, secondary, above secondary). These three factors become important in terms of whether an individual would work in a non-agricultural occupation, which generally are not in close vicinity to the place of residence in the village. An individual might also have to commute daily to the peripheral urbanized area for non-agricultural work like construction or assisting shop owners, among others.

In terms of household characteristics, dummies for caste and religion are used. These are important because caste/social groups may form a basis of social connection and networks in the job market through referrals (Munshi 2003; Munshi and Rosenzweig, 2016). Among the other household-level variables, household size, gender of the household head, and education level of the household head are included as controls (education categories for household head are taken similarly as explained earlier). Household type, which indicates the main occupation of the household, is also taken as the control. The categories are as follows: self-employed in agriculture (reference group), agricultural labour, non-agricultural labour, self-employed in non-agriculture and others (including regular wage). To control for state-level factors, state fixed effects have been used in the model. The district-level heterogeneities have been controlled for by taking standard errors clustered at the district level in the regression model. Of note is the fact that these can act as indicators of how non-agricultural opportunities are flourishing at the state and district level.

Since the outcome variables in all the regression models are dichotomous in nature, we use Probit regressions. Estimation in Probit regression is performed through the maximum likelihood method.

4 Results

4.1 Descriptive statistics

Table 11.1 lists all the variables used in the regression, along with the mean/proportion for the total rural working population in the age group 14–60 years for the 50th round (1993–94). It further gives the mean/proportion of the variables across two groups: those working in non-agriculture and those working in agriculture, also showing if the differences across the groups are statistically significant.

We find the proportion of youths in the age group 14–20 years working in agriculture is significantly higher than that for those working in the non-agricultural sector. This indicates that the young population was still drawn towards agricultural works back in 1993–94. However, as the age band increased, the proportion in the non-agriculture sector becomes significantly higher than the proportion in agriculture, indicating that with age people tended to move towards the more-profitable off-farm sector. However at higher ages (above 50 years), the pattern reverses, as we find more individuals likely to work in the agricultural sector.

As far as the data from 2011–12 are concerned, we find only 8 per cent of the individuals engaged in agriculture belong to the age group 14 to 20 years, as against about 16 per cent in 1993–94 (refer to Table 11.2). For individuals in the age group 21 to 30 years, it is only 25.5 per cent in 2011–12 in comparison to 29.4 per cent in 1993–94. Further, Figure 11.1 suggests that the percentages of individuals working in the agricultural and allied sector in 1993–94 in all the age groups are higher as compared to those in 2011–12. Of note is the fact that the difference in proportion of younger individuals (14–20 years and 21–30 years) engaged in agriculture between 1993–94 and 2011–12 is the highest among all age groups. This indicates that younger populations have increasingly moved away from working in agriculture and allied areas to the non-agricultural sector.

In terms of other variables, females are more likely to be in the agricultural sector in both years. Also, more-educated individuals are highly drawn towards the non-agricultural sector. The proportion of Muslims working in the non-agricultural sector is significantly higher in comparison to that for those working in the agricultural sector. This may be due to the fact that Muslims have fewer land holdings on average. The tribal groups are found to be more engaged in agriculture in both the earlier and recent years. Individuals belonging to SC had earlier significantly engaged in agricultural work; however, in recent years they have shifted substantially to non-agricultural work.

Table 11.1 Descriptive statistics (1993–94)

	Total	Not in agriculture	In agriculture	Difference
	(1)	*(2)*	*(3)*	*(2)-(3)*
Individual characteristics				
Age bands				
14–20 years	0.158	0.123	0.157	−0.034*
21–30 years	0.300	0.321	0.294	0.027*
31–40 years	0.250	0. 280	0.240	0.039*
41–50 years	0.179	0. 184	0.183	0.0004
51–60 years	0.113	0.092	0.125	−0.033*
Female	0.291	0.173	0.313	−0.141*
Married	0.766	0.755	0.766	−0.010*
Education				
Illiterate	0.540	0.275	0.549	−0.275*
Below primary	0.129	0.127	0.131	−0.003
Primary and middle	0.229	0.307	0.234	0.072*
Secondary	0.057	0.139	0.052	0.087*
Above secondary	0.045	0.152	0.033	0.119*
Household characteristics				
Caste				
ST	0.125	0.099	0.170	−0.071*
SC	0.209	0.165	0.176	−0.011*
Upper caste	0.666	0.736	0.654	0.081*
Religion				
Hindu	0.876	0.799	0.829	−0.031*
Muslim	0.075	0.111	0.059	0.053*
Others	0.049	0.091	0.112	−0.022*
Household type				
Self-employed in non-agriculture	0.120	0.380	0.028	0.352*
Agricultural labour	0.319	0.057	0.309	−0.251*
Non-agricultural labour	0.079	0.198	0.029	0.169*
Self-employed in agriculture	0.415	0.134	0.596	−0.463*
Others	0.067	0.231	0.038	0.193*
Household size (mean)	5.662	5.884	6.134	−0.250*
Household head characteristics				
Female head	0.061	0.064	0.061	0.003
Education				
Illiterate	0.558	0.338	0.565	−0.227*
Below primary	0.160	0.167	0.160	0.007*
Primary and middle	0.206	0.279	0.208	0.070*
Secondary	0.044	0.106	0.041	0.065*
Above secondary	0.033	0.111	0.026	0.085*
Observations	124,798	31,348	93,353	

Note: * indicates significance at 5 per cent level.

Source: Authors' calculation based on the employment-unemployment schedule of the 50th round (1993–94).

Table 11.2 Descriptive statistics (2011–12)

	Total	Not in agriculture	In agriculture	Difference
	(1)	*(2)*	*(3)*	*(2)-(3)*
Individual characteristics				
Age bands				
14–20	0.090	0.066	0.078	−0.012*
21–30	0.267	0.277	0.255	0.022*
31–40	0.293	0.309	0.272	0.037*
41–50	0.217	0.228	0.231	−0.003
51–60	0.133	0.120	0.164	−0.044*
Female	0.242	0.159	0.328	−0.169*
Married	0.839	0.83	0.849	−0.019*
Education				
Illiterate	0.335	0.176	0.309	−0.133*
Below primary	0.122	0.094	0.119	−0.025*
Primary and middle	0.318	0.331	0.335	−0.004
Secondary	0.114	0.153	0.128	0.025*
Above secondary	0.111	0.249	0.111	0.138*
Household characteristics				
Caste				
ST	0.129	0.156	0.215	−0.059*
SC	0.209	0.182	0.147	0.035*
OBC	0.440	0.398	0.39	0.008*
Upper caste	0.222	0.264	0.248	0.016*
Religion				
Hindu	0.852	0.749	0.79	−0.041*
Muslim	0.104	0.138	0.077	0.061*
Others	0.045	0.113	0.134	−0.021*
Household type				
Self-employed in non-agriculture	0.154	0.407	0.084	0.323*
Agricultural labour	0.224	0.016	0.158	−0.142*
Non-agricultural labour	0.137	0.227	0.058	0.169*
Self-employed in agriculture	0.385	0.066	0.606	−0.540*
Others	0.101	0.284	0.094	0.190*
Household size (mean)	5.189	5.184	5.727	−0.543*
Household head characteristics				
Female head	0.078	0.081	0.072	0.009*
Education				
Illiterate	0.414	0.266	0.360	−0.094*
Below primary	0.143	0.127	0.147	−0.020*
Primary and middle	0.278	0.302	0.305	−0.003
Secondary	0.089	0.129	0.106	0.023*
Above secondary	0.077	0.177	0.082	0.095*
Observations	93,250	49,576	43,674	

Note: * indicates significance at 5 per cent level.

Source: Authors' calculation based on the employment-unemployment schedule of the 68th round (2011–12).

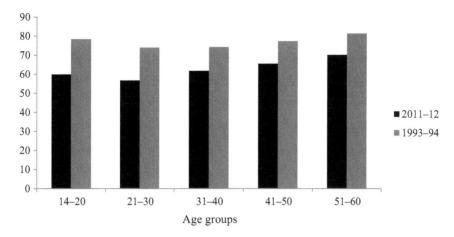

Figure 11.1 Distribution of rural workers (14 to 60 years) in agricultural and allied areas

Source: Authors' calculation based on 50th round and 68th round data

4.2 Regression results

Table 11.3 presents the regression results for both the 50thand 68th rounds. The table contains all three types of regressions indicated earlier for both the rounds:

(i)   Estimation of the probability of working in agriculture and allied areas versus working in non-agriculture
(ii) Estimation of the probability to be engaged as a self-employed individual in agriculture and allied areas versus being self-employed in non-agriculture
(iii) Estimation of the probability to be engaged as a labourer in agriculture and allied areas versus being a casual labour in non-agriculture

   Estimations from the 1993–94 (50th round) dataset (columns (1), (2) and (3)) suggest that individuals in the younger age bands were significantly less likely to be engaged in agriculture on a whole and also as self-employed or casual labourers in comparison to the individuals in the highest age band (51 to 60 years). However, coefficients for the individuals in the youngest age group (14–20 years) are found to be statistically indistinguishable from zero, indicating they were not less likely to be engaged in agricultural activities as compared to older individuals. However, in 2011–12 (indicated by columns (4), (5) and (6)) all the individuals in the younger age band are significantly less likely to be engaged in agricultural and allied areas as self-employed individuals as well as casual labours. This holds for individuals in the youngest age band also. The significant movement of the youngest age band away from agricultural and allied activities in the recent period could possibly be attributed to increased risks and vulnerability in the agricultural sector with lower relative profitability. This has been argued in a number of

Table 11.3 Regression results: estimated probability of rural, working individuals (14 to 60 years) to be employed in agricultural and allied areas (1993–94 and 2011–12)

	1993–94 (50th round)			2011–12 (68th round)		
	All	Self employed	Labourer	All	Self employed	Labourer
	(1)	(2)	(3)	(4)	(5)	(6)
Individual characteristics						
Age band (ref. 51–60 years)						
14–20 years	-0.009	-0.016***	-0.033***	-0.017**	-0.025***	-0.018*
	(0.006)	(0.004)	(0.009)	(0.007)	(0.007)	(0.010)
21–30 years	-0.025***	-0.035***	-0.031***	-0.032***	-0.046***	-0.038***
	(0.004)	(0.003)	(0.007)	(0.005)	(0.005)	(0.010)
31–40 years	-0.025***	-0.025***	-0.020***	-0.049***	-0.057***	-0.037***
	(0.004)	(0.004)	(0.005)	(0.004)	(0.005)	(0.010)
41–50 years	-0.019***	-0.013***	-0.010	-0.037***	-0.039***	-0.025**
	(0.004)	(0.003)	(0.006)	(0.004)	(0.004)	(0.010)
Female	0.050***	0.017*	0.055***	0.139***	0.078***	0.187***
	(0.013)	(0.010)	(0.008)	(0.005)	(0.006)	(0.011)
Married/Others	0.019***	0.017***	0.010**	0.002	-0.007	0.019**
	(0.004)	(0.004)	(0.004)	(0.005)	(0.007)	(0.009)
Education (ref. Illiterate)						
Below primary	-0.037***	-0.021***	-0.017***	-0.045***	-0.034***	-0.011
	(0.004)	(0.004)	(0.004)	(0.007)	(0.007)	(0.012)
Primary and middle	-0.070***	-0.038***	-0.033***	-0.081***	-0.041***	-0.034***
	(0.005)	(0.004)	(0.005)	(0.005)	(0.005)	(0.008)
Secondary	-0.170***	-0.073***	-0.067***	-0.120***	-0.058***	-0.049***
	(0.008)	(0.005)	(0.011)	(0.006)	(0.007)	(0.009)
Above secondary	-0.262***	-0.090***	-0.068***	-0.204***	-0.083***	-0.059***
	(0.014)	(0.008)	(0.015)	(0.007)	(0.008)	(0.016)

Household characteristics

Caste (ref. Upper caste)

	(1)	(2)	(3)	(4)	(5)	(6)
ST	0.027*** (0.008)	0.025*** (0.008)	0.023** (0.011)	0.030*** (0.006)	0.037*** (0.005)	0.026* (0.014)
SC	0.002 (0.006)	-0.013*** (0.005)	0.024*** (0.007)	-0.006 (0.005)	-0.017*** (0.006)	0.035*** (0.009)
OBC				0.012*** (0.004)	0.001 (0.004)	0.035*** (0.010)
Religion (ref. Hindus)						
Muslim	-0.036*** (0.008)	-0.030*** (0.007)	-0.026** (0.012)	-0.057*** (0.006)	-0.056*** (0.008)	-0.030*** (0.009)
Others	0.025*** (0.007)	0.017** (0.007)	0.025*** (0.008)	0.012* (0.008)	-0.003 (0.009)	0.006 (0.023)
Household type (ref. self-employed in non-agriculture)						
Agriculture labour	0.687*** (0.013)	0.526*** (0.018)	0.278*** (0.023)	0.695*** (0.006)	0.496*** (0.027)	0.457*** (0.014)
Non-agriculture labour	0.089*** (0.023)	0.518*** (0.025)	-0.356*** (0.035)	0.695*** (0.006)	0.496*** (0.027)	0.457*** (0.014)
Self-employed in agriculture	0.706*** (0.012)	0.776*** (0.025)	0.064** (0.031)	0.703*** (0.006)	0.775*** (0.027)	0.026 (0.021)
Regular wage/salary/ others	0.238*** (0.019)	0.605*** (0.010)	0.048 (0.035)	0.097*** (0.005)	0.516*** (0.005)	-0.005 (0.014)
Household size	-0.001*** (0.000)	-0.001** (0.000)	-0.003*** (0.001)	0.009*** (0.001)	0.006*** (0.001)	0.002 (0.002)

(Continued)

Table 11.3 (Continued)

	1993–94 (50th round)			2011–12 (68th round)		
	All	Self employed	Labourer	All	Self employed	Labourer
	(1)	(2)	(3)	(4)	(5)	(6)
Household head characteristics						
Female head	−0.010*	−0.000	−0.020***	−0.036***	−0.015**	−0.049***
	(0.005)	(0.006)	(0.006)	(0.006)	(0.007)	(0.008)
Education of head (ref. illiterate)						
Below primary	0.001	0.002	−0.002	0.020***	0.011*	0.012
	(0.004)	(0.005)	(0.005)	(0.005)	(0.006)	(0.012)
Primary and middle	0.005	0.010**	0.001	0.030***	0.015***	0.014**
	(0.004)	(0.004)	(0.006)	(0.004)	(0.006)	(0.007)
Secondary	0.009	0.015***	0.005	0.033***	0.016**	0.013
	(0.006)	(0.006)	(0.011)	(0.006)	(0.008)	(0.011)
Above secondary	0.010	0.020***	−0.036	0.042***	0.023**	−0.008
	(0.007)	(0.005)	(0.025)	(0.008)	(0.009)	(0.012)
State dummies	Yes	Yes	Yes	Yes	Yes	Yes
Observations	1,24,683	74,782	38,227	93,204	53,963	23,595
Pseudo R²	0.483	0.580	0.507	0.467	0.572	0.511
Log pseudo-likelihood	−36356.15	−15304.84	−8939.962	−34359.269	−15497.568	−7912.596

Note: Marginal effects are presented in the table. The standard errors clustered at district level are given in the parenthesis. The unit of regression is rural, working individuals in the age group 14 to 60 years. * $p < 0.10$, ** $p < 0.05$, *** $p < 0.01$.

Source: Based on authors 'calculations using NSS 50th and 68th round survey data.

studies from India and outside (Ahaibwe et al., 2013, p. 6; Gupta, 2005, p. 761; Leavy and Hossain, 2014, p. 1; Sharma, 2007, p. 27).

In terms of other controls, females in 1993–94 as well as in 2011–12 are more likely to work in agricultural and allied areas. Married individuals who were highly likely to work in agricultural sector earlier are no more drawn towards the agricultural sector. The reason for this is probably because marriage involves dependency and financial constraints which may not be fulfilled if one works in the less-profitable agricultural sector. This again implies increased movement away from agriculture due to the high risk and vulnerability along with less profitability.

As expected, educated individuals sought to move out from agriculture to non-agricultural work, and this holds true even now as well. Individuals belonging to tribal groups (STs) are significantly likely to be engaged in agriculture and allied areas; however, Muslims were less likely, as inferred from Tables 11.1 and 11.2.

4.3 Local polynomial regression

Analysis through traditional regressions through structured equations have many advantages, one of the main being the ability to control for a host of factors that may affect the individual choice of engaging in agricultural and allied work. However, one main disadvantage of regression, including Probit models, is the fact that it gives out average effects, and one is not being able to gauge the association throughout the distribution of an independent variable. Though in our analysis, for this specific reason, we categorized age into five bands, it may not be possible for us to look at the heterogeneous association, if any, within the age bands. For this purpose, we use local polynomial regression to examine the relationship between the probability of rural, working individuals in the age group of 14 to 60 years to be engaged in agricultural and allied areas and their age. Local polynomial regression uses a non-parametric kernel-weighted local polynomial regression of the dependent variable on an independent variable and displays a graph of the smoothed values with (optional) confidence bands. The methodology has been developed by Fan and Gijbels (1996).

Figure 11.2 presents the plot from the local polynomial regression for the year 1993–94. It is found from the plot that starting from 14 years, the probability of being employed in agriculture is almost constant. It is only after an age of around 20 years that the probability starts falling, and then after 40 years, it starts increasing once more.

Figure 11.3, which presents the local polynomial regression plot for 2011–12, suggests that the probability for all individuals to be engaged in agriculture is low as compared to that for 1993–94. Further it is observed that individuals even at lower ages of around 14 years are drawn away from agriculture to get employment in the non-agricultural sector. These findings are similar to those obtained from the regression estimates and hence can be considered robust.

Anecdotal evidence from field surveys conducted by us at various times from 2012 to 2015 in various parts of the country indicates findings similar to the ones inferred. For example, a rickshaw van puller in the Haldibari block of the Cooch Behar district of West Bengal back in 2012 said that agriculture was no

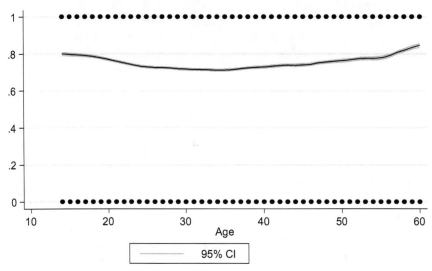

Figure 11.2 Local polynomial regression plot for 1993–94

Source: Authors' calculation based on 50th round of NSS data.

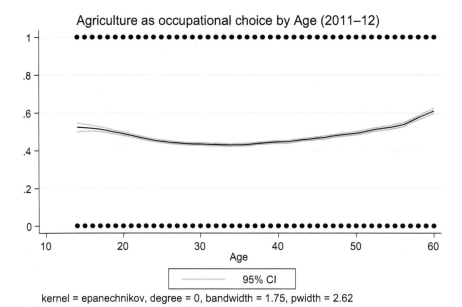

Figure 11.3 Local polynomial regression plot for 2011–12

Source: Authors' calculation based on 68th round of NSS data

longer profitable and had been plagued with various issues, including rising input costs. Hence, despite owning more than four acres of cultivable land, he earned more as a rickshaw puller and would migrate to Kerala for construction work in the coming year (2013). Similarly, a young individual of 15 years of age from the Udaipur block of the Surguja district of Chhattisgarh said that after completion of secondary examinations, he was unwilling to follow the footsteps of his father, who was engaged in agriculture and cultivated about five acres of land. The individual mentioned the vagaries in weather and rising input costs, which had negatively affected profitability in agriculture. Hence he was willing to commute daily to an adjoining urban area (the city of Ambikapur) for work. Likewise, a young mother of two from the Araria district in Bihar suggested that in recent years the burden of agricultural effort disproportionately fell on females in the household. She attributed this to increased uncertainties associated with agriculture. This, as per her account, was attributable to increase in male migration, especially towards the construction sector in Punjab and Haryana and had an adverse impact on the health of women in her village. It should be noted that in our regressions, females have been found to be more likely to work in agriculture as compared to males, even after controlling for other factors.

5 Conclusion

In the post-liberalization era, employment opportunities in the non-farm sector have increased, especially for the young and educated (Binswanger-Mkhize, 2012, p. 2). Moreover, owing to increasing vulnerability in the agriculture sector on account of a host of reasons (Mishra, 2008, p. 50), agricultural employment, as self-employed or as labour, has increasingly become less lucrative, driving people, especially younger ones, away from agriculture (Ahaibwe et al., 2013, p. 6; Gupta, 2005, p. 761; Leavy and Hossain, 2014, p. 1; Sharma, 2007, p. 27).

In this chapter, we substantiate these claims by using two nationally representative rounds of the NSS data for the years 1993–94 and 2011–12. Using Probit and local polynomial regressions, we find that the probability of being employed in the agricultural sector across different age groups vis-à-vis the group in age band 51 to 60 years declined across the duration of the study. Moreover, this is particularly true for rural youth, who are increasingly moving away from agricultural occupation. Also, we find that access to education is associated with a reduced likelihood being employed in the agricultural sector. Anecdotal evidence from the field reinforces these findings. In addition, just as in 1993–94, females are more likely than males to be employed in agriculture.

It might be argued that such a trend of movement away from agriculture is a harbinger of a much-needed change in Indian agriculture, given that the sector accounts for about 18 per cent of the gross domestic product (GDP) but about 47 per cent of employment (The Economic Survey, 2015–16, p. 83, 120). However, it is rather important to distinguish between the movement that emanates from rising literacy, aspirations and employability in other sectors as against decline in agricultural profitability and the rise in agrarian distress. The former may lead to increased capital investments and rise in wages in agriculture, whereas the latter is likely to result in the opposite, thus endangering the long-term food security of India. In this light, the chapter might be considered as a base for further examination of this paramount question.

References

Ahaibwe, G., Mbowa, S. and Lwanga, M. M., 2013. *Youth Engagement in Agriculture in Uganda: Challenges and Prospects.* Unpublished Thesis, Makerere University, pp. 1–48.

Binswanger-Mkhize, H. P., 2012. *India 1960–2010: Structural Change, the Rural Non-Farm Sector, and the Prospects for Agriculture, Department of Agricultural and Resource Economics,* University of California, Berkeley, CA, May, available at http://are.berkeley.edu/documents/seminar/Binswanger.pdf.

Chowdhury, S., 2011. Employment in India: What Does the Latest Data Show? *Economic and Political Weekly,* 46(32), pp. 23–26.

Economic Survey, 2015. Government of India, Ministry of Finance, Department of Economic Affairs, Ch. 5, New Delhi.

Fan, J. and Gijbels, I., 1996. *Local Polynomial Modelling and Its Applications,* Chapman and Hall, New York.

Faridi, M. Z., Chaudhry, I. S. and Anwar, M., 2009. The Socio-Economic and Demographic Determinants of Women Work Participation in Pakistan: Evidence From Bahawalpur District. *South Asian Studies,* 24(2), pp. 353–369.

Ferber, M. A., 1982. Labour Market Participation of Young Married Women: Causes and Effects. *Journal of Marriage and Family,* 44(2), pp. 457–468.

Government of India, 1997. *Employment and Unemployment in India, 1993–94.* National Sample Survey Organization, Ministry of Statistics and Programme Implementation Report 409.

Government of India, 2013. *Key Indicators of Employment and Unemployment in India, 2011–12.* National Sample Survey Organization, Ministry of Statistics and Programme Implementation Report KI (68/10).

Gupta, D., 2005. Whither the Indian Village: Culture and Agriculture in 'rural' India. *Economic and Political Weekly,* 40(8), pp. 751–758.

Leavy, J. and Hossain, N., 2014. Who Wants to Farm? Youth Aspirations, Opportunities and Rising Food Prices. *IDS Working Papers,* 2014(439), pp. 1–44.

Mishra, S., 2008. Risks, Farmers' Suicides and Agrarian Crisis in India: Is There a Way Out? *Indian Journal of Agricultural Economics,* 63(1), pp. 38–54.

Munshi, K., 2003. Networks in the Modern Economy: Mexican Migrants in the U.S. Labor Market. *Quarterly Journal of Economics,* 118(2), pp. 549–599.

Munshi, K. and Rosenzweig, M., 2016. Networks and Misallocation: Insurance, Migration, and the Rural-Urban Wage Gap. *The American Economic Review,* 106(1), pp. 46–98.

Powers, E. T., 2003. Children's Health and Maternal Work Activity: Static and Dynamic Estimates Under Alternative Disability Definitions. *Journal of Human Resources,* 38(3), pp. 522–556.

Sharma, A., 2007. The Changing Agricultural Demography of India: Evidence From a Rural Youth Perception Survey. *International Journal of Rural Management,* 3(1), pp. 27–41.

12 Environmental consequences of the Green Revolution in India[1]

Surya Bhushan

1 Introduction

In its simplest form, agricultural production activity can be visualized as a system wherein biotic resources (primarily domesticated crops and animals, but also soil micro-organisms) interact with abiotic resources (such as the atmosphere, soil, water and energy). The Green Revolution (GR), implemented in the mid-1960s in India, intensified the agricultural production system through an increase in the use of modern inputs, such as high-yielding varieties (HYVs) seeds, agro-chemicals like fertilizers, pesticides, assured irrigation and agricultural machinery. These inputs are used to create more optimal conditions for crops than nature can offer.[2] In other words, irrigate if it is dry; fertilize if soil fertility is low; spray or dust if pests and weeds invade crops; or mechanize and use fossil fuels if more energy is needed to till the land.

GR-induced agriculture intensifies and extensifies the interactions among the biotic and abiotic constituents of resources, such as people, land, water, biodiversity and air (climate), and in the process both causes and suffers from environmental degradation. As a result of GR-induced agriculture, agriculture has become the largest consumer of water and accounts for 70–90 per cent of freshwater withdrawals from rivers, lakes and aquifers in some developing countries (UNESCO, 2009, p. 98); the main source of nitrate pollution of groundwater and surface water (i.e., eutrophication); and the principal source of ammonia and phosphate pollution of waterways and of the release of greenhouse gases (GHGs; 15 per cent) methane and nitrous oxide into the atmosphere. The positive spillovers of agriculture, on the other hand, are the provision of environmental services and amenities, for example through water storage and purification, carbon sequestration and the maintenance of rural landscapes. Further, research-driven intensification saves 'new land from conversion to agriculture, a known source of greenhouse gas emissions and driver of climate change' (Pingali, 2012, p. 12304).

There is a litany of evidence from the literature (see Table 12.1), with case studies based on field experiments that focus on the environmental impacts associated with agriculture in general and modern technologies (such as HYVs, irrigation, chemical fertilizers and pesticides) in particular, both in industrialized and

Table 12.1 Estimates of negative externalities of productivity-enhancing technology in developing countries: evidence from the literature

Negative Externality	Evidence	Estimates of area/extent of a given problem	Environmental/economic implications
Genetic variability	Some evidence, but not substantiated	No quantitative estimates available	Biodiversity loss; declining crop yield
Salinity and waterlogging	Evidence of this problem in irrigated areas available and well documented	45 million ha globally suffer from salinity and water logging problems	Land abandoned; declining land productivity
Groundwater table	Mixed evidence of both increase and decrease in water table level is found in the literature; evidence scattered and location specific.	Water table increase reported in the range of 0.1 to 3.0 meters per year in some irrigated project areas. Reported water table decline range from 0.4 to 1.0 meters per year in some regions.	Declining land productivity
Soil erosion	Evidence found for rice production and soil erosion in Asia; evidence of such linkages in other crops not substantiated	Sporadic local estimates available, but no global estimates available	Declining land productivity
Water pollution	Most evidence found in developed countries; scattered evidence in less developed countries (LDCs)	Sporadic local estimates are available, but global estimates are available	Increased health costs; loss of aquatic flora and fauna
Air pollution	Discussed but not substantiated in LDCs	No global quantitative estimates available	Increased health costs; lower factor productivity
Impacts on human and animal health due to pests	Case-specific evidence on this linkage available. Most evidence relates to pesticides and their health effects.	Globally, 3 million cases of pesticide poisoning each year, resulting in 220,000 deaths	Increased health costs and social/economic costs associated with lower labour productivity

Source: Adapted from FAO, 2001 (p. 6).

in developing countries, including India (e.g., Conway and Pretty, 1991; Sehgal and Abrol, 1994; Pingali et al., 1997; Pingali and Rosegrant, 1994; Joshi, 1987; Chopra, 1989; Abler et al., 1994; Singh and Singh, 1995; Tilman et al., 2001; Singh et al., 2002).

In the context of India, the country has witnessed unprecedented growth in food grain production, from 72.35 million tonnes in 1965–66, the introductory year of GR technology, to 264.04 million tonnes in 2013–14 and 253.2 million tonnes in 2015–16. This was possible due to intensification and extensification of agricultural production. Consequently, the consumption of chemical fertilizers increased from 0.292 million tonnes in 1960–1961 to 27.56 million tonnes in 2011–12. The net irrigated area increased from 21 million hectares in 1950–51 to more than 66 million hectares, by 2012–13. Punjab and Haryana were the GR star states in India; their contribution to total national food grain production increased from 3 per cent before the GR to 20 per cent at present. Punjab and Haryana had contributed more than 50 per cent and 85 per cent of government procurement of rice and wheat, respectively (Singh, 2000).[3] The phenomenal increase in agricultural production in these states, however, may have come at the cost of the eco-system, and this concern has been expressed even at the policy-making level. The environment statistics released by the government of Punjab echo this concern:

> The quality of soil is getting depleted due to this mono-cultivation of Paddy-Wheat rotation. Both Paddy and Wheat have heavy water requirements and the continuous usage of ground water is depleting the water level and this is already a cause of concern. . . . It is important to take cognizance of the fact that central Punjab has 72 per cent area under paddy cultivation, out of which only 21 per cent area has canal water irrigation facility. The tube wells in the central districts of the state constitute around 70 per cent of total tube wells in Punjab (over 6 per cent of the total tube wells of India are in Punjab), which have increased from 1.92 lacs (0.91 electric and 1.01 diesel operated) in 1970–71 to 12.76 lacs (9.96 electric and 2.80 diesel operated) in 2008–09 and during 2009–10 number of tube wells has reached 13.15 lacs (10.65 electric and 2.50 diesel operated) . . . consumption of chemical fertilizers has increased more than eight times in the past 35 years. . . . The state is having a very high per hectare usage of fertilizers (192.5 kg) and pesticides (923 gm) in the country. The overuse of fertilizer and pesticides could result in degradation of soil, water and crop quality.
>
> (Environment Statistics of Punjab, 2011, p. 89)

As farming practices involve the (ab)use of water, soil and biodiversity, environmental impacts arising from agriculture are therefore presented in relation to these components of the environment. With a focus on India, this chapter critically reviews and identifies the available evidence related to environmental consequences of intensified and productivity-enhancing GR technology based agriculture.

2 Soil resources[4]

Soil is fundamental to agricultural production. It is finite and fragile, and can be either healthy or sick. A healthy soil has a rich diversity of biota and a high content of non-living soil organic matter. The absence of these makes soil sick and degraded. Functional interactions of soil biota with organic and inorganic components, air and water determine a soil's potential to store and release nutrients and water to plants, and to promote and sustain plant growth. Loss of nutrients not only reduces productivity, but also results in silting of water bodies. An inadequate and imbalanced nutrient use coupled with neglect of organic manures results in multi-nutrient deficiencies in soils.

The intensive cropping systems introduced by the GR impose much heavier demands on crop nutrients than do traditional systems. Various studies have pointed out the loss in productivity as directly linked to the severity of soil erosion. Den Biggelaar et al. (2004) analyzed six crops – maize, wheat, soy beans, sorghum, millet and potatoes – and estimated a mean loss in production/value of a half per cent per year across the continents due to soil erosion. Tan et al. (2004) observed that in both developing and least developed countries, the rate of increase in crop yield has decreased with increasing fertilizer use since the 1960s. The greatest decline in the yield/chemical fertilizer ratio was observed in least developed countries, which is a result of high depletion of nutrients out from soils. Low response can in fact be attributed to two reasons: the limited yield potential of a crop and the effect of the limited availability of nutrient elements. Obviously, the yield potential of a crop should not become a limit to the four crops considered in this study since their actual yield levels in both developing and least developed countries were much lower than those in developed countries.

Yield losses may accelerate, remain constant or decelerate as soil nutrient erodes, depending on soil type and crops. If nutrient additions do not keep pace with nutrient removal by crops, the fertility status of soils may decline faster under intensive agriculture. A pertinent question to be asked in this context is whether the higher levels of fertilizer application under intensive agriculture necessarily contribute to an increase in the crop yield. In the Indian context, using generalized additive models (GAMS), we estimated the average marginal response of chemical fertilizer use on the average yield of wheat and paddy for the period 2000–1010 (Figures 12.1 and 12.2).[5] Figure 12.1 shows the average and marginal response of chemical fertilizer use across five major wheat-producing states. Figure 12.2 looks at the same for paddy-producing states. The size of the bubble corresponds to crop productivity of wheat and paddy. Both figures clearly show lower responsiveness of yields of wheat and rice to fertilizer use in highly productive states like Punjab and Haryana. And at the same time, the less productive states show a higher responsiveness. The lower responsiveness of yield to fertilizer use in the higher productivity states may be due to application of chemical fertilizers in higher doses in the past, which might have resulted in lower availability of soil nutrients.

Sidhu and Byerlee (1992) reported that in some districts of Punjab (for instance, Ludhiana, Jalandhar) the chemical fertilizer use has already exceeded the recommended dose. Hence, its marginal contribution to the yield is expected

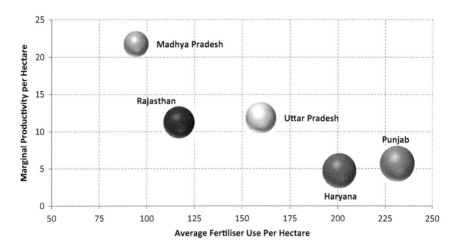

Figure 12.1 Marginal response of chemical fertilizer vs. average wheat yield
Source: Author's calculation.

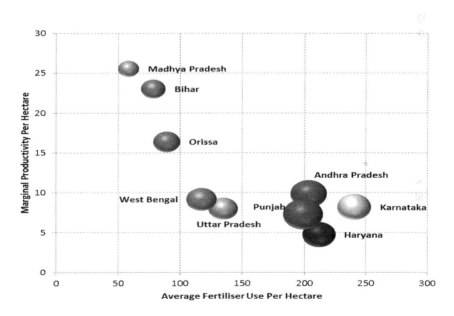

Figure 12.2 Marginal response of chemical fertilizer vs. average paddy yield
Source: Author's calculation.

to be substantially lower in the future than what was realized in the past. The lower and subsidized price of chemical fertilizer may be leading to excessive use, which in turn could be causing a backward shift in the production function. This is inconsistent with the hypothesis, proposed by Yamada and Ruttan (1980), that the incremental contribution of fertilizer to output per hectare was greatest in those countries that were already using relatively high levels of fertilizer per hectare. Although it is true that Punjab and Haryana are using higher levels of fertilizer, the responses of yield and production to fertilizer use have been found to be lower in these states. It may be the case that higher levels of fertilizer use reduce the soil fertility, which in turn forces the farmers to apply even more chemical fertilizer to maintain the production. Datta et al. (2004), in a field experiment in Haryana, demonstrated the negative response of chemical fertilizer due to soil degradation, which severely affected the soil salinity and alkalinity. They also estimated 10 to 15 per cent loss in the wheat production per hectare due to soil salinity by comparing non-affected land.

In addition to chemical fertilizer-induced soil degradation, the adverse impacts of irrigation induced soil salinity and waterlogging are also evident at the farm level in the form of declining crop productivity (Joshi, 1987; Chopra, 1989; Singh and Singh, 1995; Singh et al., 2002). Singh and Singh (1995), using a Cobb-Douglas production function for a sample of 248 respondents in Western Jamuna and Bhakra Canal in Haryana, observed a huge cost in terms of non-land resource use on problem soils (salt affected) as compared to normal soils. This consequently resulted in low farm production and income.

Further, the GR replaced the traditional rotation of leguminous crops (pulses and so on) with soil-exhaustive crops like rice, wheat, maize, bajra and cotton. Rice and wheat are heavy users of nutrients. Nutrient imbalance and mining by these cereal crops had led to nutrient deficiencies and poor soil quality in some areas. The rice-wheat systems are enormously complex, with numerous productivity and sustainability problems. Some of these problems are late sowing, low water and nutrient use efficiency, groundwater depletion in some areas or waterlogging in some other areas, salinity and sodicity (in specific areas), and build-up of weeds, pests, and diseases.

3 Water degradation

The GR-induced agricultural practices, cropping pattern, use of biological and mechanical inputs, incentives such as credit for irrigation equipment and subsidies for electricity supply resulted in the increased use of water resources and massive expansion in irrigated area. India witnessed a 'boom' in the exploitation of groundwater resources since the GR technology was introduced in the 1960s (Figure 12.3).

Irrigated agriculture is the largest abstractor and consumer of groundwater, as the groundwater-irrigated area since 1960 has increased by 500 per cent (Shah, 2009), and the share of groundwater irrigation through wells has risen from 28 per cent to 62 per cent in recent time. The severe gap between the supply of and demand for groundwater extraction and recharge has led to over-exploitation. There had been an almost 6 per cent point dip in share of groundwater wells within the threshold level of 10 meters below the ground during 1993–94 and 2000–01, making water difficult to access (Figure 12.4).

More than one-fifth of groundwater aquifers are overexploited in Punjab, Haryana, Rajasthan and Tamil Nadu, and groundwater levels are falling (World Bank,

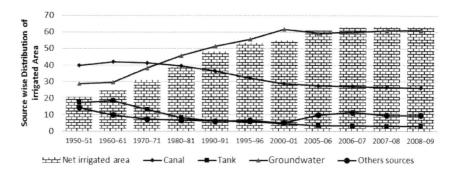

Figure 12.3 Sources of irrigation in India

Note: The bars and lines represent net irrigated area (in million hectares) and percentage share of different sources, respectively.

Source: Adapted from various issues of *Agricultural Statistics in India*, Government of India

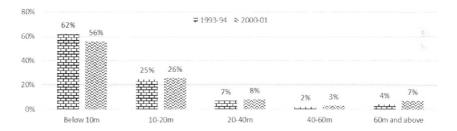

Figure 12.4 Water tables in India

Source: Adapted from various issue of annual reports, Ministry of Water Resources, Government of India

2005; Postel, 1993). The number of irrigation blocks considered over-exploited is increasing at an alarming rate of 5.5 per cent per year (CGWB, 2006). Table 12.2 shows the distribution of different talukas/blocks in India with respect to the status of groundwater. The situation is alarming in GR star states such as Punjab and Haryana. In these locations, the incidence of groundwater exploitation is high, and the situation is becoming critical. The average fall in water tables in these states was found to be one meter a year (Vaidyanathan, 1994). Over-exploitation has three obvious consequences: increase in pumping depths, reduction in tube well productivity and rise in the cost of pumping groundwater. A fall in groundwater level forces farmers to deepen their wells and install pumps with more power. Rich farmers may cope with this challenge, but small and marginal farmers, many of whose wells are supported by shallow aquifers, often find it difficult.

Another fallout of groundwater over-exploitation has been contamination of groundwater due to geogenic factors (i.e., because of particular geological formations at deeper levels), resulting in increased levels of fluoride, arsenic and

Table 12.2 Extent of groundwater exploitation

States	Number of assessed units		Semi-critical (%)		Dark/critical (%)		Over-exploited (%)	
	2004	2011	2004	2011	2004	2011	2004	2011
Andhra Pradesh	1231	1110	14	9	6	1	18	7
Bihar	515	533	0	2	0	0	0	0
Gujarat	223	223	31	6	5	2	14	11
Haryana	113	116	4	6	10	13	49	61
Karnataka	208	270	8	13	2	8	37	23
Kerala	151	152	20	15	10	1	3	1
Madhya Pradesh	312	313	6	21	2	1	8	8
Maharashtra	318	353	7	5	0	1	2	3
Punjab	137	138	3	1	4	3	75	80
Rajasthan	237	243	6	8	21	10	59	71
Tamil Nadu	385	1129	15	21	9	4	37	33
Uttar Pradesh	803	820	11	10	2	8	5	14
West Bengal	269	271	37	20	1	0.37	0	0

Notes: Unit of assessment: Mandals – Andhra Pradesh; talukas – Maharashtra, Gujarat, Karnataka; blocks – rest of the states.

$$\text{Stage of ground water use} = \frac{Annual\ groung\ water\ draft}{Net\ ground\ water\ availability} \times 100$$

Categorization of groundwater exploitation are as follows, with the stage of groundwater use indicated in parentheses: semi-critical (> 70 per cent and <= 90 per cent), critical (> 90 per cent and < 100 per cent), over-exploited (> 100 per cent).

Source: Adapted from various issues of annual reports of the Central Ground Water Board (CGWB)

iron. Runoff losses, groundwater depletion, waterlogging, reservoir siltation and non-point source pollution are some of the key issues related to water in Indian agriculture.[6]

In some places, deep drilling has led to saltwater intrusion into aquifers, rendering water unfit for agricultural or domestic use (Kerr, 1996). Table 12.3 shows the number of states and districts affected by geogenic contaminants as of July 2014.

While, on the one hand, over-exploitation of groundwater has become a serious problem, on the other hand, some recent studies have indicated either a decline or stagnation in yield of intensive irrigated rice systems in India, (Flinn and De Datta, 1984; Cassman and Pingali, 1995; Pingali et al., 1997; Yadav et al., 2000; Kumar and Yadav, 2001).[7] In most of these studies, the magnitude of yield decline was reported more for rice than for wheat; in fact, a few studies reported an increasing trend for wheat yields under irrigated ecosystems. The study by Singh and Hossain (2002)[8] in this context is noteworthy. This study estimated the total factor productivity (TFP) growth for rice and wheat in the context of Punjab and found that environmental degradation contributed negatively to TFP growth during 1990–91 to 1996–97. While the contribution of

Table 12.3 States and districts affected by geogenic contamination in groundwater

Geogenic contaminants	Number of affected states	Number of affected districts
Arsenic	10	68
Fluoride	20	276
Nitrate	21	387
Iron	24	297

Source: Adapted from CGWB (2014).

Table 12.4 Availability of surplus/unutilized groundwater in eastern states vis-à-vis Punjab

States	Net annual groundwater availability		Annual groundwater draft (billion m³)	Annual groundwater available as surplus/ unutilized	
	(billion m3)	m³ ha⁻¹ net sown area		(billion m³)	%
Assam	24.89	8973	5.44	19.45	78
Bihar	27.42	4921	10.77	16.65	61
Chhattisgarh	13.68	2872	2.8	10.88	80
Jharkhand	5.25	2968	1.09	4.16	79
Orissa	21.01	3661	3.85	17.16	82
West	27.46	5186	11.65	15.81	58
Punjab	**21.44**	**5053**	**31.16**	**−9.72**	**−45**

Source: Adapted from CGWB (2006). Dynamic Ground Water Resources of India, Ministry of Water Resources, Faridabad.

environmental degradation to TFP growth of paddy was −5.04 per cent (annualized), it was −1.58 per cent (annualized) in the case of wheat. The analysis shows that, in Punjab, the problem of resource degradation posed by rice is more serious than that posed by wheat.

Given that food security is the supreme national priority, loss in cultivation of rice due to over-exploitation of groundwater in northwestern India has to be compensated for elsewhere. As evidenced from Table 12.4, eastern India[9] seems to be the best bet for availability of surplus groundwater.

The loss in food grain production, especially of rice, in Punjab due to contemplated diversification has to be compensated for elsewhere to ensure national food security. Eastern India, with 2–3 times more rainfall as compared to Punjab, has the highest unexploited good quality groundwater aquifers, especially in Assam, West Bengal and Bihar.

4 Pest problems

Chemical inputs used to increase agricultural productivity, such as inorganic fertilizers and pesticides, have been associated with many negative direct and indirect human health impacts. Pesticides as such are toxic chemicals and represent risks to users. It is estimated that only 0.1 per cent of applied pesticides reach the target pests, leaving the bulk of the pesticides (99.9 per cent) to impact the environment (Pimental, 1995). Human pesticide poisonings and illnesses are clearly the largest environmental costs paid by a society for pesticide use.

A study by Rola and Pingali (1993) found that

- Pesticide use has a significant positive association with the incidence of multiple health impairments in Philippine rice farmers, even after accounting for other effects (e.g., age, smoking, drinking habits and nutritional status).
- The average health cost for farmers exposed to pesticides was approximately 40 per cent higher than that for unexposed farmers. Even after accounting for other factors, health costs increase by 0.5 per cent for every 1 per cent increase in insecticide dose above the average level.
- Health impairments lead to a loss in labour productivity.

In developing countries, where users are often illiterate and ill-trained and do not possess appropriate protective equipment, the risks are further magnified. Furthermore, comprehensive bodies of legislation to regulate the use and distribution of pesticides often do not yet exist.

In India, chemical pesticides were increasingly relied upon to limit production losses until recently. Pesticide use in India increased from a mere 15 g/ha of gross cropped area in 1955–56 to 90 g/ha in 1965–66. Introduction of GR technologies in the mid-1960s gave a fillip to pesticide use, and in 1975–76, it had increased to 266 g/ha, and reached a peak of 404 g/ha in 1990–91 (Birthal, 2003). About half of the total pesticides used in agriculture goes towards controlling insect pests and diseases of cotton. Cotton receives as many as 15–20 rounds of insecticide sprays from the vegetative stage until its maturity. According to estimates by Birthal and Jha (1997), one hectare of cotton receives 3.75 kg of pesticides. Rice, with an area share of 24 per cent, accounts for 17 per cent of the total pesticide use. Although, there is a paucity of reliable time-series information on pest-induced production losses, anecdotal evidence suggests an increase in losses in productivity despite an increase in pesticide use (Dhaliwal and Arora, 1996). The paradox is explained in terms of rising pest problems, technological failure of chemical pesticides and changes in production systems. Nevertheless, pesticide use in India has started declining since 1990–91, reaching 265 g/ha in 1998–99, without much affecting agricultural productivity (Birthal, 2003).

5 Conclusions

GR-induced intensive agriculture, which requires application of high doses of chemical inputs and irrigation, has brought significant land and water problems, such as soil degradation, over-exploitation of groundwater and soil pollution across developing countries, including India. The increasing demand for food due to population growth and improved income to purchase more varied and resource-intensive diets has further increased the competition for land, water, energy and other inputs for food production.

Given the manifested environmental consequences of GR-induced agriculture in India, the analysis here calls for a serious policy revamp which should aim at minimizing the excessive use of natural resources, improving input-use efficiency and reconstructing market forces to encourage diversification of agriculture from rice to alternative crops. An attempt should be made not only to increase production but also to sustain the increased production without further degradation of the natural resources. Possible reclamation measures should be taken up for restoration of the physical health of soils and their productivity. Such measures may include monitoring and management of integrated and sustainable agriculture and forestry, and collection and effective utilization of land and water inventory data for the following purposes: land-use planning, nutrient management, biomass productivity, diversification of cropping pattern, re-enrichment of inherent fertility and agroforestry, moisture conservation and water harvesting, recharging of groundwater reservoirs in areas of water table decline, and agro-industrial watershed-based planning.[10]

Notes

1 The motivation to understand and explore the inextricable link between political economy and environment was result of the author's first-hand observation during a village field study conducted in various stages during 2003 in Indian Punjab, Western and Eastern Uttar Pradesh, thanks to the project Role of Agriculture (RoA) of the Food and Agricultural Organisation (FAO).

2 The GR technology package included material components, such as irrigation or controlled water supply and improved moisture utilization, fertilizers and pesticides and associated management skills. For rice and wheat, the yield improvement resulted from a reduction in plant height through the incorporation of genes for short stature. This led to improvements in harvest index (grain-straw ratio) as well as to increases in biomass production. The varieties of wheat and rice available prior to the GR were tall and leafy with weak stems and had a harvest index of 0.3 (i.e. 30 per cent grain and 70 per cent straw). They could produce a total biomass of 10–12 t/ha. Thus their maximum yield potential was 4 t/ha. When nitrogenous fertilizer was applied at rates exceeding 40 kg/ha, these varieties grew excessively tall, lodged early and yielded less than they would have with lower fertilizer inputs. The improved varieties have a harvest index of 0.5, with increased biomass of 20 t/ha through fertilizer application and maximum yield potential of 10 t/ha. This improvement in harvest index was the single most important architectural change in the rice and wheat varieties that led to doubling of yield potential (Khush, 1995).

3 Shiva (1991) documented the environmental problems facing Indian agriculture due to the GR in her provocative and powerful work entitled *Violence of Green Revolution*. Among the environmental problems listed, the prominent ones are (a) reduction in soil fertility; (b) excessive use of fertilizers and imbalance of nutrient contents in soil due to changes in cropping pattern; (c) biomass availability in terms of fodder and organic manure; (d) genetic erosion; (e) waterlogging and salination; (f) depletion of the groundwater table; and (g) contamination of water bodies and soil with pesticides and fertilizers. She went one step further to term the GR as a 'failure'. It has led to the displacement of vast numbers of small

farmers from their land, rural impoverishment and increased tensions and conflicts. The beneficiaries have been the agro-chemical industry, large petrochemical companies, manufacturers of agricultural machinery, dam builders and large landowners.

4 I am grateful to T V Jayan of the Centre for Science and Environment (CSE) for useful discussion on soil degradation, which helped me to prepare this section. Jayan had written a cover story on soil degradation entitled 'The Last Action Hero *ing: Indian Soil, Up Against Heavy Odds' in the science and environment fortnightly, *Down to Earth*, 31 January 2003.

5 The procedure is based on non-parametric regression and smoothing techniques, which relax the assumption of linearity and enable us to uncover the structure in the relationship between the independent variables and the variable that might otherwise be missed. The model used here is as follows: $Y = \exp(\alpha) s\left(X^{\beta}\right) \exp(\varepsilon)$, where Y is yield, X denotes fertilizer use, α, β, are parameters to be estimated and ε is the error term normally distributed, and $s(X)$ is an unspecified smooth function (Bhushan, 2015). The data used for the estimation is from CACP (Various Volumes).

6 The report 'More Crop and Income per Drop of Water', submitted in 2006, suggested formation of water users associations (WUAs) and training of two water masters each in 5,000 villages with the help of 50 water and farm institutes to create awareness about better management of groundwater resources from this rabi season. Recommending that the year 2007–08 be declared the 'Year of More Crop and Income Per Drop of Water', the farm expert said modern technology would have to be 'married' with traditional wisdom to tackle the issue of depleting water resources, overuse of groundwater and replenishing soil health. The report is also available online at the Ministry website, http://wrmin.nic.in/writer eaddata/mainlinkFile/File722.pdf

7 Ackerman (2012) comprehensively argues that there is vast scope for improving India's crop water productivity and it can be done through crop diversification from grain to non-grain food crops, particularly in those areas where water productivity is low and by improving cropping patterns and agronomic practices (land preparation, fertilization, timing, popular agro-forestry). For wheat, there are varieties capable of escaping terminal drought. In zero tillage agriculture, wheat seed is broadcast before the kharif rice is harvested, so organic matter on the ground is maximized. A technique promoted by the National Food Security Mission is to place (rather than to randomly throw) fewer and younger wheat seedlings, with wider spacing, no continuous flooding, and using organic matter. With the same area under cultivation, this practice can triple output using a third of the amount of seeds. Similarly, in the System of Rice Intensification (SRI), younger seedlings are transplanted at wider spacing, the soil is kept moist but is not continuously flooded, a rotary weeder is used for mechanical weeding, and more organic compost is used as fertilizer. SRI produces 40–80 per cent higher yields with 85 per cent less seed and 32 per cent less water. Just-in-time water availability is critical, again pointing to groundwater as the most reliable source. Evidence of SRI's benefits is now available across a wide range of ecosystems throughout the major rice-producing areas of Asia. Recent reports suggest that SRI crops are able to withstand considerable water and temperature stress, more resistant to storm damage, and have greater resistance to pests and diseases (Uphoff and Kassam, 2009). Of late, in 2011–12, farmers from Darveshpura village in Nalanda district, in low yield state of Bihar of India sweated it out and produced 224 quintals of paddy a hectare (22.4 tons) using SRI.

8 They separately estimated technological change and technical efficiency in separate models, which is difficult to justify statistically. However, the results are threatening from the rice-wheat production system sustainability perspective. The method used to estimate was as follows: The contribution of technology was

estimated through the coefficient of the dummy variable representing different time periods, while the contribution of technical efficiency of farms at different times were estimated using the frontier analysis. The difference is attributed to the effect of environmental degradation ("unsustainability"). Recently, Bhushan (2016) also observed a similar trend.

9 Eastern India, the region having the highest poverty and high population density, representing 37.6 per cent of total country's area under rice and contributing nearly 55 per cent of rice production would be an ideal priority for investments.

10 Agro-industrial watershed management entails the development of land, water, plant, animal and human resources within the natural boundaries of a watershed so as to maximize the upstream benefits of production systems and the downstream benefits of food and sediment control along with processing of the watershed produce in co-operatively-owned industry (Kumar et al., 1996, p. 275).

References

Abler, D. G., Tolley, S. and Kripalani, G. K., 1994, *Indian Agriculture*, Westview Press, Boulder, CO.

Ackermann, R., 2012. New Directions for Water Management in Indian Agriculture. *Global Journal of Emerging Market Economies*, 4(2), pp. 227–288.

Bhushan, S., 2015. *Agricultural Productivity and Environmental Impacts in India: A Parametric and Non-Parametric analysis*. PhD dissertation (Unpublished), Jawaharlal Nehru University, New Delhi.

Bhushan, S., 2016. TFP Growth of Wheat and Paddy in Post-Green Revolution Era in India: Parametric and Non-Parametric analysis. *Agricultural Economics Research Review*, 29(1), pp. 27–40.

Birthal, P. S., 2003. *Economic Potential of Biological Substitutes for Agrochemicals*. Policy Paper 18, National Centre for Agricultural Economics and Policy Research, New Delhi.

Birthal, P. S. and Jha, D., 1997. *Socio-Economic Impact Analysis of Integrated Pest Management Programmes*. National Symposium on IPM in India – Constraints and Opportunities, IARI, New Delhi, October 23–24.

CACP, Various Volumes. *Price Policy for Kharif Crops: The Marketing Season 2013–14*, Department of Agriculture & Cooperation, Ministry of Agriculture, Government of India, New Delhi, March.

Cassman, K. G. and Pingali, P. L., 1995. Extrapolating Trends From Long-Term Experiments to Farmers' Fields: The Case of Irrigated Rice System in Asia. In Barnett, V., Payne, R. and Steiner, R. (eds.), *Agricultural Sustainability; Economic, Environmental and Statistical Considerations*, John Wiley & Sons Ltd., pp. 63–84.

Central Ground Water Board, 2014. *Annual Report, Central Ground Water Board*, Ministry of Water Resources, Faridabad.

CGWB, 2006. *Dynamic Ground Water Resources of India*, Central Ground Water Board, Ministry of Water Resources, Faridabad.

Chopra, K., 1989. Land Degradation: Dimensions and Causalities. *Indian Journal of Agricultural Economics*, 44(1), pp. 233–241.

Conway, G. R. and Pretty, J. N., 1991. *Unwelcome Harvest: Agriculture and Pollution*, Earthscan Publications, London.

Datta, K. K., Joy, C. de and Rajashekharappa, M. T., 2004. Implication of Land Degradation on Crop Productivity- Some Evidences From Saline Areas in North-West India. *Indian Journal of Agricultural Economics*, 59(1), January–March, pp. 150–163.

196   *Surya Bhushan*

Den Biggelaar, C., Lal, R., Wiebe, K. and Breneman, V., 2004. The Global Impact of Soil Erosion on Productivity (i): Absolute and Relative Erosion-Induced Yield Losses. *Advances in Agronomy*, 81, pp. 1–48.

Dhaliwal, G. S. and Arora, R., 1996. *Principles of Insect Management*, Commonwealth Publishers, New Delhi.

Environment Statistics of Punjab, 2011. Economic & Statistical Organisation, Punjab.

FAO, 2001. *Environmental Impacts of Productivity-Enhancing Crop Research: A Critical Review*. A Report from TAC's Standing Panel on Impact Assessment, TAC Secretariat, UNO.

Flinn, J. C. and De Datta, S. K., 1984. Trends in Irrigated Rice Yields Under Intensive Cropping at Philippines Research Stations. *Field Crops Research*, 5(3), pp. 201–216.

Joshi, P. K., 1987. Effects of Surface Irrigation Land Degradation: Problems & Strategies. *Indian Journal of Agricultural Economics*, 42(3), pp. 416–423.

Kerr, J. M., 1996. *Sustainable Development of Rainfed Agriculture in India*. EPTD Discussion Paper No. 20, IFPRI, Washington, DC.

Khush, G. S., 1995. Breaking the Yield Frontier of Rice. *Geojournal*, 35(3), pp. 329–332.

Kumar, A. and Yadav, D. S., 2001. Long-Term Effects of Fertilizers on the Soil Fertility and Productivity of a Rice-Wheat System. *Journal of Agronomy Crop Science*, 186(1), pp. 47–54.

Kumar, K., Dhyani, P. P. and Palni, L. M. S. (eds.), 1996. *Land Utilization in the Central Himalaya: Problems and Management Options*, G B Pant Institute of Himalayan Environment & Development, Kosi, Almora (UP), Indus Publishing Company, New Delhi.

Pimentel, D., 1995. Amounts of Pesticides Reaching Target Pests: Environmental Impacts and Ethics. *Journal of Agricultural and Environmental Ethics*, 8(1), pp. 17–29.

Pingali, P. L., 2012. Green Revolution: Impacts, Limits, and the Path Ahead. *Proceedings of the National Academy of Sciences (PNAS) of the United States of America*, 109(31), pp. 12302–12308.

Pingali, P. L., Hossain, M. and Gerpacio, R. V., 1997. *Asian Rice Bowls: The Returning Crisis?* CAB International, in Association with the International Rice Research Institute, Wallingford.

Pingali, P. L. and Rosegrant, M. W., 1994. *Confronting the Environmental Consequences of the Green Revolution in Asia*. EPTD Discussion Paper No. 2, August, IFPRI, Washington, DC.

Postel, S., 1993. Water and Agriculture. In Gleick, P. H. (ed.), *Water in Crisis: A Guide to the World's Fresh Water Resources*, Oxford University Press, New York.

Rola, A. C. and Pingali, P. L., 1993. *Pesticides, Rice Productivity, and Farmers' Health – An Economic Assessment*, IRRI-World Resources Institute (WRI), Los Baños, Laguna, Philippines.

Sehgal, J. and Abrol, I. P., 1994. *Soil Degradation in India: Status and Impact*, Oxford and IBH, New Delhi.

Shah, T., 2009. *Taming the Anarchy? Groundwater Governance in South Asia*, RFF Press, Washington, DC.

Shiva, V., 1991. The Green Revolution in the Punjab. *The Ecologist*, 21(2), pp. 57–60.

Sidhu, D. S. and Byerlee, D., 1992. *Technical Change and Wheat Productivity in the Indian Punjab in the Post-Green Revolution Period*. CIMMYT Economics Working Paper 92–02, CIMMYT, Mexico, DF.

Singh, G., Babu, R., Narain, P., Bhushan, L. S. and Abrol, I. P., 1992. Soil Erosion Rates in India. *Journal of Soil and Water Conservation*, 47(1), pp. 97–99.

Singh, J., Hone, P. and Kundu, K. K., 2002. Measuring Inefficiencies in Crop Production on Degraded Lands. *Indian Journal of Agricultural Economics*, 57(1), January–March, pp. 65–76.

Singh, J. and Hossain, M., 2002. Total Factor Productivity Analysis and Its Components in a High-Potential Rice-Wheat System: A Case Study of the Indian Punjab. In Sombilla, M., Hossain, M. and Hardy, B. (eds.), *Developments in the Asian Rice Economy*, IRRI, pp. 409–418.

Singh, J. and Singh, J. P., 1995. Land Degradation & Economic Sustainability. *Ecological Economics*, 15(1), pp. 77–86.

Singh, R.B., 2000. Environmental Consequences of Agricultural Development: A Case Study from the Green Revolution State of Haryana, India. *Agriculture, Ecosystem and Environment*, 82, pp. 97–103.

Tan, Z. X., Lal, R. and Wiebe, K. D., 2004. Global Soil Nutrient Depletion and Yield Reduction. *Journal of Sustainable Agriculture*, 26(1), pp. 123–146.

Tilman, D., Fargione, J., Wolff, B., DÁntonoio, C., Dobson, A., Howarth, R., Schindler, D., Schlesinger, W., Simberloff, D. and Swackhamer, D., 2001. Forecasting Agriculturally Driven Global Environment Change. *Science*, 292(5515), April 13, pp. 281–284.

UNESCO, 2009. *Water in a Changing World*, The United Nations World Water Development Report 3, available at http://unesdoc.unesco.org/images/0018/001819/181993e.pdf#page=121, accessed 14/03/2017.

Uphoff, N. and Kassam, A., 2009. *Case Study: The System of Rice Intensification*, (IP/A/STOA/FWC/2005-28/SC42), Annex 3 in European Parliament: Science and Technology Options Assessment (STOA), June.

Vaidyanathan, A., 1994. Performance of Indian Agriculture Since Independence. In Basu, K. (ed.), *Agrarian Questions*, Oxford University Press, New Delhi.

World Bank, 2005. *India's Water Economy: Bracing for a Turbulent Future*, World Bank Report, Washington, DC, available at http://go.worldbank.org/QPUTPV5530.

Yadav, R. L., Dwivedi, B. S. and Pandey, P. S., 2000. Rice-Wheat Cropping System: Assessment of Sustainability Under Green Manuring and Chemical Fertilizer Inputs. *Field Crops Research*, 65, pp. 15–30.

Yamada, S. and Ruttan, V. W., 1980. International Comparison of Productivity in Agriculture. In Kendrick, J. and Vaccara, N. (eds.), *New Development in Productivity Measurements and Analysis*, Chicago University Press, Chicago.

13 Climate change and Indian agriculture

Impacts on crop yield

Raju Mandal and Hiranya K. Nath

1 Introduction

There has been indisputable evidence of changes in temperature, precipitation, and extreme weather events. However, there is less of a consensus as to what causes these climatic changes. Since agriculture depends critically on the climatic factors, it is expected that such changes in the climate would have impacts on different aspects of agriculture. The anticipated drastic changes in temperature and rainfall patterns around the globe over the next century are likely to exacerbate the impact on agricultural productivity. Furthermore, people adapt their agricultural practices and cropping patterns in response to the evolving weather patterns. These adaptations too have an impact on agriculture. Thus, there are direct as well as indirect impacts of climate change. The study of the impacts of climate change on agriculture is extremely important particularly in the context of developing countries where a sizable portion of the population relies on agriculture for life and livelihood.

Agriculture plays a vital role in the Indian economy. Together with fishery and forestry, it accounts for about 18 per cent of its gross domestic product (GDP). Over 58 per cent of the rural households depend primarily on agriculture for their livelihood. Thus, it is extremely important to know the impacts of changes in weather conditions and the climate on agricultural productivity and growth. It is in this context that this chapter reviews the extant literature on climatic impacts on agriculture focusing on the studies that have been conducted on India. The empirical evidence on the effects of climate change on agriculture has been mixed. Applying nonparametric median regression technique to state-level time series data on average yield of rice and wheat, and on temperature and rainfall, the present study further investigates the impacts of changes in these climate variables on the yields of these two crops. The results indicate that rising temperature has a significant negative impact while rising rainfall variability has a significant positive impact on the average rice yield. Furthermore, increasing temperature variability over the crop year appears to have a significant positive impact on wheat yield.

The rest of the chapter is organized as follows. In section 2, we discuss empirical evidence of climate change effects on agriculture in different parts of the world as documented in the extant literature. Section 3 presents evidence of the impacts of climate change on Indian agriculture from existing literature. We organize and discuss these empirical studies according to the methodological strands to which they belong. In section 4, we report and discuss the results from our own estimate of climatic impacts on agriculture using state-level data. The final section includes our concluding remarks.

2 The impacts of climate change on agriculture: empirical evidence from across the globe

There is a substantial empirical literature on how climate changes impact agriculture using data on various crops from different parts of the world. The initial studies mostly focused on developed countries (e.g., Kaiser et al., 1993; Mendelsohn et al., 1994; Adams et al., 1998; Lewandrowski and Schimmelpfennig, 1999). However, some of the relatively recent studies examine climatic impacts on agriculture in developing countries as well (e.g., Sanghi and Mendelsohn, 2008; Moula, 2009; Deressa and Hassan, 2009; Sarker et al., 2012; Poudel and Kotani, 2013). This section reviews this literature that investigates the climate change impacts on agriculture drawing empirical evidence from both developed and developing countries. It especially focuses on the nature of impacts and its geographical characterization.

The empirical literature demonstrates that there have been considerable variations in the impacts of climate change on crop yield across regions and crops. These variations are primarily due to differences in the current levels of climatic conditions across geographical regions and also because of the fact that different crops have varied sensitivities to climatic conditions. An increase in temperature, for example, can have both positive and negative impact on crop yields depending on the latitude of a region and the temperature sensitivity of a particular crop. In the middle and high latitudes, increased temperatures lengthen growing seasons and expand crop producing areas pole-ward, thereby benefiting countries in these regions (Rosenzweig and Hillel, 1995). Further, as Parry et al. (1999) show, climate change increases yields in high and mid-latitudes and decrease yields at lower latitudes. Rosenzweig and Iglesias (1994) further note that for a 4°C warming and assuming CO_2 fertilization effect, yields in mid and high latitude countries (e.g., the northern United States and Canada) may increase, but yields in low latitude countries (e.g., Brazil) decline. Magrin et al. (2005) in a study on Argentina find a positive impact of climate change on crop yields. Overall, the biophysical effects of climate change on agricultural production will be positive in some agricultural systems and regions, and negative in others, and these effects will also vary through time (Parry et al., 2004).

However, several other studies find temperature to have a negative impact on crop yields. This is mainly because an increase in temperature leads to higher respiration rates, speeding up of seed formation, and, consequently, to lower biomass production resulting in lower yields (Adams et al., 1998). This negative effect of temperature rise is especially pronounced in semi-tropical and tropical conditions because many crops are already at their tolerance limits of temperature in those regions (Jayaraman, 2011). Ortiz et al. (2008) present evidence in support of this for wheat in certain zones of the Indo-Gangetic plains where optimal temperatures already exist. Even in high latitudes, temperature increases beyond 1–3°C would result in lower yields. Increase in precipitation, on the other hand, may benefit semi-arid and other water-short areas by increasing soil moisture while it may aggravate problems in regions with excessive water (Adams et al., 1998). Some of these results are also validated by Rosenzweig and Parry (1994) who find that while some countries in the temperate zone would benefit from climate change, many countries in the tropical and subtropical zones would be vulnerable to its adverse impacts.

The positive impacts of climate change as documented in some studies are mainly associated with the augmentation of CO_2 concentration and partly due to moderate temperatures in high altitudes. An increase in CO_2 concentration in the atmosphere enhances water use efficiency and net photosynthesis rate by crops thereby contributing to crop yield. Luo et al. (2003) present evidence of increase in wheat yield under all scenarios of CO_2 levels in South Australia. Climate change may indirectly affect crop production via changes in the incidence and distribution of pests and pathogens, increased rates of soil erosion and degradation, and increased tropospheric ozone levels due to rising temperatures and water run-off (Adams, 1986; Adams et al., 1998).

Attavanich and McCarl (2014) study the effects of increases in CO_2 concentration and projected climate change on the mean and variance of U.S. yield for corn, sorghum, soybeans, winter wheat and cotton. In general, an increase in CO_2 concentration leads to higher mean yields for these crops. Furthermore, increases in climate variability decreases mean crop yields and increases their variance. The effect of CO_2 fertilization is generally found to be outweighing the effect of climate change on mean crop yields in many regions resulting in an increase in the yields of these crops.

Al-Bakri et al. (2010) in their study on Jordan find the responses of wheat and barley to be different under different climate change scenarios. For both crops, there is a positive relationship between a change in rainfall and a change in expected yield. An increase in air temperature is expected to reduce yield of barley. In contrast, an increase in temperature is likely to increase wheat yield in most cases.

For South Africa, Benhin (2008) reports that a 1 per cent increase in temperature leads to about US$80.00 increase in net crop revenue while a 1 mm/month fall in precipitation leads to US$2.00 fall with significant seasonal differences in impacts. Using selected climate scenarios, the study predicts that crop net revenues are expected to fall by as much as 90 per cent by 2100 with small-scale farmers being most affected.

Researchers have also examined the effects of changes in temperature and rainfall variability on crop yield. Variability is measured either by temporal variations in these climate variables or by extreme (maximum and minimum) temperature or rainfall measures. For example, Cabas et al. (2010) note that average crop yield increases with warmer temperatures and a longer growing season which is only partially offset by the decreases due to a rise in the variability of temperature and rainfall in Southwestern Ontario, Canada. The positive impact of a longer growing season offsets the negative effect of greater heat and rainfall variability resulting in higher average yields in the future.

Sarker et al. (2012) in a study on climate change impact on yields of different varieties of rice in Bangladesh find that maximum temperature and rainfall have positive impact on *Aus* yield while maximum temperature and rainfall have positive impact and minimum temperature has negative impact on *Aman* yield. In contrast, they find that maximum temperature has a negative impact and minimum temperature has a positive impact on *Boro* yield.

Welch et al. (2010) find that minimum temperature has negative and maximum temperature has positive impacts on rice yields in Asia. The negative impact could be explained by increased respiration losses during vegetative phase and reduced grain-filling duration and endosperm cell size during ripening phase. Chen et al. (2004) while examining the impacts of annual average climate conditions on major agricultural crops across the United States find the effects to differ by crop. More rainfall causes corn yield levels to rise while decreasing yield variance. Temperature has the reverse effects. For sorghum, higher temperatures reduce yields and yield variability. More rainfall increases sorghum yields and yield variability.

Knox et al. (2012) assess the projected impacts of climate change on the yield of eight major crops in Africa and South Asia using a systematic review and meta-analysis of data from 52 original publications. They show that the projected mean change in yield of all crops is –8 per cent by the 2050s in both regions. Across Africa, estimated mean yield changes are found to be of the magnitudes of –17 per cent(wheat), –5 per cent per cent (maize), –15 per cent(sorghum) and –10 per cent(millet) and across South Asia of –16 per cent(maize) and –11 per cent(sorghum). However, no mean change in yield is detected for rice.

Mendelsohn et al. (1994) in their pioneering study note that higher winter and summer temperatures are harmful for crops while higher fall temperatures and higher winter and spring rainfall are beneficial for crops. Additionally, higher summer or fall rainfall is found to be harmful. Furthermore, they find evidence of non-linear impacts of climatic factors.

According to Mendelsohn (2007), the estimated global combined impacts of temperature and precipitation changes vary from a loss of 0.05 per cent to a gain of 0.9 per cent of agricultural GDP. The greenhouse effect is responsible for between 2.6 per cent and 5.4 per cent of the increase in agricultural production between 1960 and 2000. Most of this impact is due to the beneficial impacts of carbon fertilization. Consistent with the findings discussed above, climate change has also made some small contributions, generally helping mid and high latitude countries and slightly damaging low latitude countries. The percentage gains from warming, however, have been larger in developed countries (3–6 per cent) compared to developing countries (0.4–2 per cent).

A study on the climate sensitivity of Brazilian and Indian agriculture by Sanghi and Mendelsohn (2008) reports that temperature has a more powerful effect on farm values and net revenues than does precipitation. The study finds that if temperature rises by 2° C with an 8 per cent increase in precipitation, agricultural net revenue may fall 12 per cent in India and 20 per cent in Brazil without carbon fertilization. Given a broader range of possible climates, global warming could cause annual damages in Brazil between 1 per cent and 39 per cent and between 4 per cent and 26 per cent in India by the end of the next century, although some of these effects may be potentially offset by carbon fertilization.

Seo et al. (2005) find that while warming is harmful, increases in rainfall are beneficial for agriculture in Sri Lanka. The expected benefit ranges from 11 per cent to 122 per cent of the current net revenue. In contrast, the loss due to increases in the temperature ranges from 18 per cent to 50 per cent of the current agricultural productivity.

Isik and Devadoss (2006) examine the impact of climate change on crop yield and yield variability for wheat, barley, potato, and sugar beet yields in the state of Idaho in the United States. Their results show that climate change has modest effects on the mean crop yields, but it significantly reduces the variance and covariance for most of the crops considered. Precipitation has a negative impact on the mean yield of wheat, barley, potato and sugar beets. Temperature has a positive impact on the mean yield of wheat, sugar beets and potato while it has a negative impact on the mean yield of barley and potato. Furthermore, increases in the rainfall and temperature tend to reduce the variability of wheat yields and barley. The effect of precipitation on potato yield variability is positive. The precipitation has a negative impact and the temperature has a positive impact on variance of sugar beet yields.

Poudel and Kotani (2013) examine the impact of climatic variations on yield and its variability for rice and wheat in central region of Nepal. An increase in the variance of both temperature and rainfall has adverse effects on crop production. But a change in the mean level of temperature and rainfall induces heterogeneous impacts depending on growing seasons, altitudes and types of crops grown. Moreover, climate variations induce greater impacts on rice yields while they do not seem to have much of an effect on wheat yields.

Deschenes and Greenstone (2007) predict that climate change will lead to a 4 per cent increase in annual agricultural profits in the United States. Moreover, the estimates of the effect of climate change on the value of agricultural land range from –18 per cent to 29 per cent.

Schlenker and Roberts (2009) find evidence of a non-linear impact of temperature rise on the crop yields in the United States. According to them, yields increase up to a particular level of temperature beyond which the same decline. More specifically, yields increase with temperature up to 29° C for corn, 30° C for soybeans, and 32° C for cotton but temperatures above these thresholds are very harmful.

Schlenker and Lobell (2010) investigate the impact of climate change on five important African crops in sub-Saharan Africa (SSA) using the panel data model. They estimate that, by mid-century, the mean of aggregate production changes in SSA would be –22, –17, –17, –18, and –8 per cent for maize, sorghum, millet, groundnut, and cassava respectively. Furthermore, that the countries with the highest average yields have the largest projected yield losses, suggesting that well-fertilized modern seed varieties are more susceptible to heat related losses.

Overall, the empirical evidence on climatic impacts on agriculture has been mixed. There are wide variations in the impacts of climate change on agriculture across different regions and crop varieties.

3 The impacts of climate change on Indian agriculture

Against the backdrop of a huge population size along with changes in land use patterns, the Indian economy is faced with the enormous challenge of food and nutrition security. The challenge has been exacerbated due to ongoing global climate change that has the potential of adversely affecting the agricultural sector of the country where majority of the population depends on it for their life and livelihood and who, being poor, have the limited capacity to adapt to the adverse effects.

There are several recent studies that investigate climatic impacts on agriculture in India. The results reported in these studies that use different methodologies and datasets on a variety of crops are mixed. This section reviews this literature.

Most studies examining the impacts of climate change on Indian agriculture use crop simulation models. Several of them find evidence of a negative impact of climate change on crop yields. Soora et al. (2013) while examining regional vulnerabilities of rice yields to climate change in India find that rice yield would decline in all three climate change scenarios that they consider. Irrigated rice yields are projected to decline by 4 per cent by 2020, 7 per cent by 2050 and 10 per cent by 2080. Rainfed rice yields, on the other hand, are likely to decline by 6 per cent by 2020, and marginally (<2.5 per cent) by 2050 and 2080 under the projected climate change scenarios. They also find evidence of spatial variation in the magnitude of climate change impacts. Singh et al. (2017) projects an overall reduction in productivity of rice crop in all main rice producing states in India. Due to an increase in temperature the crop will mature early and yield will decrease in the future decades. Likewise, the study by Aggarwal et al. (2010) on the Upper Ganga Basin reveals that climate change is likely to adversely affect rice and wheat yields. Irrigated rice yield is likely to decline up to 23 per cent in several parts of the study region and the yield loss is projected to be higher in the high rainfall zones where rainfall is projected to increase further. Climate change is also likely to adversely affect the wheat yields in nine out of eleven districts under consideration. The projected increase in CO_2 will not be enough to compensate for the adverse effects of temperature rise. Furthermore, a study by Mishra et al. (2013) shows a decrease in the rice and wheat yields in the upper and middle Indian Ganga Basin (IGB) during 2011–2040. The results for lower IGB, however, are somewhat contradictory. In the upper IGB the projected rate of change in rice yield ranges from –5.9 to –43.2 per cent while in the lower IGB it ranges between +1.2 and –22.6 per cent. Similarly, the projected rate of change in wheat yield varies from –6.1 to –20.9 per cent in the upper IGB as compared to 5.4 to –1.7 per cent in the lower IGB.

Aggarwal and Sinha (1993) show that an increase of 2°C in temperature would reduce grain yields in most places. Moreover, they find evidence of heterogeneous climatic impacts across latitudes. In sub-tropical (above 23°C) environment, there is a small decrease in yields (1.5–5.8 per cent). However, in tropical locations the decrease of 17–18 per cent is substantial. Irrigated yields increase slightly for latitudes with temperature greater than 27°C but decrease in all other areas. The decrease in yield is much higher in lower latitudes. Using a crop growth simulation model, Mall et al. (2004) indicate that a rise in surface air temperature along with doubling of CO_2 concentration could pose a serious threat to soybean growth and hence the yield under three future climate change scenarios. The simulated decline in soybean yield due to thermal stress ranges between 12 per cent and 21 per cent.

A study of the impact of projected climate change on Indian mustard by Boomiraj et al. (2010) shows that mustard yields are likely to decline in both irrigated and rainfed conditions with spatial variations in magnitude across different mustard growing regions of the country. Under both irrigated and rainfed conditions, yield reductions would be higher in eastern India (67 and 57 per cent) followed by central (48 and 14 per cent) and northern India (40.3 and 21.4 per cent). This is due to the fact that the eastern part of the country is projected to experience the maximum temperature rise by 2080. In contrast, the northern region is expected to experience relatively lower temperature during the crop growing period. But rainfed crop is more susceptible to changing climate in north India due to projected reduction in rainfall under the future climate change scenarios.

Kumar et al. (2015) study climate change impact on potato yield in the Indo-Gangetic Plains and predict that climate change would reduce potato yields by ~2.5, ~6 and ~11 per cent in the study region in 2020 (2010–2039), 2050 (2040–2069) and 2080 (2070–2099) time periods.

In contrast to the above, some other crop simulation studies document evidence of a positive impact of climate change on Indian agriculture. For example, Saseendran et al. (2000) report a projected increase of 12 per cent in rice yield due to climate change. According to this study, the negative impact of a rise in temperature would be more than compensated by the positive impacts of the fertilization effect of projected elevation of CO_2 and increase in rainfall. Likewise, Lal et al. (1998) project wheat and rice yields to increase by 28 per cent and 15 per cent respectively under doubling of CO_2. However, the positive impact of elevated CO_2 on these two crops would nearly be cancelled out for an increase in temperature by 3°C and 2°C respectively. While wheat is sensitive to an increase in maximum temperature, rice is vulnerable to a rise in minimum temperature. The study also reports that the combined effect of rising CO_2 and temperature increase is an increase in wheat and rice yield by 21 per cent and 4 per cent respectively under existing irrigation practice.

Aggarwal and Mall (2002) further predict that direct effect of climate change on rice crops in different agro-climatic regions in India would always be positive irrespective of the various uncertainties. They consider the following climate change scenarios: an increase of 0.1°C in temperature and 416 parts per million (ppm) in CO_2 (2010 scenario) and an increase of 0.4°C in temperature and 755 ppm in CO_2 (2070 scenario) as the optimistic scenarios whereas an increase of 0.3°C in temperature and 397 ppm in CO_2 (2010 scenario) and an increase of 2°C in temperature and 605 ppm in CO_2 (2070 scenario) as the pessimistic scenarios of climate change. They find that the rate of increase in rice yields ranges between 1.0 and 16.8 per cent under the pessimistic scenarios depending on the level of management and model used. These increases range between 3.5 and 33.8 per cent under the optimistic climate change scenario.

The study by Abeysingha et al. (2016) on the Gomti River Basin of India reveals that there would be an increase in mean annual rice yield in the range of 5.5–6.7 per cent, 16.6–20.2 per cent and 26–33.4 per cent during the 2020s, 2050s and 2080s, respectively. Similarly, mean annual wheat yield is also likely to increase by 13.9–15.4 per cent, 23.6–25.6 per cent and 25.2–27.9 per cent for the same future time periods. In a study on northwest India, Attri and Rathore (2003) find that under a modified climate (i.e., increase in maximum and minimum temperatures by 1.0°C and 1.5°C respectively along with doubling of CO_2) there would be yield enhancements of the order of 29–37 per cent and 16–28 per cent under rainfed and irrigated conditions respectively. However, they further add that any increase of maximum temperature beyond 1°C and of minimum temperature over 1.5°C may reduce grain yield even under enhanced CO_2. Dubey et al. (2014) in their study on northwest plains of Uttarakhand report that the yields of all varieties of wheat would increase significantly under elevated CO_2 concentration but would decrease significantly with increasing temperatures.

Kumar et al. (2011) show that due to climate change irrigated rice and potato in the northeastern region, rice in the eastern coastal region and coconut in the Western Ghats (WG) are likely to gain. However, irrigated maize, wheat and mustard in the northeastern and coastal regions and rice, sorghum, and maize in the WG may lose.

The studies that use methodologies other than crop growth simulation models have also found mixed evidence of climate change impact on Indian agriculture. Burney and Ramanathan (2014) investigate the impact of climate change and air pollution on Indian agriculture applying the panel regression method to data on rice and wheat yield, temperature, precipitation, pollution variables for some selected states. Their results indicate that a 1°C increase in temperature leads to a yield decline, on average, of 4 per cent for wheat and 5 per cent for rice. According to this study, the majority of losses in rice and wheat yields are attributable to short-lived climate pollutants.

Guiteras (2009) examines the impact of temperature and rainfall on combined yield (in monetary terms) of five major food and one cash crop, namely, rice, wheat, jowar, bajra, maize and sugarcane using panel data for 200 districts of India for 40 years (1960–1999). According to this study, the projected climate change would reduce major crop yields by 4.5 to 9 per cent over the medium term (2010–2039) and by 25 per cent or more over the long-term (2070–2099) in the absence of long-run adaptation.

Barnwal and Kotani (2013) study the impact of climate change on rice yield in Andhra Pradesh using quantile regression. They find evidence of substantial heterogeneity in the impacts of climatic variables across the yield distributions. The direction of the climatic impacts on rice yields is found to be highly dependent on the agro-climatic zones. In most agro-climatic zones kharif rice yield is found to increase with an increase in average temperature. Moreover, the monsoon-dependent kharif rice is more sensitive to temperature and precipitation, while the winter season rabi rice is largely resilient to changes in the levels of climate variable. Mandal and Nath (2017) conduct a similar study for Assam and show that there is substantial heterogeneity in the impacts of changes in temperature and rainfall across seasonal rice varieties (autumn, winter and summer), agro-climatic zones and the distribution of rice yield.

Applying the Ricardian approach to farm-level data, Kumar (2011) examines the impact of climate change on farm level net revenue in India. The estimated climate response function is found to be non-linear. The temperature coefficients are larger in magnitude than the precipitation coefficients indicating relatively higher sensitivity of crop growth to temperature changes. Higher precipitation is beneficial in winter and autumn seasons but harmful during spring and summer. With a 2°C increase in temperature along with 7 per cent increase in precipitation, the results from the study indicate an annual decline of 3 per cent in farm level net revenue. The estimates of climatic impacts with India-specific climate change scenarios along with regional distributions of the impacts reveal that with the exception of the eastern states of Bihar and West Bengal and the inland region of Karnataka, climate change is likely to have an adverse impact on agriculture in the rest of the country. Likewise, in a separate study Kumar and Parikh (2001) report that under the climate change scenario of a +2°C temperature and +7 per cent rainfall change the total farm net revenue would decline by about 8.4 per cent. The negative impacts of temperature change more than compensate for the small positive impacts due to precipitation change.

Using data from nine rice-producing states Auffhammer et al. (2006) show that rainfall has a positive impact on rice harvest while minimum temperature has a negative impact. They further note that the simultaneous reductions in atmospheric brown clouds and greenhouse gases (GHGs) would have complementary positive impacts on rice harvests. Rao et al. (2014) find a negative impact of rising minimum temperature on kharif paddy yields in India. As per their estimates, the decline in kharif paddy yield ranges between 411 and 859 kg per hectare for every 1°C rise in minimum temperature across regions. Gupta et al. (2012) observe that rainfall increases rice yield at a decreasing rate whereas maximum temperature reduces it at an increasing rate. The net effect will depend on the relative strength of these two effects. In case of pearl millet and sorghum also, rainfall increases yield at a decreasing rate.

Using the Just-Pope stochastic production function framework, Gupta et al. (2013) further examine the impact of climate change on mean and variability of yield of rice and millets in India. The study shows that an increase in temperature decreases yield and its variability of rice and sorghum. But variability of temperature increases the variability of their yields. In contrast, an increase in rainfall increases their mean yield and reduces their variability. Variability of rainfall has positive and negative impacts respectively on average yield and its variability in case of rice. For sorghum, rainfall variability reduces mean yield but increases its variability. In case of pearl millets, an increase in temperature decreases mean yield but increases its variability. Variability of temperature raises variability of its yield. An increase in rainfall increases its yield but reduces its variability. Variability of rainfall reduces mean yield but increases its variability for pearl millets.

Krishnamurthy (2012) studies the impact of climate change across yield distributions of rice and wheat in India using quantile regression technique. The results indicate significant reduction in wheat yields of up to 12 per cent in all regions and at most quantiles under scenarios with a reasonable temperature increase. The reductions are found to be larger at upper quantiles. However, in case of rice there is a very modest (up to 2 per cent) increase in yield at the intermediate quantiles and a modest reduction in yield (up to 3 per cent) at upper and lower quantiles. There are significant regional differences in impacts at different quantiles.

From the above discussion it is clear that there is mixed evidence of climatic impacts on agricultural productivity and growth in India. While some studies provide evidence of positive impacts others present that of negative impacts. The heterogeneity in terms crops, topography, existing and projected agro-climatic conditions, and agronomic characteristics across different regions plays a very important role in generating these mixed results.

4 Climatic impacts on rice and wheat yield in India: further evidence from state-level data

In this section, we examine the impacts of climate variables (i.e., temperature and rainfall) on the average yield of rice and wheat, the two most important staple food crops of the country, using state-level time series data.[1] We consider annual average temperature and total rainfall during a crop year (July to June) as our main climate variables. Additionally, we include annual temperature variability (as measured by the standard deviation of monthly temperature) and annual rainfall variability (as measured by the standard deviation of monthly rainfall). To see the impact of these climate variables on average yield of rice and wheat we use median regression. For robustness of the results, we also apply pooled least square (PLS) technique.[2]

Table 13.1 presents our regression results of climate change impacts on rice and wheat yield across the states of India. Our results indicate that an increase in average temperature reduces rice yield. This is consistent with the findings of several previous studies. However, rainfall variability has a positive impact on rice yield indicating that more variations in rainfall over the crop year are beneficial to this crop. When we use PLS method, average temperature is found to have a negative impact on rice yield. Thus, the result with respect to the impact of rising temperature on rice yield is robust to the use of different estimation techniques. As for wheat yield, temperature variability has a significant positive impact on its yield and this result is also robust. It implies that a higher variability in temperature over the crop year is good for wheat yield. Average temperature has a negative effect on wheat yield but it is statistically significant only when we use PLS to

Table 13.1 Regression results (Sample Period: 1968–2001)

Explanatory variables	Rice yield		Wheat yield	
	Median regression	Pooled regression	Median regression	Pooled regression
	(1)	(2)	(3)	(4)
Constant	2755.83***	3932.85***	779.87	1834.83**
	(688.47)	(734.14)	(1132.00)	(758.33)
Trend	26.95***	27.93***	24.95***	29.50***
	(0.97)	(1.69)	(1.33)	(2.50)
Average	−43.74*	−91.48***	−37.29	−82.57***
Temperature	(24.22)	(28.06)	(37.78)	(26.09)
Total rainfall	−0.07	0.09	0.02	0.08
	(0.07)	(0.18)	(0.17)	(0.25)
Temperature	26.96	38.72	127.98***	180.06**
variability	(34.90)	(55.09)	(47.74)	(73.83)
Rainfall	1.54***	−0.02	0.71	−1.07
variability	(0.58)	(1.58)	(1.39)	(2.25)
Pseudo-R^2/R^2	0.60	0.69	0.58	0.65
No. of states	23	23	21	21
No. of observations	765	765	659	659

Note: The standard errors are in parentheses: ***significant at the 1% level; **significant at the 5% level; *significant at the 10% level.

estimate the regression model.[3] The reasons for the findings with regard to the impact of rainfall and temperature variability are not readily comprehensible. For a better understanding of these results further agronomic research will be helpful.

Note that these results are indicative at the best. We have used aggregate data and it would be desirable to use more disaggregate data. Further, we would like to include other inputs such as fertilizer, irrigation etc. that are important for yields. However, relevant data are not consistently available.

5 Conclusions

The empirical evidence on the effects of climate change on agriculture has been mixed: while some studies find evidence of adverse impacts others report evidence of positive effects. Applying nonparametric median regression technique to state-level time series data on average yield of rice and wheat and on temperature and rainfall from 1968 to 2001, the present study further investigates the impacts of changes in these climate variables on rice and wheat yields in India. The results indicate that rising temperature has a significant negative impact and rising rainfall variability has a significant positive impact on the average rice yield. Furthermore, an increase in temperature variability over the crop year appears to have a significant positive impact on wheat yield.

The studies discussed above show that different aspects of climate change (i.e., changes in temperature, rainfall, CO_2) may have differential effects on agriculture in India. Furthermore, the impacts are conditional on so many confounding factors: type of crops, topography, existing agro-climatic conditions, agronomic characteristics, available technology, and peoples' coping strategies. It seems to suggest that aggregate studies covering a large geographic region may gloss over these heterogeneities that are so critical for investigating climatic impacts. Therefore, it is imperative that researchers conduct more micro-level region-specific studies so that coping strategies and policies can be customized according to these specificities. Since collection, storage, and dissemination of data have become much easier now than before due to the unprecedented advances in the information and communication technologies (ICTs), researchers may take advantage of the enormous information to investigate climatic impacts. In fact, using real time data they may constantly update such analysis and may provide useful information to those who are involved in innovation and designing strategies and policies to cope with the adverse impacts of climate change.

Appendix I

Climate change impact on Indian agriculture: empirical model and data

We examine the impact of climate variables (temperature and rainfall) on the yield of rice and wheat using state-level time series data. The empirical model is specified as follows:

$$yield_{it} = \beta_0 + \beta_1 T_t + \beta_2 temp_{it} + \beta_3 rain_{it} + \beta_4 temp\_var_{it}$$
$$+ \beta_5 rain\_var_{it} + \sum_{(i=1)}^{(n-1)} \gamma_i dum_i + \varepsilon_{it} \tag{1}$$

where T is the time trend, $temp$ denotes average temperature, $rain$ denotes total rainfall, $temp\_var$ is the temperature variability, $rain\_var$ is the rainfall variability, dum_i is the dummy variable for state i, and ε is the white-noise error term; i indexes states ($i = 1, 2, \ldots, n$) and t indexes time period. We use median regression to estimate equation (1).[4] Median regression (more generally, quantile regression) is a nonparametric regression technique that does not require classical assumptions regarding the distribution of the regression error terms and therefore appropriate for heteroscedastic data. For robustness of the results, we also estimate a pooled least square (PLS) regression.

The dataset covers 23 major states of India from 1968 to 2001.[5] We obtain data on average yields of rice and wheat (output in kilogram per hectare) from the Directorate of Economics and Statistics (DES), Government of India. The data are extracted and compiled from the official website of DES (http://eands.dacnet.nic.in/StateData_66-76Year.htm, accessed on 4 July 2014). The climate data on temperature and rainfall used in this study are obtained from www.indiawaterportal.org/met_data/ (accessed on 25 March 2017) that provides district level monthly data on different weather variables.[6] The district-level data thus sourced are aggregated to construct state level average temperature and rainfall data. Using the state-level weather data obtained above, we construct data on four weather variables. From the temperature data, we calculate mean and standard deviation of average temperature during a crop year. From the monthly rainfall data, we calculate annual rainfall and standard deviation of rainfall for the respective states. Note that the agricultural data are reported for the crop year that begins in July and ends in June of the subsequent calendar year. For consistency, we map the constructed annual data on climatic variables to corresponding crop year.[7]

Table 13.A.1 Unit root test results

Variable	Levin-Lin-Chu (LLC) Test		Im-Pesaran-Shin (IPS) Test	
Exogenous variables in the test equation →	Intercepts only	Intercepts and trends	Intercepts only	Intercepts and trends
	(1)	(2)	(3)	(4)
Rice yield	–2.27 **	–11.65***	–3.14***	–11.72***
Wheat yield	–1.56*	–11.93***	–3.57***	–12.06***
Average temperature	–13.46***	–20.04***	–12.12***	–19.17***
Total rainfall	–22.44***	–21.68***	–20.68***	–18.91***
Temperature variability	–19.60***	–16.09***	–21.01***	–19.15***
Rainfall variability	–24.64***	–24.91***	–22.01***	–21.49***

Note: ***significant at the 1% level; **significant at the 5% level; ***significant at the 10% level

We first conduct panel unit root tests to examine if the variables are stationary so that we do not have to worry about the issue of spurious regression. In particular, we perform two most commonly used panel unit root tests: Levin-Lin-Chu (LLC) and Im-Pesaran-Shin (IPS) tests.[8] The test results are reported in Table 13.A.1. In each case, we reject the null hypothesis of unit root indicating that the variables are stationary and we can use them in the regression models in their levels.

Notes

1 Rice and wheat are the two major crops of India in terms of acreage share.
2 For modelling and other technical details, please refer to Appendix I.
3 Among the control variables, the time trend has a significant positive effect on both rice and wheat yield. This may have captured the beneficial effect of technological progress. Most state dummies that capture time invariant state-specific factors are statistically significant under both models suggesting that there are important differences in median yield across states. However, we do not report the coefficients in the table to save space.
4 Sarker et al. (2012) use median regression to examine the climatic impacts on rice yield in Bangladesh.
5 Those states for which a consistent data on the relevant variables are available are considered here. The sample includes Andhra Pradesh, Arunachal Pradesh, Assam, Bihar, Gujarat, Haryana, Himachal Pradesh, Jammu and Kashmir, Karnataka, Madhya Pradesh, Maharashtra, Manipur, Meghalaya, Mizoram, Nagaland, Orissa, Punjab, Rajasthan, Sikkim, Tamil Nadu, Tripura, Uttar Pradesh and West Bengal. For our analysis of wheat yield, we had to drop Manipur and Mizoram.
6 This data set is based on the publicly available Climate Research Unit (CRU) TS2.1 dataset, out of the Tyndall Centre for Climate Change Research, School of Environmental Sciences, University of East Anglia in Norwich, UK. For details, visit www.indiawaterportal.org/articles/background-meteorological-datasets.

7 For example, climatic data for the year 1968–69 refer to a period from July 1968 to June 1969.
8 These tests are described in Levin et al. (2002) and Im et al. (2003).

References

Abeysingha, N.S., Singh, M., Islam, A. and Sehgal, V.K., 2016. Climate Change Impacts on Irrigated Rice and Wheat Production in Gomti River Basin of India: A Case Study. *SpringerPlus* (Open Access), 5, p. 1250, doi:10.1186/s40064-016-2905-y.

Adams, R.M., 1986. Agriculture, Forestry and Related Benefits of Air Pollution Control. *American Journal of Agricultural Economics*, 68, pp. 885–894.

Adams, R.M., Hurd, B.H., Lenhart, S. and Leary, N., 1998. Effects of Global Climate Change on Agriculture: An Interpretative Review. *Climate Research*, 11, pp. 19–30.

Aggarwal, P.K., Kumar, S.N. and Pathak, H., 2010. *Impacts of Climate Change on Growth and Yield of Rice and Wheat in the Upper Ganga Basin*. WWF Report.

Aggarwal, P.K. and Mall, R.K., 2002. Climate Change and Rice Yields in Diverse Agro-Environments of India, II: Effect of Uncertainties in Scenarios and Crop Models on Impact Assessment. *Climatic Change*, 52, pp. 331–343.

Aggarwal, P.K. and Sinha, S.K., 1993. Effect of Probable Increase in Carbon Dioxide and Temperature on Wheat Yields in India. *Journal of Agricultural Meteorology*, 48(5), pp. 811–814.

Al-Bakri, J., Suleiman, A., Abdulla, F. and Ayad, J., 2010. Potential Impact of Climate Change on Rainfed Agriculture of a Semi-Arid Basin in Jordan. *Physics and Chemistry of the Earth*, 35, pp. 125–134.

Attavanich, W. and McCarl, B.A., 2014. How Is CO_2 Affecting Crop Yields and Technological Progress? A Statistical Analysis. *Climatic Change*, 124(4), pp. 747–762, doi:10.1007/s10584-014-1128-x.

Attri, S.D. and Rathore, L.S., 2003. Simulation of Impact of Projected Climate Change on Wheat in India. *International Journal of Climatology*, 23, pp. 693–705.

Auffhammer, M., Ramanathan, V. and Vincent, J.R., 2006. Integrated Model Shows That Atmospheric Brown Clouds and Green House Gases Have Reduced Rice Harvests in India. *Proceedings of the National Academy of Sciences*, 103(52), pp. 19688–19672.

Barnwal, P. and Kotani, K., 2013. Climatic Impacts Across Agricultural Crop Yield Distributions: An Application of Quantile Regression on Rice Crops in Andhra Pradesh, India. *Ecological Economics*, 87, pp. 95–109.

Benhin, J.K.A., 2008. South African Crop Farming and Climate Change: An Economic Assessment of Impacts. *Global Environmental Change*, 18, pp. 666–678.

Boomiraj, K., Chakrabarti, C., Aggarwal, P.K., Choudhary, R. and Chander, S., 2010. Assessing the Vulnerability of Indian Mustard to Climate Change. *Agriculture, Ecosystems and Environment*, 138, pp. 265–273.

Burney, J. and Ramanathan, V., 2014. Recent Climate and Air Pollution Impacts on Indian Agriculture. *Proceedings of the National Academy of Sciences*, 111(46), pp. 16319–16324.

Cabas, J., Weersink, A. and Olale, E., 2010. Crop Yield Response to Economic, Site and Climatic Variables. *Climatic Change*, 101, pp. 599–616.

Chen, C.C., McCarl, B.A. and Schimmelpfenning, D.E., 2004. Yield Variability as Influenced by Climate: A Statistical Investigation. *Climatic Change*, 66, pp. 239–261.

Deressa, T.T. and Hassan, R.M., 2009. Economic impact of climate change on crop production in Ethiopia: evidence from cross-section measures. *Journal of African Economies*, 18, pp. 529–554.

Deschenes, O. and Greenstone, M., 2007. The Economic Impacts of Climate Change: Evidence From Agricultural Output and Random Fluctuations in Weather. *American Economic Review*, 97(1), pp. 354–385.

Dubey, S.K., Tripathy, S.K., Pranuthi, G. and Yadav, R., 2014. Impact of Projected Climate Change on Wheat Varieties in Uttarakhand, India. *Journal of Agrometeorology*, 16(1), pp. 26–37.

Guiteras, R., 2009. *The Impact of Climate Change on Indian Agriculture*, Department of Economics, University of Maryland, College Park, MD.

Gupta, S., Sen, P. and Jain, P., 2013. *Impact of Climate Change on the Foodgrain Yields and Their Variability in India*. Paper presented at the Fourth National Research Conference on Climate Change, IIT Madras, October 27.

Gupta, S., Sen, P. and Srinivasan, S., 2012. *Impact of Climate Change on the Indian Economy: Evidence From Foodgrain Yields*. Working Paper No. 218, CDE, Delhi School of Economics.

Im, K.S., Pesaran, M. H. and Shin, Y., 2003. Testing for Unit Roots in Heterogeneous Panels. *Journal of Econometrics*, 115, pp. 53–74.

Isik, M. and Devadoss, S.C., 2006. An Analysis of the Impacts of Climate Change on Crop Yields and Yield Variability. *Applied Economics*, 38, pp. 835–844.

Jayaraman, T., 2011. Climate Change and Agriculture: A Review Article With Special Reference to India. *Review of Agrarian Studies*, 1(2), pp. 16–78.

Kaiser, H.M., Riha, S.J., Wilks, D.S., Rossiter, D.G. and Sampath, R., 1993. A Farm-Level Analysis of Economic and Agronomic Impacts of Gradual Climate Warming. *American Journal of Agricultural Economics*, 75, pp. 387–398.

Knox, J., Hess, T., Daccache, A. and Wheeler, T., 2012. Climate Change Impacts on Crop Productivity in Africa and South Asia. *Environmental Research Letters*, 7, 034032 (Open Access), doi:10.1088/1748-9326/7/3/034032

Krishnamurthy, C.K.B., 2012. *The Distributional Impacts of Climate Change on Indian Agriculture: A Quantile Regression Approach*. Working Paper 69/2012, Madras School of Economics.

Kumar, K.S.K., 2011. Climate Sensitivity of Indian Agriculture: Do Spatial Effects Matter? *Cambridge Journal of Regions, Economy and Society*, 4, pp. 1–15.

Kumar, K.S.K. and Parikh, J., 2001. Indian Agriculture and Climate Sensitivity. *Global Environmental Change*, 11, pp. 147–154.

Kumar, S.N. and Aggarwal, P.K., 2013. Climate Change and Coconut Plantations in India: Impacts and Potential Adaptation Gains. *Agricultural Systems*, 117, pp. 45–54.

Kumar, S.N., Aggarwal, P.K., Rani, S., Jain, S., Saxena, R. and Chouhan, N., 2011. Impact of Climate Change on Crop Productivity in Western Ghats, Coastal and Northeastern Regions of India. *Current Science*, 101(3), pp. 332–341.

Kumar, S.N., Govindakrishnan, P.M., Swarooparani, D.N., Nitin, C., Surabhi, J. and Aggarwal, P.K., 2015. Assessment of Impact of Climate Change on Potato and Potential Adaptation Gains in the Indo Gangetic Plains of India. *International Journal of Plant Production*, 9(1), pp. 151–170.

Lal, M., Singh, K.K., Rathore, L.S., Srinivasan, G. and Saseendran, S.A., 1998. Vulnerability of Rice and Wheat Yields in NW India to Future Changes in Climate. *Agricultural and Forest Meteorology*, 89, pp. 101–114.

Levin, A., Lin, C. and Chu, C.J., 2002. Unit Root Tests in Panel Data: Asymptotic and Finite-Sample Properties. *Journal of Econometrics*, 108, pp. 1–24.

Lewandrowski, J. and Schimmelpfennig, D., 1999. Economic implications of climate change for U.S. agriculture: assessing recent evidence. *Land Economics*, 75, pp. 39–57.

Luo, Q., Williams, M., Bellotti, W. and Bryan, B., 2003. Quantitative and Visual Assessments of Climate Change Impacts on South Australian Wheat Production. *Agricultural Systems*, 77(3), pp. 173–186.

Magrin, G.O., Travasso, M.I. and Rodriguez, G.R., 2005. Changes in Climate and Crop Production During the 20th Century in Argentina. *Climatic Change*, 72, pp. 229–249.

Mall, R.K., Lal, M., Bhatia, V.S., Rathore, L.S. and Singh, R., 2004. Mitigating Climate Change Impact on Soybean Productivity in India: A Simulation Study. *Agricultural and Forest Meteorology*, 121, pp. 113–125.

Mandal, R. and Nath, H.K., 2017. Heterogeneous climatic impacts on agricultural production: evidence from rice yield in Assam, India. *Asian Journal of Agriculture and Development* (forthcoming).

Mendelsohn, R., 2007. Past Climate Change Impacts on Agriculture. In Evenson, R. and Pingali, P. (eds.), *Handbook of Agricultural Economics*, Vol. 3, Ch. 60, pp. 3010–3031.

Mendelsohn, R., Nordhaus, W.D. and Shaw, D., 1994. The Impact of Global Warming on Agriculture: A Ricardian Analysis. *American Economic Review*, 84(4), pp. 753–771.

Mishra, A., Singh, R., Raghuwanshi, N.S., Chatterjee, C. and Froebrich, J., 2013. Spatial Variability of Climate Change Impacts on Yield of Rice and Wheat in the Indian Ganga Basin. *Science of the Total Environment*, 468–469, pp. S132–S138.

Moula, E.L., 2009. An empirical assessment of the impact of climate change on smallholder agriculture in Cameroon. *Global Planetary Change*, 67, pp. 205–208.

Ortiz, R., Sayre, K.D., Govaerts, B., Gupta, R., Subbarao, G.V., Ban, T., Hodson, D., Dixon, J.M., Ortiz-Monasterio, J.I. and Reynolds, M., 2008. Climate Change: Can Wheat Beat the Heat? *Agriculture, Ecosystems and Environment*, 126(1–2), pp. 46–58.

Parry, M., Rosenzweig, C., Iglesias, A., Fischer, G. and Livermore, M., 1999. Climate Change and World Food Security: A New Assessment. *Global Environmental Change*, 9(Supplement 1), pp. S51–S67.

Parry, M.L., Rosenzweig, C., Iglesias, A., Livermore, M. and Fischer, G., 2004. Effects of Climate Change on Global Food Production Under SRES Emissions and Socio-Economic Scenarios. *Global Environmental Change*, 14, pp. 53–67.

Poudel, S. and Kotani, K., 2013. Climatic Impacts on Crop Yield and Its Variability in Nepal: Do They Vary Across Seasons and Altitudes? *Climatic Change*, 116, pp. 327–355.

Rao, B.B., Chowdary, P.S., Sandeep, V.M., Rao, V.U.M. and Venkateswarlu, B., 2014. Rising Minimum Temperature Trends Over India in Recent Decades: Implications for Agricultural Production. *Global and Planetary Change*, 117, pp. 1–8.

Rosenzweig, C. and Hillel, D., 1995. *Climate Change and the Global Harvest: Potential Impacts on the Greenhouse Effect on Agriculture*, Oxford University Press, New York.

Rosenzweig, C. and Iglesias, A. (eds.), 1994. *Implications of Climate Change for International Agriculture: Crop Modeling Study*. EPA 230-B-94-003, U.S. EPA Office of Policy, Planning and Evaluation, Climate Change Division, Adaptation Branch, Washington, DC.

Rosenzweig, C. and Parry, M.L., 1994. Potential Impact of Climate Change on World Food Supply. *Nature*, 367, pp. 133–138.

Sanghi, A. and Mendelsohn, R., 2008. The Impacts of Global Warming on Farmers in Brazil and India. *Global Environmental Change*, 18, pp. 655–665.

Sarker, A.R., Alam, K. and Gow, J., 2012. Exploring the Relationship Between Climate Change and Rice Yield in Bangladesh: An Analysis of Time Series Data. *Agricultural Systems*, 112, pp. 11–16.

Saseendran, S.A., Singh, K.K., Rathore, L.S., Singh, S.V. and Sinha, S.K., 2000. Effects of Climate Change on Rice Production in the Tropical Humid Climate of Kerala, India. *Climatic Change*, 44, pp. 495–514.

Schlenker, W. and Lobell, D.B., 2010. Robust Negative Impacts of Climate Change on African Agriculture. *Environmental Research Letters*, 5, 014010, doi:10.1088/1748-9326/5/1/014010.

Schlenker, W. and Roberts, M.J., 2009. Nonlinear Temperature Effects Indicate Severe Damages to U.S. Crop Yields Under Climate Change. *Proceedings of the National Academy of Sciences*, 106(37), pp. 15594–15598.

Seo, S.N., Mendelsohn, R. and Munasinghe, M., 2005. Climate Change and Agriculture in Sri Lanka: A Ricardian Valuation. *Environment and Development Economics*, 10, pp. 581–596.

Singh, P.K., Singh, K.K., Bhan, S.C., Baxla, A.K., Singh, S., Rathore, L.S. and Gupta, A., 2017. Impact of Projected Climate Change on Rice (*Oryza sativaL*) Yield Using CERES-Rice Model in Different Agroclimatic Zones of India. *Current Science*, 112(1), pp. 108–115.

Soora, N.K., Aggarwal, P.K., Saxena, R., Rani, S., Jain, S. and Chauhan, N., 2013. An Assessment of Regional Vulnerability of Rice to Climate Change in India. *Climatic Change*, 118(3), pp. 683–699.

Welch, J.R., Vincent, J.R., Auffhammer, M., Moya, P.F., Dobermann, A. and Dawe, D., 2010. Rice Yields in Tropical/Subtropical Asia Exhibit Large But Opposing Sensitivities to Minimum and Maximum Temperatures. *Proceedings of the National Academy of Sciences*, 107(33), pp. 14562–14567.

14 The way forward

M. P. Bezbaruah

1 Introduction

Diffusion of Green Revolution technology across the country and the strata of farmers of different size classes over the two decades since its initial success in the Punjab-Haryana-Western UP belt in the late 1960s transformed India from a country of chronic food shortages to a food-secure nation, at least in the macro sense. However, this remarkable achievement of post-independence India did not come without a price. The fatigue and stress building up during the successful run of the Green Revolution that had surfaced during the 1980s was further accentuated to a crisis point by the mid-1990s. While at the aggregate level growth rate slowed down and productivity stagnated, at the micro level financial performance of the farms turned adverse, leading to growing indebtedness of farmers to the financers in both institutional and non-institutional categories. Farmers in many parts of the country found it difficult to cope with the stress, and some even resorted to the extreme step of taking their own lives.

The root cause of the crisis can be summed up as policy mismanagement. The investments in large irrigation projects made during early development plans in India had kept the conditions ready in parts of the country for adoption of the high-yielding variety (HYV) seeds when the technological breakthrough was finally achieved. Thus, in no time the farmers in Punjab, Haryana and Uttar Pradesh could turn the new opportunity into the famous Green Revolution. Expansion of irrigation capacity in the major and medium sectors, however, could not be sustained in the post-Green Revolution period for reasons discussed in Chapter 10. Consequently, farmers have been forced to depend increasingly on groundwater-based minor irrigation systems, which has had very adverse consequences in the dryer regions in the form of lowering the groundwater tables and increasing the need to dig deeper for drawing water. Secondly, the input subsidy-price support regime brought in for the well-intended purpose of promoting adoption of the HYV and agro-chemical package also had inherent undesirable consequences for the agro-ecological environment. Hence these support measures should have been moderated and phased out as the new technology got rooted, stabilized and started spreading. But this was not done, and the distortionary effects of the policy were allowed to be accentuated, leading to serious environmental damage. Eventually, when price corrections became unavoidable, the burden of adjustment on the farmers had telling effects. Meanwhile extension services, which had earlier enabled farmers to turn the Green Revolution into a resounding success, were allowed to slacken, leaving many farmers at the mercy of input sellers for guidance and advice. This obviously was a recipe for conflict of interest from which some early adopters of Bt cotton in Maharashtra suffered badly. On top of these problems, opening up of international trade in agricultural products, limited as the move was, was pursued without adequate precaution for enabling farmers to cope with the increased uncertainty of price that would go with it.

In contrast to the much publicized narratives of agrarian distress and farmers' suicides, the resilience that farmers displayed in the adversity and the inherent dynamism within Indian agriculture which enabled the sector to secure for itself a turn-around from the depth of the crisis have not received the attention they deserve. Revival in the growth of farmers' income, which has contributed to the mitigation of farmers' suicide rate post-2005, has come primarily from diversification of farming into the horticulture and livestock sub-sectors, which have the potential of returning higher value per unit of resource engaged. The shift in product composition in favour of horticultural and livestock products and away from cereals corresponds to a similar change in consumers' preferences in the food baskets across all expenditure strata (Birthal et al., 2013, Table 14.2, p. 17). This correspondence indicates that farmers sensed market signals correctly and have acted upon them to change their cropping patterns accordingly. Agrarian reforms that remained unimplemented and/or ineffective for decades, and have by now even outlived their relevance, have been substituted by endogenously evolving market institutions. It is true that in the recent years, a shift of the workforce from agriculture to non-agricultural occupations has become somewhat quicker.[1] On whether these exits are induced by the push factor of low returns from cultivation, particularly of traditional crops like food grains, or the pull of greener pastures in non-agriculture sectors, the jury is still out. It is quite possible that both types of factors have been at work and decisions to exit are actually influenced by a combination of the factors. But this trend needs to be viewed as an opening of new opportunities in agriculture rather than as putting a death nail into it. Reduced population pressure on land and a consequent rise in agricultural wages can make conditions conducive for furthering mechanization of farm processes. This, in turn, can lead to an increase in labour productivity and even higher returns from cultivation for those who stay in the sector. Moreover, higher agricultural wages mean a higher benchmark for wages in rural non-farm and even urban labour markets, which works to mitigate poverty.

The task now is to create the enabling environment through uplift of the relevant infrastructure and institutions for building on these positive developments so that Indian agriculture comes out strong to stand up to the impending challenges of the 21st century. What follows next is a discussion of the areas and nature of relevant policy interventions.

218   M. P. Bezbaruah

2 Some critical areas of intervention

2.1 Infrastructure including irrigation

It is an imperative to continue strengthening general rural infrastructure, comprised primarily of roads, power supply and telecommunication, if farmers are to be empowered with enhanced market connectivity and improved delivery of various other support services. A lot has been achieved in connecting the interiors of India with the network of state and national highways under the Pradhan Mantri Gram Sarak Yojana (PMGSY), or Prime Minister's village road programme.[2] This is a job which is not finished as yet. Moreover, maintenance of the constructed roads is equally important and the task holds additional challenges in hilly and high rainfall areas where deterioration can be quicker. As for the specific agricultural infrastructure of irrigation, the emphasis right now seems to be on more efficient use of the available water by adopting methods like drip irrigation.[3] The initiative is laudable, especially in dry areas where groundwater depletion and fall in the water tables have already assumed alarming proportions. To induce wider adoption of these methods among farmers, it may be necessary to subsidize equipment. Unlike in the case of agro-chemicals or electricity, a subsidy in this context can be justified on the ground that the use of these methods are expected to yield considerable positive externalities in conserving the natural resource base in the dry areas. The quantum of subsidy to farmers in different agro-climatic conditions needs to be carefully calculated. While the subsidy should be large enough to induce farmers to adopt the methods, it should not be so large as to induce diversion of the equipment to secondary markets in less subsidized locations. In the longer run, reviving public investments in major and medium irrigation projects can bring about a more permanent solution. But adding capacity in the major-medium irrigation sector would require more than just mobilizing and deploying the necessary finances, which can indeed be substantial. It will also be necessary to identify new sources of water, such as run-off of monsoon precipitation in eastern India and the Western Ghats, designing the engineering for harnessing such sources and taking on the anti-dam lobbyists and the environmentalists in debates on the consequences of alternative strategies and action plans, including non-intervention.

2.2 Reorienting agrarian reforms

One of the concerns of academics and policymakers regarding the future of Indian agriculture has been the falling size of holdings of farmers and the consequent disproportionate rise in the number of holdings in the marginal size class. It cannot be denied that the small holding size, getting smaller over the years, can come as a serious constraint for continuing as a viable production unit. Hence, agrarian reforms will have to be designed and taken up to keep such constraints at bay. Traditional thinking in this regard runs in terms of redistribution of land owned by those in larger holding size classes to those who form the lower holding size classes. In today's context, such a scheme of redistribution of land ownership may not be effective or even viable. Past experience shows that land redistribution is politically difficult to implement. In addition, recent studies have shown that even farmers in the higher size classes have been losing assets (Das, 2015). Hence, there simply may not be enough land to redistribute and bring all units to a minimum threshold size. Redistribution may thus result in pulling down all rather than pulling up the marginal ones. Moreover, a static redistribution may cure the symptom but will not address the root cause, which means that the problem may resurface post-redistribution.

In this context, what assumes importance is reforming tenancy laws to facilitate the efficient function of the land lease market. Conventional tenancy laws adopted in Indian states after independence were induced by concern for the plight of the tenant farmers, who often suffered at the hands of landlords from the threat of eviction and seemingly usurious rents. Well-meaning as these laws were, it has been found that in practice the laws have had the unintended consequence of driving tenancy underground to avoid the stringent provisions of the acts. Consequently, despite tenancy remaining an active and widespread phenomenon in the countryside, all of it is virtually informal, mostly short term and outside government records. Tenancy regulations now need to be revised not only to make them more effective but also to attune them to the changed circumstances. Land owners – big, small or marginal – should be able to lease out land without the fear of losing ownership. This will facilitate many unviable marginal cultivators and absentee land owners to exit the sector. Besides adopting alternative occupations elsewhere, marginal land owners will be able to appropriate some rent income from their land ownership. By facilitating the exit of people from agricultural to non-agricultural occupations, these laws can act as catalysts in completing the structural transformation of the Indian economy by bringing down the dependence of the work force on agriculture more to the tune of its contribution to GDP. At the ground level, it will open up opportunity for pushing up mechanization of agricultural processes and thereby increasing labour productivity in the sector. Those who want to stay back and even scale up their operations to take advantage of emerging opportunities in the sector can expand their holdings without the pitfalls of informal and underground tenancy contracts. With more and more land likely to be available for leasing, the balance of bargaining strength in the land lease market is likely to shift in favour of the leasees, which should have a moderating effect on the rent.

Meanwhile emerging factor markets of groundwater for irrigation and rental of capital goods have made lumpy farm capital goods like power tillers, tractors and irrigation pump sets effectively divisible and usable for cultivating units of any size. These developments have largely substituted for the difficult and long under-implemented reform of consolidation of holdings. Scholars and policy makers now need to be vigilant about possible market failure in these emerging markets so that efficiency and equity of resource use are not adversely affected.

2.3 Broadening and deepening of financial inclusion

With the onset of the Green Revolution, the financing needs of farms in India increased. The HYV seeds and fertilizer technology were intensive in purchased inputs, so their adoption meant that farmers needed more funds for carrying out agricultural operations. The banking sector in India responded to the growing demand for finances in agriculture by extending its presence and operations in rural India after nationalization of most of the major commercial banks in 1969. Though traditional co-operative credit institutions also played their roles in some parts of the country, what gave nationwide momentum to the spread of institutional financial services to the rural economy in general and agriculture in particular was the advent of the regional rural banks (RRBs). Later, in 1982, the National Bank for Agriculture and Rural Development (NABARD) was set up as the apex institution of the structure of institutional rural finance in the country. To ensure inflow of institutional credit to sectors, including agriculture, which were otherwise under-served by financial institutions, the Reserve Bank of India came up with the restriction on the banking system that each bank would have to direct a minimum of 40 per cent of its credit to 'priority sectors'. Within the priority sectors, there have also been sub-targets for specific sub-sectors, such as agriculture.

Expansion and penetration of formal financial institutions no doubt played an important role in the rural economy in the post-Green Revolution period. However, the expansion being mostly supply driven, the system left a large segment of demand for financial services of rural households unattended. This segment was left to be catered to by informal operators, including traditional money lenders. These informal suppliers have generally been demand driven and have product range to match the different credit needs of farmers and rural households. But supply from these sources usually comes at much higher rates of interest, and many farmers resorting to informal supply end up becoming severely indebted. One of the reasons why small and marginal farmers have often lagged behind larger farmers in exploiting full potentials of farm technology is that their credit need has been largely unserved by institutions of rural credit.

Post-reform, rural financial markets in India have undergone changes. Financial sector reforms brought in as a component of India's post-1991 overall economic reforms process required banks to fulfil more stringent prudential norms. Profitability came to be recognized as an important performance indicator of the banks. In the process of restructuring banks and their financial profiles, branch expansion to rural areas virtually stopped and was even rolled back in some cases. RRBs were regrouped into bigger entities for better financial consolidation. Meanwhile many private and foreign banks, which are generally metropolitan and urban oriented, started operating. As these banks found meeting priority sector lending requirement difficult, they were allowed to lend the balance to the Rural Infrastructure Development Fund (RIDF) administered under NABARD. While this escape route for banks might have left government agencies with financial resources for spending on rural infrastructure, the direct institutional credit flow to rural and agricultural units got at the same time limited. Moreover within agriculture, allocation of bank credit has gradually shifted away from seemingly riskier crop loans to other segments, such as term loans.

Meanwhile the less formal part of India's rural financial system underwent innovation and expansion. Micro-finance institutions (MFI), non-bank financial companies (NBFC) and other local institutions like thrift societies (notwithstanding some unscrupulous fly-by-night operators) entered rural financial markets to give competition to the traditional moneylenders. A linkage between formal and non-formal segments emerged as banks, encouraged by NABARD, started to reach out to borrowers at the grassroots level through linkage programmes with MFIs, NBFCs, non-governmental organizations (NGOs), self-help groups (SHGs) and joint liability groups (JLGs). A recent initiative of the RBI to issue licenses to open and operate small banks[4] has further strengthened the process of convergence of formal and informal financial institutions serving the rural and unorganized sectors of the economy. Introduction of the negotiable instrument of priority sector lending certificates (PSLC)[5] is yet another recent initiative of the RBI to enable financial institutions to efficiently and meaningfully fulfil their priority sector lending obligation.

The developments in the rural financial market in the forms of entry of new institutions and stronger linkages among formal, semi-formal and informal institutions augur well for the rural economy of India. As the operations of semi-formal and informal institutions and also of the new small banks are more demand driven, these institutions are better placed for customizing products and procedures for the rural masses. Since funds are made available at a lower cost than through the traditional moneylenders, the risk of borrowers falling into a debt trap simply because of the burden of the interest payment will be reduced. With credit supply being available from multiple sources, a farmer or a rural entrepreneur now has the option of choosing a credit provider and even sourcing credit from multiple sources. However, therein lies a potential pitfall too. A farmer defaulting to one creditor can go to another for more credit. But defaults everywhere may finally close all the escape routes from the state of growing indebtedness. Drawing from available case studies Rao reconstructs the typical case of such a farmer in the following words:

> He/she carries a heavy accumulated burden of debts to many creditors with none ready to lend any further and all insisting on immediate repayment. The proximate cause is low/negative returns over a successive run of years due to crop losses caused by weather, pests, etc. and crash in prices. Given his/her strong urge to move upwards, he/she persists in borrowing and investing in the hope of having a good season helping him/her to clear all debts and earn handsome returns.
>
> (Rao, 2009, p 120)

When this turns out to be a mirage, the desperation can easily drive a farmer to suicide.

While it is necessary to support a revival of agricultural growth by making finances available to farmers at fair rates, the old way of reaching the interiors through branch expansion is unlikely to be revived. Indeed, technology has obviated the need for the bank to be physically present in brick-and-mortar structures everywhere. The information technology (IT)-based systems of delivering financial services have perhaps not yet fully stabilized. But with the push towards a digital India[6] and with the practice of transferring benefits from government's welfare schemes electronically to the bank accounts of target beneficiaries directly,[7] more and more people, including farmers, are likely to be financially included through electronic mediums.

IT-based information sharing systems among credit providers need to be strengthened to address the information asymmetry problem faced by them. The system is imperative for enabling a creditor to distinguish prime borrowers from the subprime ones.

Left to market operators, credit supply to agriculture will be inherently constrained by the weather, pests and market-related risks to which the sector is typically exposed. The interest on whatever credit is advanced may also be high due to higher risk perception. State interventions for ensuring adequate credit flow to the sector, hence, will have to continue. The initiatives of the RBI to make priority sector lending more effective assume importance in this context. Moreover, the revamped crop insurance scheme under Pradhan Mantri Fasal Bima Yojana (PMFBY) has in it an inbuilt mechanism of insuring crop loans advanced by banks to farmers. Expanding coverage of this scheme will thus help expand credit delivery by banks to farmers.

2.4 Strengthening the post harvest value chain

Indian agriculture has already started diversifying away from cereals towards higher value commodities such as fruits, vegetables and livestock products. The shift is in conformity with changes in consumers' preferences across the spectrum of income categories. The process can potentially reward farmers with better returns. But farm output from these sub-sectors being relatively more perishable, realization of higher returns depends critically on connecting producers to effective value chains. The chain involves several links, from aggregation, storage and processing to retailing. Farmers may be inducted into a value chain through any or many of the alternative routes, such as a producer cooperative, a producer company, a contract farming agreement and/or simply direct retailing. Policy interventions are required for putting enabling infrastructure and institutions in place to strengthen the links in the chain wherever they are weak or even absent. Physical infrastructure of connectivity and cold storage are the basic requirements. For these infrastructures to be effectively utilized, some supporting facilities need to exist. For instance, effective markets for 'warehouse receipts'[8] can be crucial for fuller appropriation of benefits of storage facilities by farmers. Similarly, the system for certification and labelling of the processed and packaged farm products needs to be in place for these products to be widely marketed in domestic and foreign retail outlets.

2.5 Technology, research and extension

Technology options

In the longer run, a significant step-up in productivity, which is important for sustaining higher farm income, has to come from a technological breakthrough. Since the HYV seeds of the Green Revolution, whatever technological improvements have taken place have mostly been incremental in nature. System of Rice Intensification (SRI), developed in Madagascar in 1980s, has been hailed as a 'potential source of technological revolution for small and marginal farms' by the Task Force on Agricultural Development constituted by NITI Aayog, Government of India.[9] It is a labour-intensive water economizing method that reportedly improves the yield of rice by 30 to 50 per cent. The method has gained some popularity in the states of Tamil Nadu, Bihar and Tripura, though it has yet to be adopted extensively in all rice-growing parts of the country. Proponents and critics of SRI continue to debate the claimed benefits of the method (Glover, 2011). Whether SRI constitutes a real technological breakthrough or merely a set of good crop husbandry practices can also be debated. But to the extent it improves yield while reducing pressure on environmental and natural resources, its practice should be undoubtedly promoted.

What promise to emerge as a disruptive and game changing development in the technology front are genetically modified (GM) seeds. Developed through genetic engineering, these seed varieties promise high crop productivity, lower use of fertilizers and pesticides, and even nutritional health benefits. Over the last couple of decades, these crops have gained increasing acceptance among farmers around the world. In India, the resounding success of Bt cotton after a few initial hiccups has already demonstrated the potency of the technology. Unfortunately India has been hesitant to extend the new technology to other crops such as Bt brinjal and golden rice, which promise not only high productivity and low environmental cost but also significant health benefits (Birthal, 2013).

The concerns about GM crops range from human health safety issues to the market power of the large bio-technology firms producing and distributing the seeds (Robbins, 2014). These debates should be welcomed as they can play a constructive role in shaping the future course of development and dissemination of this promising technology by suitably modifying the research agenda and laying out the regulatory framework. But getting stuck in endless debates and not taking the issues forward by yielding to the pressure of unreasonable activist groups may cost the country dearly. Exploring the use of GM varieties with the necessary safeguards, especially in areas such as pulses and oil seeds, where conventional technology has not been yielding significant gains, has been recommended by the Task Force on Agricultural Development mentioned above.

Revamping research and extension

This brings us to the issue of rejuvenating agronomic research and extension service in the country. While the breakthrough in HYV seeds of wheat and rice were made in CYMMAT in Mexico and IRRI in the Philippines, respectively, the work of scientists in India's domestic research institutions had a stellar role in not only adapting the technology to local conditions but also taking it forward by developing newer breeds better suited to the diverse agro-economic environments of this large country. Extension workers played an equally important role by counselling farmers regarding the nuances of application of the technology and acting as conduit between the scientists' laboratories and farmers' fields in respect of specific problems that sprang up from time to time and place to place. In the subsequent period, as government-provided extension services started slackening, farmers were often left at the mercy of input dealers for advice – a state of affairs rife with the hazards of conflict of interests.

The time has come to re-energize research and extension. Research is imperative, first for ascertaining health and environmental safety of new varieties, then to adapt the new varieties to the Indian agro-environmental conditions, and finally to indigenously develop safe and effective GM crops to give multinational seed companies a run for their money. The extension service will have to re-enact its role in the success of the Green Revolution by being the effective couriers of the technology from laboratories to farmers' fields and facilitate successful adoption with informed advisory inputs. This time around the extension workers will be able to do the job with reduced leg work as it will be possible to reach out to farmers and communicate with them through ICT-enabled devices and modes.

3 A concluding comment

In the ultimate analysis, Indian agriculture in the 21st century has to evolve in a way so as to sustain the food security of the country's residents, improve nutritional standards across all income strata, check resource depletion and environmental degradation, acquire resilience to cope with exogenous challenges such as climate change effects, and most importantly, honour the farmers by ensuring a decent and dignified living out of farming.

Notes

1 In the Situational Assessment Survey 2002–03 of National Sample Survey Office (NSSO), 40 per cent of farmers surveyed stated that they would prefer to quit farming if there was a choice. As the survey was done at a time when the agrarian crisis was nearly at its peak, the percentage may have had some upward bias. But as per estimates for the subsequent period from 2004–05 to 20012–13 during which the farmers' suicide rates steadily declined indicating that the worst of the agrarian crisis was over, workforce in Indian agriculture declined by 34 million at an average annual rate of 2.04 per cent. Further the decline was observed in both the categories of cultivators and agricultural labourers (Chand, 2017, p. 16).
2 Launched in 2000, PMGSY is a fully centrally funded nationwide scheme to provide good all-weather road connectivity to unconnected villages. Since its inception during the National Democratic Alliance government led by Prime Minister Atal Bihari Bajpayee, successive governments at the centre held by different political configurations have been pursuing the scheme with undiminished importance. Target for the financial year 2016–17 was to add 48,812 kilometres of road (source: http://pmgsy.nic.in/circulars/JH19122016.pdf)

3 The thrust of the Pradhan Mantri Krishi Sinchayee Yojana (Prime Minister's Scheme for Irrigating Agriculture), launched in 2015 by amalgamating the different ongoing government programmes for irrigation, has been to expand cultivable area under assured irrigation by improving on-farm water use efficiency through wider adoption of precision-irrigation and other water saving technologies.

4 Small Banks are meant to provide basic banking services of acceptance of deposit and delivery of credit to sections of the economy such as unorganized sector entities of small business units, small and marginal farmers etc. which are underserved by the scheduled commercial banks. In September 2015, RBI granted 10 licenses to open small finance banks geared towards expanding access to financial services in rural and semi-urban areas.

5 In April 2016 the RBI released guidelines for PSLCs with which banks are expected to manage their priority sector lending limits more effectively and at a lower overall cost for the economy. In the event of shortfall in priority sector lending targets and sub-target, a bank can fulfil its obligation by buying PSLCs, which will be sold by institutions that over-achieve their own targets. There will, however, be no transfer of loan or risks, from the certificate selling institutions to buying institutions. Further a certificate will expire at the end of the financial year in which it is to be used for in covering a shortfall. Small banks, MFIs, NBFCSs and RRBs, which may lend to the priority sectors in access of their minimum stipulated limit, will now be able to sell their excess credit points in the form of PSLCs to city oriented institutions like foreign and large private sector banks which usually find it difficult to meet their own stipulations. More these institutions find it difficult to meet the requirements, higher will be the demand for the PSLCs, and accordingly better will be the rewards to the institutions that are more geared to priority sector lending at the ground level. This prospective reward should work as an additional incentive for these operators to more intensively serve the credit needs of small businesses and small and marginal farmers.

6 Launched in July 2015 Digital India is a campaign launched by the Government of India to ensure that government services are made available to citizens electronically by strengthening and broadening of internet connectivity.

7 Direct Benefit Transfer (DBT) initiative rolled out from 1 January 2013 aims to ensure that benefits of relevant welfare schemes go directly to bank accounts of beneficiaries electronically, minimizing stages involved in fund flow thereby reducing delay in payment, ensuring better targeting and curbing leakages.

8 A warehouse receipt is a document that certifies ownership and guarantees existence of a commodity of a particular quantity, type, and quality in a named storage facility. Negotiable warehouse receipts allow transfer of ownership of that commodity without having to deliver the commodity physically. Thus a farmer who acquires the receipt upon depositing the product in a warehouse can encash the receipt at any point of time in the market at its ongoing price. The final dealers of the commodity can secure its physical delivery by submitting the receipts acquired in the market.

9 'Raising Agricultural Productivity and Making Farming Remunerative for Farmers, An Occasional Paper', NITI Aayog, Government of India, 16 December 2015, p 22.

References

Birthal, P. S., 2013. Application of Frontier Technologies for Agricultural Development. *Indian Journal of Agricultural Economics*, 68(1), pp. 20–38.

Birthal, P. S., Joshi, P. K., Negi, D. S. and Agarwal, S., 2013. *Changing Sources of Growth in Indian Agriculture: Implications for Regional Priorities for Accelerating Agricultural Growth*. IFPRI Discussion Paper, International Food Policy Research Institute, New Delhi.

Chand, R., 2017. Doubling Farmers' Income: Strategy and Prospect. *Indian Journal of Agricultural Economics*, 72(1), pp. 1–23.

Das, D., 2015. Changing Distribution of Land and Assets in Indian Agriculture. *Review of Radical Political Economics*, 47(3), pp. 412–423.

Glover, D., 2011. Science, Practice and the System of Rice Intensification in Indian Agriculture. *Food Policy*, 36(6), pp. 749–755.

Rao, V. M., 2009. Farmers' Distress in a Modernizing Agriculture – The Tragedy of the Upwardly Mobile: An Overview. In Reddy, D. N. and Misra, S. (eds.), *Agrarian Crisis in India*, Oxford University Press, New Delhi, Ch.5.

Robbins, J., 2014. Can GMOs Help End World Hunger? *Huffington Post*, January 12.

Index

Note: Page numbers in italics indicate figures; those in bold indicate tables.

Farmer Water Melon Co-operative 90
farm income insurance scheme (FIIS) 68, 69
financial inclusion, broadening and deepening 220–2
fixed rent lease arrangements 29, 30, 42–3
Food Bazar 87
Food Corporation of India 157
food grains *vs.* non-food grain crop sector, changes in 12, 14
foreign direct investment (FDI) 131
formal water markets 47–8
Foster, P. 46

General Agreement on Tariffs and Trade (GATT) 2, 5
genetically modified (GM) seeds 223
geogenic contamination in groundwater in India 191
Gijbels, I. 179
Global Hub Procurement Program 90
Godrej 87
Goswami, B. 35, 36, 38, 39, 40, 41, 43
government as food grains purchaser 82
Government of India 40, 223
Green Revolution (GR): environmental consequences of, in India (*see* environmental consequences, Green Revolution in India); financial inclusion and 220–2; future for 216–24; groundwater-based irrigation and 47; Indian agriculture after 8–25; negative effects of 2; positive effects of 1–2; success of 8; technology (*see* technology adoption by farmers)
Green Revolution, Indian agriculture after 8–25; *see also* environmental consequences, Green Revolution in India; irrigation; compositional changes in 11–14; cropping pattern/crop diversification changes 14–19; cultivation costs, farm income and 21–3; growth trends in 9–11; introduction to 8–9; investment trends *19*, 19–21, *21*; success of 8; terms of trade and 23–5, *24*
Greenstone, M. 202
gross capital formation (GCF) *19*, 19–21, *21*
gross domestic product (GDP): from agriculture *9*, 10; India's, overall growth of *9*, 9–10
gross irrigated area (GIA) 97, 98; ratio of, to total cropped area 100–2, 101

groundwater exploitation in India: extent of 189–91, *190*; geogenic contamination in groundwater 191; surplus/unutilized groundwater 191
growth trends, Indian agriculture 9–11; across regions/states 10–11; in overall/agricultural GDP *9*, 9–10
Guiteras, R. 205
Gulati, A. 98, 155
Gupta, S. 51, 52, 206

Hariyali Kisaan Bazaar 87
Herring, R. J. 114
high-yielding variety (HYV) seeds 183, 216, 220
HOPCOMS 80
Hossain, M. 190–1

Iglesias, A. 199
income terms of trade (IoT) 23
India: agricultural exports 140–8, 141, *142–3*, *144*; agricultural imports 138–40, 139; agricultural marketing in (*see* agricultural marketing in India); agronomic research and extension service in, revamping 223–4; co-operatives in 80–1; free trade agreements (FTAs) 140; geogenic contamination in groundwater in 191; groundwater exploitation in, extent of 189–91, *190*; irrigation sources in *189*; land leasing decision in, determinants of 36–8, *37*; percentage distribution of area under lease in *34*, 35; pesticide use in 192; price movements of exports 143–4, 145, *146–7*, *148*; surplus/unutilized groundwater in 191; tariff rate quotas (TRQs) 134; tenancy across major states of 33; tenant holdings, in total holdings and leased-in area 32; trade policies, evolution of 131–4; water tables in *189*
Indian agriculture: agrarian crisis and 6, 21; climate change impact on 203–7, 210–11, *211*; crop sector growth in 12, 14; factor markets in 46–57 (*see also* factor markets in Indian agriculture); globalization and 2; Green Revolution and 1–2, 8–25 (*see also* Green Revolution, Indian agriculture after); growth trends in 9–11; infrastructure and, strengthening 218; introduction